BEST of the BEST
AIR FORCE
COOKBOOK

AIR FORCE
COOKBOOK

Favorite Recipes from USAF Families

COMPILED BY
Karen Tosten

EDITED BY
Gwen McKee & Barbara Moseley

QUAIL RIDGE PRESS
Preserving America's Food Heritage

*I would like to acknowledge Gwen and Barney McKee
for their support in writing this cookbook. Without their encouragement,
it wouldn't have been possible. Their zest for life and passion for
sharing what's most important in life—faith, family and food—
have inspired me. I also want to thank my family for their unconditional
love and support. They endured many years of taste-testing recipes,
both good and bad, and lived to tell about it!*

Library of Congress Cataloging-in-Publication Data

Best of the best Air Force cookbook : favorite recipes from USAF families / compiled by Karen
   Tosten.
     p. cm. —
   Includes index.
   ISBN-13: 978-1-934193-08-2
   ISBN-10: 1-934193-08-9
   1. Cookery. 2. United States. Air Force. I. Title.
     TX714.T6755 2008
     641.5--dc22   2007047905

ISBN-13: 978-1-934193-08-2 • ISBN-10: 1-934193-08-9

First printing, April 2008 • Second, September 2008
Printed by Tara TPS in South Korea

On the cover: Photos courtesy of U.S. Air Force; Thunderbirds by Staff Sgt. Josh Clendenen;
HH-60 Pave Hawk by Senior Airman Jeremy McGuffin; B-52 Stratofortress by Staff Sgt.
Bennie J. Davis III; C-130J Hercules by Senior Master Sgt. Dennis Goff.

Back cover photo by Greg Campbell

QUAIL RIDGE PRESS
P. O. Box 123 • Brandon, MS 39043 • 1-800-343-1583
email: info@quailridge.com • www.quailridge.com

CONTENTS

Ten Commandments
for Military Wives

1. Thou shalt not write in ink in thy address book.

2. Thou shalt not covet choice assignments of other uniformed branches of the service.

3. Love thy neighbor. ('Tis easier if thou buyest a house on a corner.)

4. Honor thy Commissary and Exchange for as long as they both shall live.

5. Thou shalt not ridicule a local politician, for mighty senators from local politicians grow.

6. Thou shalt look for the best in every assignment, even though the best may be "world's biggest cockroaches" or "record snow in one month's time" or "most childhood diseases experienced in one year."

7. Thou shalt remember all thy friends from all thy assignments with greetings at Christmas, for thou never knowest when thou might like to spendeth the night with them en route to a new base.

8. Be kind and gentle to retired, white-haired Exchange and Commissary customers, because thou, too, will be a retiree someday.

9. Thou shalt not curse thy husband when he's off TDY on Moving Day.

10. Thou must never arrive at a new base and constantly brag about how everything was much better at thy last base.

Submitted by Laurie Smith – Seattle, Washington
Wife of Lt. Colonel Bruce Smith

PREFACE

Good times, good friends, good food are synonymous with Air Force family living.

It has been twenty-two years since my husband, William "popped the question" and changed my name and my life forever. His proposal came in the form of a two-fold question. First he actually asked me to marry him, but then he asked me to consider what our life would be like together as he was planning to fly for the Air Force. I thoughtfully considered the question, reflecting on my own life growing up in corporate America. My father's job forced us to move on the average of every two to three years, and so I really felt I could relate to life in the military. While I did not always enjoy having to leave my friends, I was always able to adapt to each location and made new friends and found new adventures. I decided life in the Air Force could not be any worse, and with the love of my life by my side, I knew I could answer without any reservations. This carefully thought-out answer of "YES" actually came out in about two seconds, and immediately our future life in the Air Force became a challenge and an adventure that we both looked forward to starting together.

Our life in the Air Force began at Mather Air Force Base in Sacramento, California. My husband would typically call me on his way home from work with two questions, "What's for dinner?" and "Can my 'Crew Dawgs' come?" I quickly learned to cook what I considered fairly good meals in mass quantities. Constantly cooking for others challenged me to find new and interesting dishes. I found that I could always call on a friend to help find just the right recipe. This was all part of understanding life in the Air Force, which in reality is quite simple. When you are the spouse of someone in the Air Force, you, too, become part of the big Air Force family.

You share life together in an incredibly unique way. While you may not always be near your own family when holidays roll

around, your Air Force family is always there. We are around for each other's weddings, baby showers, high school graduations, funerals, and more importantly, everyday life: soccer games, *Monday Night Football*, piano and ballet recitals, getting up at three o'clock in the morning to watch the Super Bowl from overseas. . . . Whatever life has in store for us at the time, we share it together. We laugh together, cry together, vent together, and celebrate together. And what I discovered was that most of these things happen around the dinner table. Good food and good friends can get you through the good times as well as the difficult ones. Life in the military certainly has its challenges, but when it is faced head-on with the strength you can only get from "family," it is an incredibly fulfilling one.

Life over the last twenty years hasn't really changed too much for me. I am still gathering recipes and cooking for friends. Over the years I have collected quite a few recipes, which really got me thinking. With all of the magnificent recipes collected from my military family, I decided it was time to share them (and recipes from others) with the rest of the world.

Once again, I enlisted the help of my Air Force family, asking them to send recipes, particularly from family and friends they have met in the military. People from all over the world have sent me their favorite recipes to share with you. Together we have traveled the world and learned to cook some of the most interesting and tasty dishes. Pride in our military heritage and the knowledge learned from our travels can be found in *Best of the Best Air Force Cookbook*. It is with great pride that I share with you this collection of recipes from my special family to yours.

Happy cooking,
Karen Tosten

Pre-Flight Appetizers

An Air Force crew chief inspects the cockpit of an **A-10 Thunderbolt II** at a forward-deployed Operation Iraqi Freedom location.

A-10s have excellent maneuverability at low air speeds and altitude, and are highly accurate weapons-delivery platforms. Their wide combat radius and short takeoff and landing capability permit operations in and out of locations near front lines. The aircraft can survive direct hits from armor-piercing and high-explosive projectiles up to 23mm. Their self-sealing fuel cells are protected by internal and external foam.

Spooky Dip

This is called Spooky Dip because it is a strange color and has who-knows-what-kind of chunks in it. It is really easy and tasty and goes with tortilla chips, pretzels, and veggies or on tacos, taco salads, or hamburgers.

1 cup sour cream
1 cup salsa
2 green onions, chopped

½ cup shredded Cheddar
cheese (or more)

Mix all ingredients and serve with whatever you like to dip with.

Mrs. Melinda Smith – Monument, Colorado
Wife of Lt. Colonel (Ret.) Fred Smith

Italian Vegetable Dip

1 cup mayonnaise
1 cup sour cream
1 (6-ounce) package Good
  Seasonings Zesty Italian
  Salad Dressing Mix

¼ cup chopped mixed red and
  green peppers

Mix mayonnaise, sour cream, seasoning mix, and peppers together. Chill. Serve with crackers.

Mrs. Eleanor Eells – Rowlet, Texas
Wife of Tech Sergeant (Ret.) Robert Eells

The United States Air Force is the aerial warfare branch of the United States armed forces and one of the seven uniformed services. Previously part of the United States Army, the USAF was formed as a separate branch of the military on September 18, 1947. Prior to 1947, the responsibility for military aviation was divided between the Army (for land-based operations) and the Navy (for sea-based operations from aircraft carrier and amphibious aircraft). The stated mission of the USAF today is to "deliver sovereign options for the defense of the United States of America and its global interests — to fly and fight in air, space, and cyberspace."

Chili Cheese Dip

1 onion, chopped
1 tablespoon butter
1 (10-ounce) can Ro-Tel
   tomatoes, drained

1 (2-pound) box Velveeta
1 (15-ounce) can chili without
   beans
1 (15-ounce) can tamales, mashed

Sauté onion in butter. Add tomatoes, cheese, chili, and tamales; stir and heat till cheese is melted. Serve warm with Fritos Scoops.

Mrs. Frances Anderson – Pineville, Louisiana
Wife of Lt. Colonel (Ret.) Andy Anderson

Hot Sausage Dip

1 pound Jimmy Dean (mild
   or hot) sausage
1 (10-ounce) can Ro-Tel
   tomatoes, undrained

2 (8-ounce) packages cream
   cheese, softened
1–1½ cups shredded Cheddar
   cheese

Preheat oven to 350°. Brown sausage in skillet and drain. Combine undrained Ro-Tel and softened cream cheese. Combine sausage with cream cheese mixture. Spoon sausage mixture into quiche or casserole dish. Top with Cheddar cheese. Bake until heated through, approximately 20–25 minutes. Serve with crackers or tortilla chips.

Mrs. Mary Ranger – St. Louis, Missouri
Wife of Colonel Kelly Ranger

Chicken Enchilada Dip

This spicy baked chicken and cheese dip is a real crowd-pleaser, and tastes great with chips or crackers. Any cheese will work with this recipe.

1 pound skinless, boneless chicken breast halves	1 (8-ounce) package shredded Cheddar cheese
1 (8-ounce) package cream cheese, softened	1 (4-ounce) can diced green chile peppers
1 cup mayonnaise	1 jalapeño pepper, finely diced

Preheat oven to 350°. Place chicken breast halves on a medium baking pan. Bake in preheated oven 20 minutes, or until no longer pink. Remove from heat; cool and shred. Place shredded chicken in a medium bowl. Mix in cream cheese, mayonnaise, Cheddar cheese, green chile peppers, and jalapeño pepper. Transfer chicken mixture to a medium baking dish. Bake uncovered 30 minutes, or until edges are golden brown. Makes 30 servings.

Mrs. Sandra Hauenstein – Byron, Georgia
Wife of Master Sergeant Charles Hauenstein

Hot Artichoke Dip

1 (14-ounce) can artichoke hearts, drained, chopped	¾ cup mayonnaise
2 garlic cloves, smashed	½ teaspoon Worcestershire
	Ground pepper to taste

Preheat oven to 350°. Combine all ingredients and bake in casserole dish 20–25 minutes. Serve with favorite crackers or chips. Makes about 2 cups.

Colonel (Ret.) Ronald G. Noland – Baton Rouge, Louisiana

Artichoke and Chili Dip

1 (14-ounce) can artichoke
   hearts, drained, chopped
1 cup mayonnaise

1 cup grated Parmesan cheese
1 (4-ounce) can chopped green
   chiles

Preheat oven to 350°. Combine artichoke hearts, mayonnaise, Parmesan cheese, and green chiles. Pour into a 9-inch-round pie pan. Bake about 20 minutes, or until hot and bubbly. Serve with tortilla chips or crackers. Makes about 2½ cups.

Major Rhonda Donze – Melbourne, Florida
Wife of Lt. Colonel (Ret.) Robert Donze

Crab Dip

Very easy and very pretty!

12 ounces cream cheese, softened
2 tablespoons Worcestershire
½ onion, grated
Garlic salt to taste
1 tablespoon lemon juice

2 tablespoons mayonnaise
1 (8-ounce) bottle chili sauce
2 (7-ounce) cans crabmeat,
   drained

Combine first 6 ingredients, mixing smooth with mixer. Spread on round platter about the size of a pizza pan. On top of this, spread chili sauce. Then spread crabmeat.

Mrs. Billie Neese – New Orleans, Louisiana
Wife of Lt. Colonel (Ret.) Robert Neese

Simply Sensational Salsa

2 (14½-ounce) cans diced or
  stewed tomatoes
3 sprigs cilantro

1 (4-ounce) jar jalapeños with
  a little juice
1 medium onion, quartered

Combine all in a food processor or chopper and blend to desired consistency.

Mrs. Marcia Allen – Benton, Arkansas
Wife of Senior Airman Gregory Allen

Fresh Roma Salsa

10 fresh Roma tomatoes
5 jalapeños
1 teaspoon crushed or minced
  fresh garlic

⅓ cup chopped onion
Salt and pepper

Boil tomatoes and jalapeños in water to cover until tomatoes split open; drain water. Cut tops off jalapeños and remove seeds. Slowly blend tomatoes, jalapeños, garlic, and onion. Add salt and pepper to taste. Makes approximately 1½ quarts.

Master Sergeant Joel Bertrand – Tucson, Arizona

Hoppin' HOT Stuffed Jalapeños

Our lives changed when we first tried this recipe—it is that good and so simple. It takes a brave person to seed the jalapeños, but the results are worth it.

25 jalapeños
1 pound Jimmy Dean regular
  sausage

1 (8-ounce) package cream cheese,
  softened
½ cup grated Parmesan cheese

Preheat oven to 400°. Clean and cut jalapeños lengthwise. With a spoon, scoop out seeds and discard them. Lay jalapeños on a foil-lined cookie sheet. Fry sausage, drain grease, and break into small chunks. Mix cream cheese and Parmesan cheese into sausage. Fill each jalapeño half with the sausage mixture till flush with the side, and return to pan. Bake 20–25 minutes. Serve alone or with Spooky Dip (see page 10). Great with cold beer. Every once in a while someone will get a super hot jalapeño (you never know with jalapeños—some are mild and some are hot), so eat at your own risk!

Note: Wear gloves when seeding jalapeños—one whiff of the seeds can make your eyes water, and if the juice gets in your eye, you must flush with cold water. I use baggies to cover my hands.

Mrs. Melinda Smith – Monument, Colorado
Wife of Lt. Colonel (Ret.) Fred Smith

Chile Omelet Appetizer

8 eggs
½ cup milk
Salt and pepper to taste
2 dashes Worcestershire

1 (4-ounce) can chopped green
  chile peppers, drained
1 (10-ounce) can Ro-Tel, drained
2 cups shredded Cheddar cheese

Preheat oven to 350°. Beat eggs, milk, salt and pepper, and Worcestershire. Set aside. Lightly grease a baking dish. Mix together chiles and Ro-Tel and spread on bottom of pan. Spread shredded cheese over chili mix, and then pour eggs over chiles and Ro-Tel. Bake 40 minutes.

Mrs. Mary Ranger – St. Louis, Missouri
Wife of Colonel Kelly Ranger

Baked Raspberry Brie

1 sheet puff pastry, thawed
  according to package
1 (8-ounce) round Brie cheese

¼ cup raspberry jam
¼ cup sliced almonds

Preheat oven to 350°. Place pastry sheet on lightly greased baking sheet. Place Brie cheese into center of pastry and spread jam on the top of the cheese round. Sprinkle with almonds. Wrap Brie with pastry. Trim excess pastry. Seal seams by brushing with water and pressing together. Bake 35 minutes or until pastry is golden brown. Serve with crackers or toasted bread points. Serves 6–8.

Mrs. Karen Tosten – Hattiesburg, Mississippi
Wife of Major (Ret.) William Tosten

Marinated Feta Cheese

This recipe is a "must have" at all our family functions and holidays. It is best when served as a spread with fresh French bread rounds. It can also be served as a topping for grilled chicken or pork loin.

8 ounces feta cheese, crumbled	1 teaspoon oregano
½ (8-ounce) jar sun-dried tomatoes in oil, chopped	1 teaspoon Italian seasoning
	5 cloves fresh garlic, minced
⅓ cup chopped Italian parsley	⅔ cup olive oil (no substitutions)
½ teaspoon thyme	

Mix all ingredients and add olive oil last. The olive oil should cover the mixture completely. Cover and let the ingredients "get acquainted" for at least one hour. If you make it the night before and refrigerate, then let it sit out to bring to room temperature before serving. Serve with French bread pieces and a glass of red wine. Avoid kissing for 2 days . . . but worth it!

Mrs. Jackie McWhorter – Monument, Colorado
Wife of Colonel (Ret.) "Mac" McWhorter

Aircraft flown by the United States Air Force:
• Attack and observation planes aid ground troops with air support.
  F-15E, F-117, A-10, Lockheed AC-130
• Bombers are the "big guns" of the Air Force. Their job is to drop explosives on enemy targets. B-52H, B-1B, B-2
• Electronic warfare aircraft search for, intercept, identify, and locate any immediate threat. E-3, E-8, EC-130, EC-135
• Fighters shoot down enemy combat aircraft and attack ground targets.
  F-22, F-15C, F-16
• Reconnaissance and special-duty aircraft observe and photograph enemy bases and positions and survey weather conditions. U-2, RC-135, Q-4, Q-1
• Trainers are used to instruct pilots and navigators. T-6, T-37, T-38, T-43, T-1, TG-10
• Transports and tankers keep the Air Force flying with personnel and supplies. They can refuel other Air Force planes in midair. C-17, C-5, C-130, C-135, VC-25, C-32, C-9, CV-22, C-37, C-21, C-12, C-40, KC-10, KC-135 Stratotanker
• Helicopters are used to transport troops into battle and behind enemy lines, and for rescuing downed pilots at sea and other special missions. HH-60, MH-53, UH-1N

Holiday Veggie Tree

I made this for the first time this year and took it to a Christmas Eve party. For Christmas, I used only broccoli and radishes to give it a green and red garnish to go with the season. I got lots of compliments on it, because it was so dang cute! This recipe is a nice replacement for the traditional veggie pizza, because the crescent rolls make for a more chewy crust. Also, you can play with the dough to make different shapes for different events . . . an Easter egg, American flag, or whatever suits you!

1 (8-count) can crescent rolls
1½ tablespoons mayonnaise
2 (3-ounce) packages cream
  cheese, softened

¾ cup chopped vegetables
  and cheese (carrots, broccoli,
  cauliflower, peppers, radishes)

Fold crescent rolls as directed on can. Place the rolls in the shape of a Christmas tree on a cookie sheet, starting with 1 on top, 2 in the row underneath that so on and so forth, making sure to press the dough together where each roll touches the other. If you have an odd roll left after making all of your rows, use it as the "stem" of the Christmas tree. Bake as directed on can. When done baking, let the "tree" cool until cool to the touch. Mix mayonnaise and cream cheese together in a bowl, then spread evenly over crescent roll tree, leaving ¼ inch from the edge "unfrosted," so you can see the shape of the tree. Then, evenly spread the chopped-up cheese or veggies of your choice on top of the cream cheese. Refrigerate 1 hour.

Mrs. Lisa Hook – Minot, North Dakota
Wife of Captain Patrick Hook

Toasted Almond Crab Spread

1 (8-ounce) package cream
 cheese, softened
1 1/2 cups shredded Swiss cheese
1/3 cup sour cream
1/8 teaspoon ground nutmeg
1/8 teaspoon pepper
1 (6-ounce) can crabmeat,
 drained, flaked, cartilage
 removed (or 1/2 cup real or
 imitation crabmeat, chopped)

3 tablespoons finely chopped
 green onions, divided
1/3 cup sliced almonds, toasted
Assorted crackers

Preheat oven to350°. In a mixing bowl, combine the first 5 ingredients. Stir in crab and 2 tablespoons onions. Spread into an ungreased 9-inch pie plate. Bake 15 minutes or until heated through. Sprinkle with almonds and remaining onions. Serve with crackers.

Mrs. Samantha Laidlaw – Ft. Walton Beach, Florida
Wife of Captain Brian Laidlaw

Sensational Shrimp Spread

1 (8-ounce) package cream
 cheese, softened
3 tablespoons mayonnaise
1 (4 1/4-ounce) can tiny shrimp,
 drained and chopped

1 tablespoon minced onion
1/2 teaspoon Worcestershire
Salt and pepper to taste

In medium bowl, combine cream cheese and mayonnaise. Mix well. Stir in shrimp, onion, Worcestershire, salt and pepper. Mix well. Cover and refrigerate 2–3 hours. Serve with crackers. Serves 12.

Mrs. Monetta Noland – Mobile, Alabama
Wife of Colonel (Ret.) Ronnie Noland

Shrimp Mold

This is great to have at parties and you can make this a day or so ahead of time. Keeps well for up to a week.

1 (10¾-ounce) can tomato soup
1 (8-ounce) package cream
cheese, softened
1 (.25-ounce) package plain
gelatin, dissolved in 3
tablespoons water
½ pound precooked frozen
shrimp, thawed, finely
chopped (more, if desired)

½ cup finely chopped onion
½ cup finely chopped celery
1 cup mayonnaise
Juice of ½ lemon
½ teaspoon salt

Heat soup and cheese; whisk until smooth. Remove from heat and add gelatin. Whisk again until smooth. Add all other ingredients; mix well. Pour into lightly oiled mold. Let mixture chill in fridge till set. Unmold and serve with Chicken in a Bisket Crackers.

Staff Sergeant Tara M. Borton – Fayetteville, North Carolina
Wife of Tech Sergeant Randy Borton

Mexican Caviar

1 (4-ounce) can chopped
ripe olives
1 (4-ounce) can chopped green
chiles
2 small or 1 large tomato,
peeled, finely chopped

2 green onions, finely chopped
2 garlic cloves, minced
3 teaspoons olive oil
2 teaspoons red wine vinegar
Dash of seasoned salt
1 teaspoon pepper

Combine olives, green chiles, chopped tomatoes, green onions, garlic, oil, vinegar, seasoned salt, and pepper in medium-size bowl. Chill overnight.

Mrs. Alice Taylor – Bann / Rheinland-Pfalz-Germany
Wife of Lt. Colonel (Ret.) Kerry Taylor

Sausage Cheese Balls with Mornay Sauce

2 pounds uncooked bulk
    sausage, crumbled
1½ cups Bisquick baking mix
4 cups grated sharp Cheddar
    cheese
½ cup finely chopped onion

½ cup finely diced celery
½ teaspoon garlic powder
¼ teaspoon salt
Dash of ground pepper
Dash of hot pepper flakes

Heat oven to 325°. In a large bowl, combine sausage, baking mix, cheese, onion, celery, garlic powder, salt, pepper, and hot pepper flakes. Mix well. Form into ¾-inch balls. Arrange on cookie sheet and bake 15 minutes, or until golden brown. Serve with toothpicks and Rich Mornay Sauce.

RICH MORNAY SAUCE:

4 tablespoons unsalted butter
4 tablespoons all-purpose flour
3 cups chicken broth
1 teaspoon salt
¼ teaspoon white pepper
¼ teaspoon grated nutmeg

½ teaspoon paprika
4 egg yolks
¾ cup heavy cream
¼ cup grated Parmesan or
    shredded Swiss cheese

In a saucepan over low heat, melt butter. Stir in flour and cook, stirring until blended and bubbly. Gradually stir in broth. Increase heat to medium-high and bring to a boil, stirring constantly. Boil for 1 minute, or until sauce thickens. Season with salt, pepper, nutmeg, and paprika. Remove from heat.

In a bowl, whisk together egg yolks and heavy cream. Pour half of the sauce into the bowl, whisking, to temper the eggs. Return this to the pan and stir well. Return pan to medium-low heat, and cook, stirring, until heated through. Add cheese gradually, stirring until cheese melts. Makes 3 cups.

Mrs. Chrisi McGlone – Colorado Springs, Colorado
Wife of Captain Kevin McGlone

Easiest Ever Cheese Ball

1 package Hidden Valley
  Original Ranch Dressing
  mix

1 (8-ounce) package cream
  cheese, softened
1 cup chopped pecans

Mix dressing mix with cream cheese. Form into a ball. Roll in chopped pecans. Chill.

Mrs. Barbara McGee – Hampton, Virginia
Wife of Lt. Colonel (Ret.) Guy McGee

Bacon-Water Chestnut Wrap

1 pound bacon
2 (8-ounce) cans sliced water
  chestnuts, drained

¼ cup mayonnaise
¼ cup chili sauce
½ cup brown sugar

Preheat oven to 350°. Cut bacon into 3 sections. Wrap water chestnuts in bacon slices and secure with toothpick. Place on a cookie sheet and bake 45 minutes. To make sauce, mix mayonnaise, chili sauce, and brown sugar. Remove wraps from oven and baste with sauce. Place on clean cookie sheet and bake 15 more minutes.

Colonel (Ret.) Ronald G. Noland – Baton Rouge, Louisiana

Wow Water Chestnuts

1 (8-ounce) can whole water
  chestnuts
4 strips bacon, cut in thirds

¾ cup ketchup
½ cup sugar

Preheat oven to 350°. Drain water chestnuts. If too large, you may cut them in half. Wrap ⅓ strip of bacon around each chestnut. Secure with toothpick. Bake 30 minutes. Drain off grease. Mix ketchup and sugar. Pour over chestnuts and bacon. Bake another ½ hour.

Master Sergeant Deb Marsh – Hubbard, Ohio

Egg Rolls

1 pound ground beef
½ cup chopped celery
1 onion, chopped
½ cup chopped carrots

Soy sauce, salt, pepper to taste
1 package egg roll wrappers
Oil for frying

Brown beef in skillet; drain. Add all vegetables. Season with soy sauce, salt and pepper to taste. Fill each wrapper with 1 tablespoon meat mixture. Roll wrappers to create an egg roll. Heat oil in skillet and fry egg rolls until brown. Drain on paper towels.

Master Sergeant (Ret.) Nelia Woods – Pasig City, Philippines

Crab Puffs

1 (12-ounce) can fancy
  crabmeat
1 (8-ounce) jar light Cheese
  Whiz

1 stick butter, softened
1 teaspoon garlic powder
8–12 whole English muffins,
  halved

Preheat oven to 400°. Combine crabmeat, Cheese Whiz, butter, and garlic powder. Mix well. Spread on muffin halves, then put on cookie sheet and freeze until almost firm, approximately 30–45 minutes. Cut muffin halves into fourths and freeze until needed. Bake on a lined or greased cookie sheet 12–20 minutes, until cheese is melted and bubbly. Makes approximately 32–48 pieces.

Mrs. Nancy Townsend – Colorado Springs, Colorado
Wife of Colonel Bruce Townsend

Cheese Puffs

1 cup grated Cheddar cheese
½ cup butter, melted
¼ teaspoon paprika

1 cup sifted self-rising flour
⅛ teaspoon salt

Preheat oven to 350°. Set cheese out on counter until room temperature. Mix cheese, butter, paprika, flour, and salt. Roll into small marble-size balls and place on baking pan. Bake 15 minutes. Makes 6 dozen.

Mrs. Barbara McGee – Hampton, Virginia
Wife of Lt. Colonel (Ret.) Guy McGee

The Nutsnacker

1¼ cups whole almonds
1 (8-ounce) package cream
cheese, softened
½ cup mayonnaise
1 tablespoon chopped green onion

5 bacon slices, crisply cooked,
crumbled
½ teaspoon dill weed
⅛ teaspoon pepper

Spread almonds in a single layer in shallow pan. Bake at 300° for 15 minutes, stirring often, until almonds just begin to turn color. Combine cream cheese and mayonnaise; mix well. Add onion, bacon, dill, and pepper; mix well. Cover; chill overnight.

Form cheese mixture into shapes of two pine cones on serving platter. Beginning at narrow end, press the almonds at slight angle into cheese mixture in rows. Continue overlapping rows until all cheese is covered. Garnish with artificial pine sprigs. Serve with crackers. Makes 1½ cups.

Mrs. Gail Teigeler – Riverside, California
Wife of Lt. Colonel (Ret.) Thomas Teigeler

Mexican Roll-Ups

1 (4-ounce) can chopped green
  chiles
½ (8-ounce) package cream
  cheese, softened

½ cup sour cream
½ teaspoon garlic salt
2 large flour tortillas

Mix first 4 ingredients. Spread over tortillas. Roll up and cover with plastic wrap. Refrigerate, preferably overnight. Just before serving, slice ¾–1 inch thick. Serve with Newman's Chunky Salsa for dipping.

Mrs. Billie Neese – New Orleans, Louisiana
Wife of Lt. Colonel (Ret.) Robert Neese

Terrific Tortilla Rolls

1 (8-ounce) package cream
  cheese, softened
1 (4-ounce) can chopped green
  chiles
1 (4-ounce) can chopped black
  olives

½ cup shredded Cheddar cheese
1 cup sour cream
1 tablespoon grated onion
1 cup shredded chicken (optional)
1 (10-count) package flour tortillas

Combine cream cheese, chiles, olives, cheese, sour cream, and onion in a bowl. Mix well. Add chicken, if desired. Spread mixture on tortillas and roll up; refrigerate. Once chilled and firm, cut into 1-inch pieces. Serve with toothpicks and salsa, if desired.

Mrs. Sara Tosten – Alexandria, Louisiana
Wife of Lt. Colonel (Ret.) Charles T. Tosten, Jr.

Symbolism of the
Air Force Coat of Arms

1. The predominant colors, ultramarine blue and gold, are the colors of the Air Force through transition from the Air Corps.

2. The thirteen stars represent the Thirteen Original Colonies of the United States. The grouping of three stars at the top of the design portrays the three Departments of the National Defense Establishment, Army, Navy, and Air Force.

3. The crest includes the American Bald Eagle, the symbol of the United States and air striking power. The eagle's head is turned to the right which symbolizes facing the enemy—looking toward the future and not dwelling on past deeds. The cloud formation depicts the creation of a new firmament, and the wreath, composed of six alternate folds of silver and blue, incorporates the colors of the basic shield design.

4. The shield, divided with the nebuly line formation, representing clouds, is charged with the heraldic thunderbolt. The thunderbolt portrays striking power through the medium of air (the sky blue background). At the honor point of the shield is a lightning bolt, conceived of as a missile cast to earth in the lightning flash. The pair of wings and smaller lightning flashes surrounding the bolt complete the design.

5. On a band encircling the whole is the inscription "United States Air Force."

Refueling Beverages

U.S. AIR FORCE PHOTO BY MASTER SGT. KEITH REED

A pair of **F-16 Fighting Falcons** from the 510th Fighter Squadron, Aviano Air Base, Italy, take fuel from a **KC-135 Stratotanker** over northern Bosnia as part of a combat air patrol mission in support of NATO's Operation Allied Force. The KC-135's principal mission is air refueling; it holds up to 30,000 gallons (200,000 pounds) of fuel.

Jo Ann's Jell-O Fruit Punch

1 (3-ounce) package Jell-O,
  any flavor
4 cups boiling water
1 (12-ounce) can frozen
  lemonade

1 (46-ounce) can pineapple juice
2 cups sugar
2 (1-liter) bottles 7-Up or
  ginger ale

Dissolve Jell-O in boiling water. Mix with juices and sugar; freeze. When ready to serve, put frozen mixture in punch bowl and add 7-Up or ginger ale.

Senior Master Sergeant (Ret.) Ray Graber – Panama City, Florida

Refreshing Pineapple Punch

2 (46-ounce) cans pineapple
  juice
1 cup lemon juice, fresh or
  bottled

1 cup sugar
1 pint cranberry juice
2 quarts ginger ale

Have ingredients well chilled. Combine first 4 ingredients in punch bowl and stir well. For lively bubbles, add ginger ale at last minute.

Mrs. Tammi Naman – Lincoln, Alabama
Wife of Major Kevin Naman

The mission of the U.S. Air Force is to defend the United States through control and exploitation of air and space. Teamed with the Army, Navy, and Marine Corps, the Air Force is prepared to fight and win any war if deterrence fails. To meet this challenge, the Air Force brings six core competencies to the fight: 1) air and space superiority 2) global attack 3) rapid global mobility 4) precision engagement 5) information superiority 6) agile combat support.

Easy Punch for Any Type Party

FOR 12 GUESTS
½ (46-ounce) can pineapple
    juice
1 quart sherbet, any flavor
½ (2-liter) bottle 7-Up

FOR 25 GUESTS
1 (46-ounce) can pineapple
    juice
1½ quarts sherbet, any flavor
1 (2-liter) bottle 7-Up

FOR 50 GUESTS
2 (46-ounce) cans pineapple
    juice
3 quarts sherbet, any flavor
2 (2-liter) bottles 7-Up

FOR 100 GUESTS
4 (46-ounce) cans pineapple
    juice
3½ gallons sherbet, any flavor
4 (2-liter) bottles 7-Up

FOR 200 GUESTS
8 (46-ounce) cans pineapple
    juice
6½ gallons sherbet, any flavor
8 (2-liter) bottles 7-Up

FOR 300 GUESTS
12 (46-ounce) cans pineapple
    juice
9½ gallons sherbet, any flavor
12 (2-liter) bottles 7-Up

Shake cans of juice to stir, then empty into whatever container you are serving from. Break sherbet into pieces and add to juice. Stir well. (You may want to save some sherbet to add shortly before serving.) Add 7-Up less than an hour before serving.

Mrs. Jennifer Willand – Northwood, Iowa
Wife of Master Sergeant Dan Willand

White Grape Punch

1 bunch green or red seedless grapes
1 (16-ounce) bottle white grape juice, chilled, divided

1 (2-liter) bottle ginger ale, chilled

A day or two before the event, remove grapes from stems and put 1–2 grapes in ice cube trays with enough juice to cover them. Freeze until firm.

When ready to serve, mix remaining white grape juice and ginger ale in pitcher. Stir well. Place ice cubes in clear wine glasses, then pour punch into glasses. You may want to double or triple ingredients and make an ice ring, and serve out of a punch bowl. Servings depend on glass size.

Mrs. Nancy Townsend – Colorado Springs, Colorado
Wife of Colonel Bruce Townsend

Ruby Red Punch

1 gallon red Hawaiian Punch
1 (46-ounce) can pineapple juice

6 scoops vanilla ice cream
4 (12-ounce) cans ginger ale

Mix punch, pineapple juice, and ice cream in punch bowl. Pour ginger ale over the top.

Mrs. Laurie Smith – Seattle, Washington
Wife of Lt. Colonel Bruce Smith

Bruce's Hot Tub Cocktails

Best if enjoyed with good friends and served in a hot tub!

**1 (16-ounce) bottle cranberry/
raspberry cocktail juice**

**4 jiggers Malibu coconut rum
1 carton fresh raspberries**

Mix together juice and rum in a pitcher. Refrigerate. Clean fresh raspberries and roll on paper towel to dry (be careful not to damage). Freeze in plastic baggie. When you're ready to serve, pour juice and rum mixture in plastic cocktail glasses using frozen berries as ice cubes.

Lt. Colonel Bruce Smith – Seattle, Washington

Lt. Colonel Bruce Smith flying his F-15E "Shagm-130"

Strawberry Daiquiri Punch

1 (6-ounce) can frozen limeade
1 (12-ounce) can frozen
   lemonade
1 (2-liter) bottle 7-Up or Sprite

30 ounces (almost a quart) water
1 fifth light rum
1½ cups strawberries, blended
   until smooth

Mix together all ingredients in pitcher. Refrigerate. Serve cold.

Mrs. Duchess Sicay – Union, South Carolina
Wife of Major (Ret.) George Sicay

Golden Champagne Punch

1 (46-ounce) can pineapple juice
1 (6-ounce) can frozen orange
   juice concentrate
1 cup lemon juice

1 cup sugar
1 fifth Sauterne
2 fifths champagne

Mix juices and sugar; chill. Pour juice mixture into punch bowl or large pitcher. Add wines. Serves 15–20.

Mrs. Barbara McGee – Hampton, Virginia
Wife of Lt. Colonel (Ret.) Guy McGee

Kahlúa Coffee Punch

This is a favorite at our Cinco de Mayo parties!

4 cups hot water
16 teaspoons instant coffee
  crystals
½ cup sugar

1½ cups half-and-half
¾ cup Kahlúa
½ gallon vanilla ice cream

Mix water, coffee crystals, sugar, and half-and-half in heat-resistant bowl on low heat. Add Kahlúa. Pour into punch bowl with ½ gallon vanilla ice cream. Enjoy!

Mrs. Diana Donnelly – Enterprise, Alabama
Wife of Lt. Colonel (Ret.) Robert Donnelly

Sweet Butter Batter Hot Buttered Rum

SWEET BUTTER BATTER:

¾ pound butter
2¼ cups brown sugar
2 cups fine white sugar

1 teaspoon vanilla
⅓ quart (approximately)
  vanilla ice cream

Melt butter in double boiler; mix in remaining ingredients except nutmeg. Refrigerate. Can keep longer in freezer.

1 jigger light rum   Dash of nutmeg

In mug, combine rum and 1 heaping tablespoon Sweet Butter Batter. Fill to top of mug with boiling water. Add a dash of nutmeg and enjoy!

Master Sergeant Deb Marsh – Hubbard, Ohio

Hot Caramel Cider

1 cup Martinelli's Sparkling
  Apple Cider
2 teaspoons Torani Caramel
  Syrup (or 1 teaspoon each
  caramel and vanilla)

Whipped cream
Ground cinnamon

Pour sparkling cider into a pot and heat on the stove (decently hot, but not boiling). Pour syrup into a mug, followed by cider. Add whipped cream to top and sprinkle some cinnamon on top of cream. Makes 1 serving.

Airman First Class Tyler Graham – Tucson, Arizona

Slow Cooker Hot Mulled Cider

⅓ cup brown sugar
2 quarts apple cider
1 teaspoon whole allspice

1½ teaspoons whole cloves
2 cinnamon sticks
2 oranges, sliced with peels on

Combine brown sugar and cider in slow cooker. Put spices in a tea strainer or tie in a cheese cloth. Add to slower cooker. Stir in orange slices. Cover and simmer on LOW at least 2 hours (more for a stronger taste). Makes 10 (1-cup) servings.

Variation: Add a dash of nutmeg.

First Lt. Kelly Russell – Minot Air Force Base, North Dakota

Hot Cinnamon Wassail

1 (46-ounce) can cranberry juice
1 (46-ounce) can cran-apple juice
1 (46-ounce) can apple juice

6 cinnamon sticks
1 tablespoon whole cloves
½ cup sugar
1 tablespoon ground cinnamon

Use a 60-cup coffee pot (or boil on top of stove in 5-quart pot). Place juices in coffee pot, then use a filter in strainer and add the dried spices (if using a pot on top of stove, you can place dried spices in a coffee filter and tie closed—if just placed in pot, you will have to strain out cloves and cinnamon sticks before serving). Plug coffee pot in and let perk just like you would if making coffee. Store the unused portion in refrigerator.

Lt. Colonel (Ret.) William and Lt. Colonel Deanna Paulk
– Panama City, Florida

U.S. Air Force aeronautical ratings are military aviation skill standards established and awarded by the United States Air Force for commissioned officers participating in aerial and space flight. USAF aeronautical badges, commonly referred to as "wings" from their shape and their historical legacy, are awarded by the Air Force in recognition of degrees of achievement and experience. Officers earning these badges are classified as rated officers. Rating standards apply equally to both fixed-wing and helicopter pilots.

The five categories of aeronautical ratings are:
• **Pilot**—rankings include Pilot, Senior Pilot, and Command Pilot.
• **Navigator**—rankings include Navigator, Senior Navigator, and Master Navigator.
• **Air Battle Manager**—rankings include Air Battle Manager, Senior Air Battle Manager, and Master Air Battle Manager.
• **Observer**—rankings include Observer, Senior Observer, and Master Observer.
• **Flight Surgeon**—rankings include Flight Surgeon, Senior Flight Surgeon, and Chief Flight Surgeon.

Plantation Almond Tea

¾ cup sugar
¼ cup lemon juice
2 (family-size) tea bags

2 cups boiling water
2 cups cold water
½ teaspoon almond extract

In a large stainless pan, add sugar, lemon juice, and tea bags. Pour boiling water over mixture. Cover and let steep for 10 minutes. Remove tea bags. Add cold water and almond extract. Stir. Cool in refrigerator. Serve over crushed ice. Make 4 (1-cup) servings.

Mrs. Sara Tosten – Alexandria, Louisiana
Wife of Lt. Colonel (Ret.) Charles T. Tosten, Jr.

Charles and Sara Tosten on their wedding day, May 9, 1958

Ora's Friendship Tea

Refreshing.

1 (21-ounce) green can TANG
5 packages unsweetened
  Kool-Aid
3½ cups instant lemonade

2½ cups sugar
5 teaspoons cinnamon
2½ teaspoons ground cloves

Mix all ingredients together and store in jar. Stir 2 or 3 teaspoons in cup of hot or cold water.

Senior Master Sergeant (Ret.) Ray Graber – Panama City, Florida

Lemon Drops

½ cup fresh lemon juice
½ cup citron vodka

3 tablespoons sugar
Ice

Mix lemon juice, vodka, sugar, and ice in a cocktail shaker. Rub lemon wedge around martini glass rim and roll in sugar. Strain into sugar-rimmed glasses and enjoy!

Mrs. Marty Holcomb – Athens, Georgia
Wife of Lt. Colonel Pete Holcomb

Gluehwein

Gluehwein is a German winter/holiday drink.

2 fifths cheap dry red wine   **5 whole cloves**
½ cup sugar   **1 lemon, thinly sliced**
5 cinnamon sticks   **1 orange, thinly sliced**

Combine wine, sugar, cinnamon sticks, cloves, lemon slices, and orange slices in large saucepan. Place over medium heat and simmer. Strain and serve hot.

Mrs. Alice Taylor – Bann / Rheinland-Pfalz-Germany
Wife of Lt. Colonel (Ret.) Kerry Taylor

Kerry standing by his Pave Hawk MH60

Holiday Eggnog

1 dozen egg yolks
2 cups Jack Daniel's bourbon
1 pound powdered sugar

1 quart heavy cream
1 quart whole milk

Beat eggs yolks until thick and lemon colored. Slowly add bourbon then sugar. Beat cream until thick but not forming peaks. Add in to the bourbon mixture. Add milk.

Mrs. Judy Tyler – Mobile, Alabama
Mother-in-law of Major (Ret.) William Tosten

Homemade Irish Cream

¾ cup good Irish whiskey
1 (14-ounce) can sweetened
  condensed milk
1½ pints heavy whipping cream
3 raw eggs

1 tablespoon chocolate syrup
1 tablespoon instant coffee (add
  more or less to suit your taste)
½ teaspoon almond extract
1 teaspoon vanilla extract

Blend all ingredients in blender on "whip" setting. Chill overnight.

Major (Ret.) William Tosten – Alexandria, Louisiana

B-52

Salute to Desert Storm Crew R-22!

½ ounce Kahlúa
½ ounce Bailey's Irish Cream

½ ounce Grand Marnier

Combine in a mixing glass with ice. Swirl ingredients gently and strain into a glass either straight up or on the rocks.

Major (Ret.) William Tosten – Alexandria, Louisiana

Robert's Breakfast Shake

1 medium banana
1 cup orange juice
½ cup vanilla yogurt

½ cup frozen or fresh
  strawberries
1 cup ice

Combine banana, orange juice, and yogurt in blender. Add strawberries and ice; blend. Serves 2.

Note: Be sure to rinse blender and glasses right away because this stuff is a real pain to wash off after it dries.

Chief Master Sergeant (Ret.) Robert Lee Young – Del Rio, Texas

Banana Shake

Good for help in reducing blood pressure.

2 bananas, sliced
2 cups skim milk
2 cups nonfat vanilla yogurt

1 cup pineapple juice
1 tablespoon honey

Process all ingredients in blender until smooth. Serve immediately. Serves 4.

Master Sergeant Deb Marsh – Hubbard, Ohio

Ballistic Breads
& Breakfast

An **LGM-30 Minuteman III** missile soars in the air after a test launch. The Minuteman is a strategic weapon system using a ballistic missile of intercontinental range (greater than 3,500 miles) typically designed for nuclear weapons delivery. The "L" indicates that the missile is silo-launched; "G" indicates ground targets; "M" means it is a guided missile. The name Minuteman comes from the Revolutionary War's Minutemen, who vowed to be ready for battle within two minutes of receiving notice.

Banana Bread

1¼ cups all-purpose flour   ½ cup Crisco
1 cup sugar   3 small bananas
½ teaspoon salt   2 eggs
1 teaspoon baking soda

Preheat oven to 350°. Mix dry ingredients. Cut in Crisco. Crush bananas with a fork. Beat the eggs and add with bananas to flour mixture. Stir only enough to mix. Put in greased loaf pan. Thump the pan to get the air out. Bake 50–60 minutes. Do not double.

First Lt. Kelly Russell – Buffalo, New York
Wife of First Lt. Patrick Applegate

Sour Cream Banana Bread

1 stick butter, softened   1 teaspoon baking soda
1 cup sugar   ½ teaspoon salt
2 eggs   1 cup mashed bananas
1 teaspoon vanilla   ½ cup sour cream
1½ cups all-purpose flour   ½ cup nuts (optional)

Preheat oven to 350°. Mix butter and sugar with eggs until fluffy. Add vanilla, flour, baking soda, salt, bananas, and sour cream. Mix until smooth. Fold in nuts, if desired. Bake in a greased loaf pan for 1 hour, or until cake tester comes out clean.

Mrs. Cathy Harvey – Georgetown, South Carolina
Wife of Lt. Colonel Joe Harvey

Chocolate Chip Banana Bread

$\frac{1}{2}$ cup margarine, softened
1 cup sugar
2 eggs
3 bananas, mashed

2 cups all-purpose flour
1 teaspoon baking soda
$\frac{1}{4}$ cup chocolate chips

Preheat oven to 350°. Mix ingredients in order. Pour into greased and floured loaf pan. Bake 35–40 minutes. Check doneness by inserting a toothpick into bread; if it comes out clean, it is done.

Mrs. Jennifer Willand – Northwood, Iowa
Wife of Master Sergeant Dan Willand

Banana Nut Bread

1 cup sugar
$\frac{1}{2}$ cup shortening
$\frac{1}{2}$ teaspoon salt
2 eggs, well beaten

3 ripe bananas, mashed
1 teaspoon baking soda
2 cups sifted all-purpose flour
$\frac{1}{2}$ cup nuts

Preheat oven to 325°. Cream sugar, shortening, and salt. Add eggs and mashed bananas. Add baking soda to flour, sift together, and combine with nuts. Mix well. Turn into greased loaf pan and bake 1 hour (longer for higher elevations) or until brown. To speed up the aging of bananas or to intensify the flavor, remove peels from bananas, place in zip-lock bags, and put in freezer until needed. Thaw (or microwave on DEFROST) to use.

Master Sergeant (Ret.) Lin Howe-Young – Fruitport, Michigan

Banana Pineapple Bread

Made with aloha from the Howe family, Banana Pineapple Bread is one of the items put into a welcome basket when new squadron members arrive on the island. I like that this recipe makes a large batch because it freezes well. I always have some on hand whether it is for a new arrival to our squadron or when friends drop in. I knew it was a hit when one of our newly welcomed ohana told me her two-year-old son loved it . . . it passed the keiki test!

4 cups all-purpose flour
1 tablespoon baking powder
1½ teaspoons baking soda
1½ teaspoons salt
2 sticks butter, softened
2 cups sugar
4 large eggs

1 (8-ounce) can crushed
   pineapple, undrained
½ cup sour cream
1 cup mashed, ripe bananas
   (about 2 medium)
Raw sugar or granulated sugar
   for topping

Combine flour, baking powder, baking soda, and salt; set aside. Cream butter and sugar until light and fluffy; mix in eggs. Add flour mixture alternating with pineapple, sour cream, and bananas, and mix until combined. Pour into 3 lightly greased regular-size loaf pans. Sprinkle with sugar and bake at 350° for 45 minutes.

Note: Hawaiian words: ohana = family (squadron members and family are considered ohana upon arrival); keiki = child

Joanie Howe – Hickam Air Force Base, Hawaii
Wife of Lt. Colonel Rob Howe, 65th Airlift Squadron Commander

---

The island of Kahoolawe in Hawaii was once used as a target by the United States Navy and Air Force. It is uninhabited and, still today, off-limits to visitors. Kahoolawe was returned to the state in 1994 and is currently being cleaned up by the U. S. Government.

Pumpkin Nut Bread

2⅔ cups sugar
⅔ cup shortening
1 (16-ounce) can pumpkin
⅔ cup water
4 eggs

3⅓ cups self-rising flour
1 teaspoon ground cinnamon
1 teaspoon ground cloves
2 teaspoons vanilla
⅔ cup coarsely chopped nuts

Heat oven to 350°. Grease bottoms only of 2 loaf pans. Mix sugar and shortening in bowl. Stir in pumpkin, water and eggs. Mix in flour, cinnamon, cloves, and vanilla. Stir in nuts. Pour into pans. Bake until wooden pick inserted in center comes out clean.

Mrs. Tammi Naman – Lincoln, Alabama
Wife of Major Kevin Naman

Spicy Pumpkin Bread

3½ cups all-purpose flour
2 teaspoons baking soda
1½ teaspoons salt
1 teaspoon cinnamon
1 teaspoon nutmeg

1 cup oil
4 eggs
⅔ cup water
2 cups pumpkin
3 cups sugar

Preheat oven to 350°. Mix flour, baking soda, salt, cinnamon, and nutmeg in large bowl. Set aside. In another large bowl, combine oil, eggs, water, pumpkin, and sugar. Mix well. Add dry ingredients. Mix well. Pour into 2 greased loaf pans. Bake 1 hour. Check doneness with cake tester.

Mrs. Melinda Smith – Monument, Colorado
Wife of Lt. Colonel (Ret.) Fred Smith

Pumpkin Muffins

½ cup oil
1 cup sugar
3 eggs
1 cup pumpkin
2 cups self-rising flour

½ teaspoon baking soda
1 (3½-ounce) box instant
   coconut cream pie filling
½ teaspoon salt
1 teaspoon cinnamon

Mix oil, sugar, eggs, and pumpkin together. Combine flour, baking soda, cream pie filling mix, salt, and cinnamon together. Stir together wet mixture with flour mixture. Pour into greased muffin tins. Bake 20–25 minutes.

Mrs. Cathy Harvey – Georgetown, South Carolina
Wife of Lt. Colonel Joe Harvey

Best Ever Light-As-A-Feather
Blueberry Muffins

⅓ cup sugar
¼ cup butter, softened
1 egg
1 cup milk
1¾ cups plus 2 teaspoons
   all-purpose flour, divided

4 teaspoons baking powder
⅛ teaspoon salt
1 cup fresh blueberries, washed,
   dried

Preheat oven to 375°. Cream sugar and butter together. Mix in egg and milk. Sift 1¾ cups flour with baking powder and salt. Combine sugar mixture with dry ingredients just until combined; don't overmix. Roll blueberries in remaining 2 teaspoons flour; fold into mixture. Fill greased muffin tins with about ⅓ cup batter. Bake 20–25 minutes.

Mrs. Karen Tosten – Hattiesburg, Mississippi
Wife of Major (Ret.) William Tosten

Breakfast English Muffins

1 pound Jimmy Dean regular
  sausage
2 sticks margarine, softened
2 jars Old English Cheddar
  cheese spread

½ teaspoon red pepper
½ teaspoon garlic powder
2 dashes seasoned salt
12 English muffins split

Preheat oven to 400°. Brown crumbled sausage until well done. Drain on paper towels. Blend softened margarine, cheese spread, and spices. Add cooked sausage and mix well. Spread this mixture on English muffins. Freeze muffin halves on cookie sheets. When frozen, put in freezer bags. When ready to serve, bake frozen muffins 10–15 minutes. Makes 24 muffins.

Mrs. Barbara Haywood – Bossier City, Louisiana
Wife of Master Sergeant (Ret.) Daniel Haywood

Broccoli Bread

½ stick margarine, melted,
  divided
1 box Jiffy Cornbread Mix
1 box frozen chopped broccoli,
  thawed

2 cups shredded sharp Cheddar
  cheese
1 small onion, finely chopped
4 eggs, beaten
½ cup milk

Preheat oven to 400°. Pour ¼ cup margarine in loaf pan. Mix cornbread mix, broccoli, cheese, onion, eggs, remaining ¼ cup melted butter, and milk together. Pour into loaf pan. Bake 33–35 minutes. Serve warm.

Mrs. De Edra Farley – Alpine, Texas
Wife of Captain Rich Farley

Bread Machine Pepperoni Bread

¾ cup water
1 tablespoon butter
½ teaspoon salt
½ teaspoon pepper
¾ teaspoon sugar
2 cups all-purpose flour
1½ teaspoons yeast

½ (3½-ounce) package
  sliced pepperoni
1 cup grated provolone
1 cup grated mozzarella
1 teaspoon olive oil
Grated cheese or Italian seasoning

This dough recipe is for bread machine dough. Use your machine's recommendations for order of first 7 ingredients. Use dough setting. Once the dough has been mixed, remove from the machine.

Roll dough flat, about 8x13 inches. Cover top surface with a single layer of sliced pepperoni (there will be spaces). Spread grated cheeses over pepperoni. Roll, jellyroll-style, being sure to pinch the ends under. Dampen edge with wet fingertips to seal. Place on cookie sheet, seam side down, cover with a towel, and let rise for 30 minutes.

Preheat oven to 350°. Before baking, remove towel and rub top of loaf with olive oil. You may sprinkle with grated cheese and/or Italian seasoning. Bake 20–30 minutes, until golden brown. Let cool slightly before cutting.

Mrs. Sandra Harrop – Crooksville, Ohio
Wife of Master Sergeant Donald Glenn Harrop, Jr.

Herman

STARTER:

2 cups lukewarm water
1 package dry yeast
Pinch of ginger

3 cups all-purpose flour, divided
½ cup sugar
1 cup milk

Dissolve lukewarm water with yeast and a pinch of ginger. Wait 15 minutes and then add 2 cups of flour. Let stand in warm place for 2 hours. Refrigerate. Stir Herman every day. On his 5th day, feed him ½ cup sugar, 1 cup flour and 1 cup milk. On his 10th day, bake Herman. Makes 4 cups. Use 2 cups for recipe below, then keep one cup and give one cup away with the recipe.

HERMAN BREAD MIX:

2 cups Starter
1 cup sugar
2 cups all-purpose flour
2 eggs
¾ cup milk
1 teaspoon cinnamon

½ teaspoon salt
¾ cup oil
2 teaspoons baking powder
1 cup nuts
½ teaspoon baking soda
1 cup raisins

Mix all together. Put in greased 9x13-inch cake pan.

HERMAN TOPPING:

¼ cup real butter
1 tablespoon all-purpose flour

1 cup brown sugar
1 tablespoon cinnamon

Cut butter into remaining ingredients and sprinkle on top of cake. Bake at 350° for 35–40 minutes.

Note: If you are given a cup of Herman, add ½ cup sugar, 1 cup flour, and 1 cup milk the day you get him. Then add the other ingredients called for on the 5th day. Don't forget to stir every day!

Master Sergeant Deb Marsh – Hubbard, Ohio

Elizabeth's Cheesy French Bread

1 (8-ounce) package shredded
  Mexican blend cheese
¾ cup mayonnaise

1½ teaspoons dried parsley flakes
⅛ teaspoon garlic powder
1 loaf French bread, split

Preheat oven to 350°. Stir cheese, mayonnaise, parsley, and garlic pow-der together. Spread over French bread halves. Put on baking pan and bake 15–20 minutes or until hot and bubbly.

Mrs. Sara Tosten – Alexandria, Louisiana
Wife of Lt. Colonel (Ret.) Charles T. Tosten, Jr.

Lefse
(Scandinavian Flatbread)

Traditionally made in the winter.

3 cups "riced" or mashed
  potatoes
½ cup whipping cream
¼ cup butter

1 teaspoon salt
1 teaspoon sugar
2 cups all-purpose flour

Mix all ingredients, except flour, while potatoes are hot. Refrigerate overnight.

Add flour and mix well. Take small amount of dough, squeeze into a ball, and roll out on floured board into very thin circle. Carefully lift with spatula and fry on hot (425°–450°) griddle for about a minute. Flip and fry other side. Lefse should look like a tortilla (but not taste like one).

Note: Scandinavians (or others) who have a Lefse stick (long, flat spatula) and Lefse griddle (large, round electric frying pan without sides) may make large Lefse. Otherwise, roll out Lefse to fit the size of your griddle or frying pan. Best to make a double batch.

Mrs. Lila Kleven – Tomah, Wisconsin
Grandmother of Cadet Andrew Teigeler

Butterhorns

1 cup milk, scalded
$\frac{1}{2}$ cup shortening
$\frac{1}{2}$ cup sugar
1 teaspoon salt

1 package yeast
3 eggs, beaten
$4\frac{1}{2}$ cups all-purpose flour
Melted butter or margarine

Preheat oven to 400°. Combine milk, shortening, sugar, and salt. Cool to lukewarm. Add yeast and stir well. Add eggs, then flour. Mix to a smooth, soft dough. Knead lightly on floured surface. Place dough in greased bowl; cover and let rise until doubled in bulk (about $1\frac{1}{2}$ hours).

Divide dough into thirds. Roll each third on lightly floured surface to 9-inch circle. Brush with melted butter or margarine. Cut each circle in 12 wedge-shaped pieces. Roll each wedge, starting with wide end and rolling to point. Arrange on greased baking pan (may make into crescents by curving each roll). Cover and let rise until very light. Bake 10 minutes, till golden brown. Makes 3 dozen.

Mrs. Gail Teigeler – Riverside, California
Wife of Lt. Colonel (Ret.) Tom Teigeler

The United States Air Force does not have an official motto, but there are numerous unofficial slogans such as "No One Comes Close" and "Un Ab Alto" (One Over All). For many years, the U.S. Air Force used "Aim High" as its recruiting motto; more recently, they have used "Cross into the Blue," "Do Something Amazing," and "Above All."

Monkey Bread

⅓ cup brown sugar
1–2 tablespoons butter or
margarine
Almonds or pecans (optional)
¾ cup sugar

2 teaspoons cinnamon
1 loaf bread dough (completely
thawed, if using frozen dough)
1 tablespoon butter or margarine,
melted

Sprinkle brown sugar in bottom of greased (or nonstick) loaf pan. Drop 2 tablespoons of margarine over sugar. Sprinkle nuts on top. Combine sugar and cinnamon in bowl. Break dough into small (1-inch) pieces, roll in hand, and then add to sugar/cinnamon mixture. Stir dough and cinnamon/sugar mixture occasionally to coat dough. When all dough coated, add melted margarine and stir. Dump dough into loaf pan and pat down flat. Cover loosely with sheet or light towel. Let rise about 2 hours. Bake 20 minutes at 375°. If dough appears very moist, cover with foil to prevent top from getting too brown; continue baking another 5–10 minutes.

When done, run knife along sides of pan. Invert on wire rack and remove pan (should put wax paper under rack to catch any drippings). Cool.

Mrs. Lila Kleven – Tomah, Wisconsin
Grandmother of Cadet Andrew Teigeler

Sour Cream Waffles

1 cup sour cream
2 eggs
3 tablespoons soft butter
1 cup sour buttermilk
2 cups all-purpose flour

1 tablespoon sugar
½ teaspoon salt
2 teaspoons baking powder
1 teaspoon baking soda

Beat sour cream, eggs, butter, and buttermilk with electric mixer, then add dry ingredients, mixing until smooth. Ladle ¼ cup batter onto lightly greased hot waffle iron. Cook until golden brown, 3–4 minutes.

Mrs. Lou Ferguson – Fruitport, Michigan
Wife of Master Sergeant (Ret.) Dale Ferguson

Hotcakes à la Belle

3 cups milk
¼ cup cooking oil
4 eggs, separated
2 tablespoons sugar

2 teaspoons salt
3 cups all-purpose flour
4 teaspoons baking powder

Combine milk, oil, egg yolks, sugar, and salt. Lightly stir in flour and baking powder. Whip egg whites separately, and lightly fold into milk mixture. Do not fold in thoroughly; leave lumps of white. Spoon onto griddle that has been slightly greased. Cook until golden brown on both sides. Makes 48 cakes.

Mrs. Frances Anderson – Pineville, Louisiana
Wife of Lt. Colonel (Ret.) Andy Anderson

Swedish Pancakes

It was always a special day when my dad made these for our family. He never measured anything, so one day I stood next to him and measured everything out as we put it together. They are much like crêpes. And with three girls in the house, my dad always said he took out all of the calories for us.

7 eggs	4 cups self-rising flour
4 cups milk	1 stick butter, melted

Mix eggs and milk. Add flour and mix well. Gradually add butter. Cook on hot griddle. The dough should be fairly runny; spread it out like a crêpe. Serve with butter, syrup, and powdered sugar. Roll up the pancake and enjoy! Makes a lot; easy to halve or quarter.

Mrs. Laurie Smith – Seattle, Washington
Wife of Lt. Colonel Bruce Smith

Fly Away Light Pancakes

2 tablespoons butter	1 cup all-purpose flour
1 egg	1 tablespoon sugar
1 cup milk	2 teaspoons baking powder
2 tablespoons oil	½ teaspoon salt

Melt butter. Combine with egg, milk, and oil. Mix flour, sugar, baking powder, and salt. Stir wet ingredients into dry. Spoon on oiled griddle and brown both sides. Serve with hot syrup.

Mrs. Tara Hansen – Ft. Worth, Texas
Wife of Captain Eydin Hansen

Nutty Orange Coffee Cake

¾ cup sugar
½ cup pecans, chopped
4 ounces cream cheese, softened
2 teaspoons grated orange rind
2 (11-ounce) cans buttermilk
  biscuits, opened, separated

½ cup butter, melted
1 cup powdered sugar, sifted
2 tablespoons orange juice

Preheat oven to 350°. Combine sugar and pecans and in a small bowl; set aside. Combine softened cream cheese and orange rind. Place about ¾ teaspoon cream cheese in center of biscuits; fold in half sealing the edges. Dip biscuits in melted butter, then dredge in sugar and pecan mixture. Place biscuits in the bottom of a tube pan. Only form a single layer. Drizzle with any remaining butter over biscuits; sprinkle with remain sugar and nut mixture. Bake 35 minutes or until done. Immediately invert pan onto a plate. Mix powdered sugar and orange juice in small bowl. Drizzle over biscuits. Serve warm.

Mrs. Tara Hansen – Ft. Worth, Texas
Wife of Captain Eydin Hansen

The United States Air Force is one of the largest and most technologically advanced Air Forces in the world, with about 6,013 manned aircraft in service (4,282 USAF; 1,321 Air National Guard; and 410 Air Force Reserve), approximately 160 Unmanned Combat Air Vehicles, 2,161 Air-Launched Cruise Missiles, and 580 Intercontinental Ballistic Missiles. As of September 30, 2006, the USAF had 334,200 personnel on active duty, 120,369 in the Selected and Individual Ready Reserves, and 107,000 in the Air National Guard. An additional 10,675 personnel were in the Standby Reserve, and the Air Force employed 168,558 civilian personnel.

Billie's Daisy Coffee Cake

1 package yeast	2½–3 cups sifted all-purpose flour
¼ cup warm water	¾ cup sugar
2 tablespoons sugar	¼ cup brown sugar
3 tablespoons shortening	2 teaspoons cinnamon
1½ teaspoons salt	¾ cup chopped nuts
¾ cup milk, scalded	½ cup butter, melted

Preheat oven to 350°. Soften yeast in warm water. Combine sugar, shortening, and salt; add milk. Cool to lukewarm. Add yeast mixture; gradually add flour to form stiff dough. Knead 3–5 minutes or until smooth. Place in a bowl and cover; let rise in warm place until doubled in bulk, about 1–1½ hours.

Combine remaining ingredients except butter. Use a 12-inch-round pizza pan (or make one from aluminum foil, dull side up). Grease the pan. Pinch off small pieces of dough, enough to roll into a 6-inch strip, ½ inch thick. Dip each strip into butter, then into cinnamon-sugar-nut mixture. Wind into a flat coil in center of pan, placing strips close together to make a round coffee cake. Cover and let rise until light.

Bake for 25–30 minutes. Cool slightly. Drizzle with powdered sugar glaze (powdered sugar, milk, vanilla).

Mrs. Billie Borders – Poquoson, Virginia
Wife of Major (Ret.) Jerry Borders

Apple Coffee Cake

FILLING:

4 cups chopped apples

1 cup water

2 tablespoons lemon juice

1¼ cups sugar

⅔ cup cornstarch

In a saucepan, combine apples and water. Simmer covered, about 5 minutes or until fruit is tender. Stir in lemon juice. Mix sugar and cornstarch; stir into apple mixture. Cook and stir until thickened and bubbly. Cool.

BATTER:

3 cups all-purpose flour

¼ teaspoon ground mace

1 cup sugar

1 teaspoon salt

1 teaspoon ground cinnamon

1 tablespoon baking powder

1 cup butter or margarine

2 eggs, slightly beaten

1 cup milk

1 teaspoon vanilla

Preheat oven to 350°. Mix together dry ingredients. Cut in butter or margarine until mixture resembles fine crumbs. Combine eggs, milk, and vanilla. Add to flour mixture, mixing until blended. Spread half the Batter into a greased 9x13x2-inch baking pan or 2 greased 8x8x2-inch baking pans. Spread cooled Filling over Batter. Spoon remaining Batter in small mounds over Filling, spreading out as much as possible.

TOPPING:

½ cup sugar

¼ cup butter or margarine

½ cup all-purpose flour

½ cup chopped walnuts

Combine ingredients except nuts until mixture resembles coarse crumbs. Stir in nuts. Sprinkle Topping over Batter in pan. Bake 45–50 minutes or until cake tests done. Cool. Makes 1 large coffee cake or 2 small coffee cakes.

Variation: Substitute apricots, peaches, pineapple, or whole blueberries for apples.

Master Sergeant (Ret.) Lin Howe-Young – Fruitport, Michigan

Fresno French Toast

2 eggs
1 cup all-purpose flour
1 cup milk
1 ½ teaspoons baking powder
½ teaspoon salt
1 teaspoon cinnamon
1 teaspoon vanilla

8–10 slices firm white bread
6 tablespoons butter, divided
3 tablespoons vegetable oil,
   divided
Powdered sugar
Apricot jam

Mix eggs in a blender until combined, then add flour, milk, baking powder, salt, cinnamon, and vanilla; mix until smooth. Pour mixture into a shallow dish. Cut bread in half to form triangles. Heat 2 tablespoons butter and 1 tablespoon oil in a wide frying pan over medium-high heat; lay bread slices in egg mixture until well soaked, then drain briefly and place in pan. Fry a few pieces at a time, adding more butter and oil as needed, until golden brown on all sides. As they are done, arrange on a serving platter and keep warm. Dust with powered sugar and pass the jam. Serves 4–6.

Mrs. Linda Rufi – Tucson, Arizona
Wife of Chief Master Sergeant (Ret.) Tony Rufi

Not all of the United States' military combat aircraft are operated by the USAF. The United States Army operates its own helicopters, mostly for support of ground combatants; the Army also maintains a small fleet of fixed wing aircraft (mostly Unmanned Aerial Vehicles). The Navy is responsible for the aircraft operating on its aircraft carriers and Naval air stations, and the Marine Corps operates its own combat and transport aircraft. The Coast Guard also maintains transport and search-and-rescue aircraft, which may be used in combat and law enforcement roles. All branches of the U.S. military operate helicopters.

Pineapple Upside Down French Toast

2 tablespoons butter
¼ cup brown sugar
¼ cup crushed pineapple,
  drained
1 egg, beaten

¾ cup milk
⅛ teaspoon salt
4 slices bread
Powdered sugar

Preheat oven to 400°. Melt butter in deep-dish pie pan. Combine brown sugar and crushed pineapple with melted butter in pie pan. Mix together egg, milk, and salt in separate bowl. Place bread on top of this mixture and let it soak up the milk mixture. Place soft bread on top of pineapple. Bake 25 minutes, until lightly browned. Cool 3 minutes before inverting onto serving platter. Sprinkle with powdered sugar.

Mrs. Jackie McWhorter – Monument, Colorado
Wife of Colonel (Ret.) "Mac" McWhorter

Sopaipillas

2 cups all-purpose flour
1 cup Bisquick
1 cup pancake mix

1½ cups warm water
Cooking oil
Honey

Mix all dry ingredients in a large bowl. Slowly add WARM water and mix by hand. Cover dough with dish towel and let stand for an hour. Take a small piece of dough (baseball size), roll out, and cut into small pieces; place a few into a large pot of HOT oil. Flip over when they puff up. Remove when they have a golden color, which normally takes a few seconds. Serve with honey or powered sugar.

Master Sergeant Joel Bertrand – Tucson, Arizona

Aunt Donna's Cinnamon Rolls

These are great to make the night before and let rise to top of pan overnight. Bake in the morning.

2 cups milk
1 package quick rise yeast
½ teaspoon plus ½ cup sugar, divided
¼ cup warm water
1 egg, beaten
2 teaspoons salt

½ cup oil
6 cups all-purpose flour
1 stick butter, softened
Cinnamon and brown sugar mixture to taste
2 cups heavy cream, divided
2 cups brown sugar, divided

Preheat oven to 350°. Boil milk; cool to lukewarm. Dissolve yeast plus ½ teaspoon sugar in ¼ cup water. Let yeast rise to full cup. Place milk in large bowl. Add egg, remaining ½ cup sugar, salt, oil, and yeast mixture. Mix well. Gradually mix in the flour until it makes a soft dough.

Let rise 45 minutes to 1 hour. Punch down; let rise 45 minutes to 1 hour.

Roll out half the dough. Spread with soft butter; sprinkle with cinnamon and brown sugar mixture to taste. Roll and cut into 16 pieces.

In a 9x13-inch cake pan, mix 1 cup cream and 1 cup brown sugar. Place cut cinnamon rolls in pan. Let rise to top of pan. Repeat with other half of dough in another 9x13-inch pan. Bake at 350° for 15–20 minutes.

Mrs. Sandra Harrop – Crooksville, Ohio
Wife of Master Sergeant Donald Glenn Harrop, Jr.

Zucchini Frittata with Roasted Red Peppers

Every summer the Gourmet Chef, a local specialty cooking store located in downtown Minot, hosts a baking contest held in conjunction with a downtown festival. The main ingredient is different every year. The year I entered, which was my first-ever cooking contest, the ingredient was zucchini. The rules stated that it must be baked in the oven. They also judged it on taste, presentation, use of ingredient, and ease of preparation. There were thirty other contestants and my entry was the last to make it in, just seconds before the time deadline. I had "lost" my car keys, so my husband had to come home from work to drive me to the contest. I really did not expect to win and was extremely surprised when my name was announced!

12 large eggs
1 cup grated Parmesan cheese, divided
Salt and pepper to taste
½ teaspoon dried marjoram
2 medium zucchini, rinsed and cut into 2-inch long julienne strips (about 3 cups)

3 tablespoons olive oil, divided
1 medium onion, chopped
3 cloves minced garlic
½ cup diced roasted red pepper

Preheat oven to 425°. In a large bowl whisk together eggs, ½ the Parmesan, salt, pepper, and marjoram. In a 12-inch nonstick skillet with an oven-proof handle, sauté zucchini in 2 tablespoons olive oil over medium heat until softened. Transfer to a separate bowl.

Add remaining oil to skillet. Sauté onions until they start to caramelize. Add garlic and cook 1 minute, then add cooked zucchini and roasted red pepper. Pour egg mixture into skillet. Shake to make sure you distribute egg mixture between vegetables; bake 7–9 minutes. Once frittata is firm around edges and still a little soft in the middle, sprinkle on remaining Parmesan, and put under broiler about 4 inches from heat for 1–2 minutes, or until cheese is bubbling and golden. Let frittata cool in skillet 5 minutes; run a thin knife around edge, and slide frittata onto a serving plate. Cut frittata into wedges and serve warm or at room temperature.

Mrs. Dianne Walbeck – Minot, North Dakota
Wife of First Lt. David T. Walbeck

Homemade White Bread

There are many things you can make with this dough besides the loaves of bread, like monkey bread, cinnamon rolls, and dinner rolls.

⅔ cup sugar
2 tablespoons salt
1 cup powdered skim milk
1 cup shortening
6 cups hot water
4 packages active dry yeast (or
  9 teaspoons from jar)

½ cup lukewarm water
3 eggs
22 cups all-purpose flour (about
  7½ pounds), sifted onto counter
  or board, divided

In very large bowl, mix together sugar, salt, and powdered milk. Add shortening and break into small pieces. Add hot water and stir; shortening should become very soft. While this mixture is cooling, put yeast in lukewarm water; stir to dissolve. Beat eggs in a separate bowl. When first mixture is lukewarm to the touch, add eggs, yeast, and 4 cups flour. Beat until smooth. Add another 4 cups flour. Beat until smooth. Continue to add flour, 2–4 cups at a time, stirring into dough until approximately 22 cups have been added. Put dough on floured board. Knead dough until flour is completely worked into dough. Knead another 2–5 minutes. It may be necessary to sprinkle dough with flour occasionally to prevent sticking.

Wash, rinse, dry, and grease bowl. Put in dough and lightly grease top of dough. Wrap bowl in clean sheet and set on counter out of draft (if cold in the house, may want to put on top of stove and turn on the hood light). Allow to rise 2 hours. Punch down dough and knead until dough is original size. Wrap again; allow to rise another 2 hours. Punch down once more. Cut dough into 8 chunks.

Knead each chunk on floured board, and holding each end, slap dough several times against board to get out air pockets. Shape into loaves and place in greased or nonstick loaf pans. Allow to rise 2 hours, covered with sheet, out of draft. Bake at 400° for 20–30 minutes until golden. When done, remove from pan and set upright under sheet (to

(continued)

(Homemade White Bread continued)

keep top from becoming too hard) to cool. Uncover and turn on sides until completely cool (to keep bottom from becoming soggy). Store in plastic bags. May be frozen. Makes 8 loaves.

Mrs. Lila Kleven – Tomah, Wisconsin
Grandmother of Cadet Andrew Teigeler

Cardamom Bread

2 cups milk	1 tablespoon cardamom
½ cup margarine or butter	2 packages dry yeast
1 teaspoon salt	¼ cup warm water
¾ cup plus 1 teaspoon sugar,	4 eggs, beaten
divided	7–8 cups all-purpose flour

Scald milk; add margarine, salt, and ¾ cup sugar. Stir until margarine is melted and sugar is dissolved. Cool slightly until warm. Add cardamom. Dissolve yeast in warm water with remaining 1 teaspoon sugar. Add eggs to cooled milk mixture. Add dissolved yeast. Add 2 cups flour and beat until smooth. Add remaining flour gradually until soft dough is formed. Knead lightly for 10 minutes. Put dough in greased bowl to rise until doubled. Punch down and braid into 2 loaves. Let rise again.

Preheat oven to 375°. Bake 20 minutes or until golden brown. Spread with melted butter or margarine. Sprinkle with sugar.

Mrs. Gail Teigeler – Riverside, California
Wife of Lt. Colonel (Ret.) Tom Teigeler

Easy Beer Bread

1 (12-ounce) can beer   2 teaspoons sugar
3 cups self-rising flour   Melted butter for top

Grease and flour loaf pan. Mix beer, flour, and sugar, and turn into the loaf pan. Brush top of bread with melted butter. Bake at 350° for 1 hour.

Mrs. Melinda Smith – Monument, Colorado
Wife of Lt. Colonel (Ret.) Fred Smith

Squash and Onion Pastry

DOUGH:

1 cup all-purpose flour   6 tablespoons unsalted butter,
⅛ teaspoon salt   cold
⅛ teaspoon sugar   ¼ cup ice water

Stir together flour, salt, and sugar. Cut in butter until mixture resembles coarse cornmeal. Spoon ice water in and mix with a fork until dough is moist. Form into a ball and cover with plastic wrap. Refrigerate.

TOPPING:

⅓ cup sliced onion   ¼ teaspoon each salt and pepper
1 cup thinly sliced yellow squash   1 tablespoon milk
1 tablespoon olive oil   ¼ cup grated Parmesan cheese
1 tablespoon thyme

Sauté onion and squash in olive oil for 5 minutes or until vegetables are tender. Add thyme, salt and pepper. Allow to cool.

Preheat oven to 400°. On lightly floured surface, roll Dough out into a 9-inch circle. Spoon vegetable mixture on top of the Dough, leaving 1-inch border. Fold Dough back onto filling, making a raised edge. Brush milk on pastry edge. Sprinkle with Parmesan cheese. Place on baking sheet. Bake 20–25 minutes. Serve warm.

Mrs. Karen Tosten – Hattiesburg, Mississippi
Wife of Major (Ret.) William Tosten

Chile Cheese Cornbread

This is a meal in itself. Everybody loves it!

2 boxes Jiffy Cornbread Mix	1 teaspoon sugar
1 (4-ounce) can green chiles,	1 onion, chopped fine
chopped	1 ½ cups shredded cheese
¼ cup oil	1 (15-ounce) can cream corn

Preheat oven to 350°. Mix cornbread according to package directions. Add remaining ingredients. Mix well. Pour into greased 9x13-inch pan and bake 45 minutes.

Mrs. Billie Neese – New Orleans, Louisiana
Wife of Lt. Colonel (Ret.) Robert Neese

Mama's Cornbread Dressing

5 cups day-old cornbread	¼ cup butter
5 slices cubed, toasted white	1 ½ teaspoons dried, rubbed sage
bread	¼ teaspoon salt
20 saltine crackers, crushed	¼ teaspoon pepper
3 cups canned vegetable broth	2 large eggs
2 cups chopped celery	1 large egg white
2 cups chopped onions	

Preheat over to 375°. Mix breads and crackers in large bowl. Combine broth, celery, onions, and butter in large saucepan; bring to a boil. Reduce heat and simmer 10 minutes. Add broth mixture to cornbread mixture, stirring well. Add remaining ingredients; stir well to combine. Pour into 7x11-inch baking dish coated with cooking spray. Bake 45 minutes; cover and bake 30 more minutes.

Mrs. Billie Neese – New Orleans, Louisiana
Wife of Lt. Colonel (Ret.) Robert Neese

Homemade Granola Cereal

1 cup chopped almonds
1 cup shredded coconut
6 cups oats
1 cup wheat germ
1 cup raisins

¼ cup dried sunflower seeds
2 tablespoons sesame seeds
½ cup honey
½ cup vegetable oil

Preheat oven to 325°. Toast nuts and coconut in oven about 5 minutes or until slightly browned. Be careful not to burn. In a large bowl, mix almonds and coconut together with oats, wheat germ, raisins, sunflower and sesame seeds. In small bowl, mix honey and oil. Pour over oat mixture and stir until well coated. Spread on baking pan. Bake 15 minutes.

Mrs. De Edra Farley – Alpine, Texas
Wife of Captain Rich Farley

Breakfast Casserole

2 (8-count) cans crescent rolls
1 pound Jimmy Dean sausage,
  crumbled and browned
1½ cups frozen hash browns,
  thawed

1½ cups shredded Cheddar
  cheese
6 eggs, beaten
¼ cup milk
½ cup grated Parmesan cheese

Preheat oven to 375°. Lay crescent rolls flat and press seams together in a 9x13-inch pan. Layer cooked sausage over crescent rolls. Add thawed potatoes on sausage layer. Cover with Cheddar cheese. Mix eggs with milk and pour over entire casserole. Sprinkle with Parmesan cheese. Bake 25 minutes.

Mrs. Karen Tosten – Hattiesburg, Mississippi
Wife of Major (Ret.) William Tosten

Sausage Mozzarella Quiche

1 (9-inch) pie crust	4 eggs, beaten
4 ounces mozzarella cheese, shredded	¾ cup milk
	½ teaspoon salt
6 ounces sausage, cooked and crumbled	¼ teaspoon pepper

Preheat oven to 375°. Line unbaked pie shell with cheese and sausage. Combine eggs, milk, salt, and pepper. Beat well. Pour egg mixture over cheese and sausage. Bake 25–30 minutes.

Mrs. Karen Tosten – Hattiesburg, Mississippi
Wife of Major (Ret.) William Tosten

Crusty Sausage Brunch

Easy and good!

2 (8-ounce) cans refrigerated crescent rolls	1 (8-ounce) package cream cheese
	1 (8-ounce) package grated cheese
1 pound pork sausage (hot or mild)	

Heat oven to 375°. Unroll 1 can of dough into 2 long rectangles. Place in ungreased 9x13-inch glass baking dish; press over bottom and ½ inch up sides to form crust. Brown sausage in large skillet over medium heat until thoroughly cooked, stirring frequently. Remove sausage from skillet; discard drippings. Add cream cheese to same skillet. Cook over low heat until melted. Add cooked sausage; stir to coat. Spoon mixture evenly over dough. Sprinkle with cheese. Unroll second can of dough on work surface. Press to form 9x13-inch rectangle; firmly press perforations to seal. Carefully place over cheese. Bake 21–26 minutes or until golden brown. Cool 15 minutes. Cut into small squares.

Mrs. Tammi Naman – Lincoln, Alabama
Wife of Major Kevin Naman

Bacon and Egg Casserole

Assemble the night before, and bake the next morning.

1 (16-ounce) loaf Hawaiian
  bread, cut into ¾-inch cubes
1 cup finely shredded Mexican
  four cheese blend
8 slices bacon, cooked,
  crumbled

8 large eggs
2½ cups milk
½ teaspoon salt
½ teaspoon pepper
1 teaspoon dry mustard
½ teaspoon Worcestershire

Arrange bread cubes in a lightly greased 9x13-inch baking dish. Sprinkle with shredded cheese and crumbled bacon. Whisk together eggs, milk, salt, pepper, mustard, and Worcestershire. Pour over prepared casserole; press down bread cubes with a spoon to allow bread to soak up the liquid. Cover and chill 8 hours. Let stand 30 minutes before baking. Bake at 350° for 35 minutes or until set and golden. Serve with salsa or sliced fresh tomatoes.

Mrs. Linda Rufi – Tucson, Arizona
Wife of Chief Master Sergeant (Ret.) Tony Rufi

Sausage and Bacon Breakfast Casserole

6 slices bread
6 slices bacon
1 pound breakfast sausage

6 eggs
1 tablespoon mustard
2 cups shredded cheese

Spray a 9x13-inch cake pan with nonstick spray. Tear up bread and spread on bottom of pan.

Cook bacon and sausage. Cut into pieces and layer on top of bread. Scramble eggs in bowl with mustard. Pour over top. Sprinkle cheese over top. (I use Cheddar or a Cheddar mix.) Refrigerate overnight. Bake the next morning at 350° about 30 minutes or until golden.

HINT: If using a glass pan, do not preheat oven. Put cold glass pan in cold oven. You may need to add a little cooking time.

Mrs. Sandra Harrop – Crooksville, Ohio
Wife of Master Sergeant Donald Glenn Harrop, Jr.

Overnight Breakfast Sausage Casserole

1½ pounds breakfast sausage
2½ cups seasoned croutons
2 cups shredded cheese
2¼ cups milk

4 eggs, beaten
¾ teaspoon dry mustard
1 cup cream of mushroom soup
1½ cups milk

Crumble and brown sausage; drain. Pour half the croutons into bottom of 9x13-inch baking dish. Sprinkle half browned sausage and half cheese over croutons. Repeat layers. Mix together milk, eggs, and mustard. Pour over top of sausage layers. Refrigerate overnight.

In the morning, combine mushroom soup and milk. Pour over casserole and bake 45–60 minutes at 350°. Let stand for 10 minutes before serving.

Mrs. Cathy Harvey – Georgetown, South Carolina
Wife of Lt. Colonel Joe Harvey

Lt. Col. Joe Harvey sits on a throne found at the Al Faw Palace, located in Baghdad, Iraq. The palace was built by Sadam Hussein as a memorial to the Iraqi soldiers who fought to free Faw from Iranian control. It now serves as headquarters for the Multi-National Corps-Iraq.

Breakfast Burritos

3 pounds sausage
4 pounds potatoes, cubed
1 dozen large eggs, scrambled
Chopped Anaheim green chile
  (optional)

3 dozen flour tortillas, warmed
2 pounds grated cheese

Cook sausage; drain. Cook potatoes separately. Mix drained potatoes with sausage; add scrambled eggs, and cook until eggs are done. Spread a small amount of chile onto each warm tortilla, if desired; add cheese, then sausage mixture. Roll up and wrap with foil. Place in oven at a low setting to keep warm. Makes 36 burritos.

Master Sergeant Joel Bertrand – Tucson, Arizona

Anytime Cheddar Cheese Soufflé

This is truly good anytime!

½ teaspoon salt
½ teaspoon dry mustard
½ teaspoon red pepper
10 slices white sandwich bread,
  cubed
3 cups shredded sharp Cheddar
  cheese

2 tablespoons butter, cut into
  small pieces
3 eggs, beaten
3 cups whole milk

In a small bowl, combine salt, mustard, and red pepper. Spray 2-quart casserole dish with nonstick cooking spray. Layer half of bread into casserole dish. Cover with half shredded cheese and half seasonings mix, and dot with 1 tablespoon butter. Repeat. In a small bowl, beat eggs and milk. Pour over layers of bread and cheese. Cover and refrigerate at least one hour or overnight.

Preheat oven to 350°. Bake 50–60 minutes until bubbly and browned. Serves 6.

Mrs. Barbara McGee – Hampton, Virginia
Wife of Lt. Colonel (Ret.) Guy McGee

Just Plane Good
Soups, Chilis & Stews

U.S. AIR FORCE PHOTO BY TECH. SGT. SEAN M. WHITE

Numbers 5 and 6 of the USAF Air Demonstration Team, also known as the **Thunderbirds**, perform a reflection pass. The team performs precision aerial maneuvers to exhibit the capabilities of modern high-performance aircraft to audiences throughout the world. The squadron performs no more than 88 air demonstrations each year.

The Thunderbirds fly specially-marked **F-16 Fighting Falcons**, a highly maneuverable fighter that has a proven record in air-to-air combat and air-to-surface attack. In addition to their air demonstration responsibilities, the Thunderbirds are part of the USAF combat force. If required, the team's personnel and aircraft can be rapidly integrated into a fighter unit at Nellis Air Force Base, Nevada.

Homemade German Potato Soup

5 medium-large potatoes
1 small carrot
1 bunch green onions
1 small onion

2–3 tablespoons butter or
    margarine
2–3 pints light cream
Salt to taste

Peel and quarter potatoes. Cut carrot into small pieces and add to large pot with potatoes. Chop green ends of green onions and add to pot. Fill water level to about ½ inch over top of potatoes. Cook until knife cuts through them easily. Drain water into a bowl—you will use this water later. Mash potatoes (some people prefer their soup with some consistency, some like it without the potato pieces). Once desired consistency is reached, pour water back onto potatoes. Keep soup over low heat. Chop onion and sauté in butter or margarine—do not let onion burn. Add onion to soup. Add light cream until soup becomes a nice beige cream color. Add salt to taste.

Tech Sergeant Candis Winslow – Panama City, Florida

The Thunderbirds were formed on June 1, 1953, as the 3,600th Air Demonstration Team at Luke Air Force Base in Arizona. The name "Thunderbirds" was soon adopted by the unit, influenced in part by the strong Indian culture and folklore of the southwestern United States where Luke is located. Indian legend speaks of the Thunderbird with great fear and respect. To some it was a giant eagle . . . others envisioned a hawk. When it took to the skies, the earth trembled from the thunder of its great wings. From its eyes shot bolts of lightning. Nothing in nature could challenge the bird of thunder, the story said, and no man could stand against its might. A more appropriate name couldn't have been selected, as it is with the same commanding presence the Thunderbirds take to the skies.

Winning Taco Soup

Use any variety of beans . . . this is good soup!

1 pound ground beef
1 onion, chopped
1 (16-ounce) can chili beans
  with liquid
1 (15-ounce) can kidney beans
  with liquid
1 (15-ounce) can whole-kernel
  corn with liquid
1 (8-ounce) can tomato sauce
2 cups water
2 (14½-ounce) cans diced
  tomatoes
1 (4-ounce) can diced green
  chile peppers
1 package taco seasoning mix

Cook beef with onion until brown; place with remaining ingredients together in slow cooker, and mix to blend. Cook on LOW for 8 hours. Top with crushed Tostitos or Fritos, shredded cheese, and sour cream.

Mrs. Laurie Smith – Seattle, Washington
Wife of Lt. Colonel Bruce Smith

Super Easy Tortilla Soup

1 (10-ounce) can Ro-Tel
  tomatoes
3 (10¾-ounce) cans chicken
  with rice soup
2 cups crushed Tostitos chips
1 avocado, cubed
1½ cups shredded Cheddar cheese
Picante sauce (optional)

Combine tomatoes and soup in pan. Simmer 10 minutes. Place ⅓ cup chips into the bottom of each bowl. Ladle soup over chips and top with avocado and cheese. Add picante to taste.

Mrs. Connie Leetsch – Abilene, Texas
Wife of Chief (Ret.) Cecil H. Leetsch
Mrs. Leetsch also served in the Women's Air Force from 1951–1954.

Winter Minestrone

2 tablespoons olive oil
1 onion, chopped
2 carrots, peeled, chopped
2 celery stalks, chopped
3 ounces thinly sliced pancetta, coarsely chopped
2 garlic cloves, minced
1 pound Swiss chard, stems trimmed, leaves coarsely chopped
1 russet potato, peeled, cubed
1 (14½-ounce) can diced tomatoes

1 fresh rosemary sprig
1 (15-ounce) can cannellini beans, drained, rinsed, divided
2 (14-ounce) cans low-sodium beef broth, divided
1 (1-ounce) piece Parmesan cheese rind
2 tablespoons chopped fresh Italian parsley leaves
Salt and pepper to taste

Heat oil in a large heavy pot over medium heat. Add onion, carrots, celery, pancetta, and garlic. Sauté until onion is translucent, about 10 minutes. Add Swiss chard and potato; sauté 2 minutes. Add tomatoes and rosemary sprig. Simmer until chard is wilted and tomatoes break down, about 10 minutes.

Meanwhile, blend ¾ cup beans with ¼ cup broth in a processor until almost smooth. Add puréed bean mixture, remaining broth, and Parmesan cheese rind to vegetable mixture. Simmer until potato pieces are tender, stirring occasionally, about 15 minutes. Stir in remaining whole beans and parsley. Simmer until beans are heated through and soup is thick, about 2 minutes. Season with salt and pepper to taste. Discard Parmesan rind and rosemary sprig (leaves will have fallen off stem.) Ladle soup into bowls and serve.

Mrs. Frances Anderson – Pineville, Louisiana
Wife of Lt. Colonel (Ret.) Andy Anderson

Egg Drop Soup

5 cups chicken broth
3 tablespoons cold water
1 tablespoon plus 1½ teaspoons
  cornstarch

1 egg, slightly beaten

Boil chicken broth. Mix water and cornstarch. Add to soup. Stir until thickened. Slowly pour beaten egg into boiling soup, stirring with a fork. Remove from heat.

Mrs. Marty Holcomb – Athens, Georgia
Wife of Lt. Colonel Pete Holcomb

Wild Rice Soup

3 cups chicken broth
1 cup uncooked wild rice
¼ pound bacon, diced
½ teaspoon salt
2 stalks celery, finely chopped
1 (7-ounce) can mushroom
  pieces, drained
½ medium onion, chopped
2 (10¾-ounce) cans cream of
  mushroom soup

1 quart half-and-half
¼ cup white wine
½ teaspoon beau monde
  seasoning
1 (10-ounce) can white chicken,
  drained
Salt and pepper to taste

Boil chicken broth. Add uncooked wild rice to broth. Add salt. Bring to a boil, reduce heat, then cover and simmer 35–45 minutes (you will know it is done when the black shells split, and you can see the white rice inside rice shells), and the broth is absorbed. Sauté bacon in large saucepan; add celery, mushrooms pieces, and onion. Cook until tender. Over low heat add soup, half-and-half, and wine; add to rice mixture with seasoning and chicken. Salt and pepper to taste.

Mrs. Judy Tyler – Mobile, Alabama
Mother-in-law of Major (Ret.) William Tosten

Vichyssoise

2 cups cubed raw potatoes
1 cup chopped onion
2 cups water
3 chicken bouillon cubes
2 tablespoons butter

¾ cup milk
⅛ teaspoon pepper
2 tablespoons parsley
½ cup heavy cream

Combine potatoes, onion, water, and bouillon cubes in saucepan on medium-high heat. Cook 15 minutes or until potatoes are tender. Do not drain; pour into blender. Add butter, milk, pepper, and parsley. Blend on HIGH 30 seconds. Pour into bowl; add cream and chill.

Mrs. Frances Anderson – Pineville, Louisiana
Wife of Lt. Colonel (Ret.) Andy Anderson

French Market Soup

1 (1-pound) package 15-bean
  mix
1 tablespoon salt
3 quarts water
1 ham hock
1 bay leaf
1 tablespoon thyme
1 quart tomatoes
2 medium onions, finely
  chopped

2 cloves garlic, minced
6 stalks celery, finely chopped
1 green pepper, finely chopped
2 tablespoons Cajun spice mix
2 tablespoons parsley flakes
1 pound smoked sausage, sliced
4 or 5 chicken breasts, cooked,
  shredded

In large stockpot, soak beans in water with salt overnight. Drain. Add 3 quarts water with ham hock, bay leaf, and thyme. Simmer 3 hours.

Remove ham bone, removing any meat; add meat back to pot. Add tomatoes, onions, garlic, celery, green pepper, spice mix, and parsley flakes. Cook 1½ hours. Add sausage and chicken. Cook until heated through. Serve.

Mrs. Connie Wilson – Minot, North Dakota
Wife of Lt. Colonel Darren E. Wilson

Sweet Potato Apple Soup

1 medium onion, chopped
3 tablespoons butter
1 tablespoon curry powder
½ teaspoon cinnamon
½ teaspoon ginger
Salt and pepper to taste

3 large sweet potatoes, peeled
and diced
2–3 Rome apples, peeled and
diced
3 tablespoons chopped parsley
3 (14-ounce) cans chicken broth

Sauté onion in butter. Add curry powder, cinnamon, ginger, salt, pepper, sweet potatoes, apples, parsley, and chicken broth. Simmer until potatoes and apples are tender. Purée. Makes 10 medium servings.

Mrs. Brenda Burrows – Yorktown, Virginia
Wife of Major (Ret.) Chris Burrows

Pumpkin Soup

1 medium onion, chopped
2 tablespoons butter
20 ounces chicken broth
1 (16-ounce) can pumpkin
1 (4-ounce) can chopped green
chiles

1 teaspoon salt
Dash of pepper
1 cup half-and-half
8 ounces shredded Cheddar cheese

Sauté onion in butter. Add broth; bring to a boil. Reduce heat to simmer. Add pumpkin, chiles, and seasonings. Stir well with wire whisk. Cover and simmer 10 minutes. Add half-and-half and cheese. Heat thoroughly; do not boil.

Mrs. Marty Holcomb – Athens, Georgia
Wife of Lt. Colonel Pete Holcomb

Crew Dawgs Favorite Chicken Soup

1 whole chicken
3 quarts reserved chicken stock
1 large onion, chopped
2 cloves garlic, minced
6 tablespoons butter
1 quart half-and-half
1 cup cooked rice

2 (4-ounce) cans chopped
  green chiles
1 pound Monterey Jack cheese,
  grated
½ pound Cheddar cheese,
  grated

Boil chicken; reserve stock. Remove chicken from bones. Sauté onion and garlic in butter; add to chicken and stock. Bring to a boil, then turn heat down to low. Add half-and-half, rice, and green chiles. Mix well. Add grated cheeses. Continue to stir well until cheese has melted. Serve with tortilla chips or Fritos.

Mrs. Karen Tosten – Hattiesburg, Mississippi
Wife of Major (Ret.) William Tosten

Potato Leek Chowder
(From Scotland)

3 large leeks (white and light
  green parts only)
5 medium potatoes
3 cups low-sodium chicken broth
Ground pepper to taste

1¼ cups whole milk
2 tablespoons dried parsley
½ cup grated sharp Cheddar
  cheese

Separate leeks and wash well. Cut into 1-inch pieces. Peel and dice potatoes. Sauté in a large saucepan for several minutes, stirring so they don't brown. Add broth and pepper and bring to a boil; simmer 15 minutes. Let cool. Purée half of mixture with chicken broth. Return to saucepan. Add milk gradually and heat chowder. Do not boil. Stir in parsley. Sprinkle with cheese.

Mrs. Linda Slater – Long Island, New York
Wife of Chief Master Sergeant Kevin G. Slater

Fish Chowder

4 slices bacon	1 (8-ounce) bottle clam juice
1 small onion, finely chopped	½ cup heavy cream
1 rib celery, finely chopped	1 large potato, peeled and diced
1 small carrot, peeled, finely	¾ pound firm white fish
chopped	(halibut or cod)
2 teaspoons all-purpose flour	Parsley
1 cup water	

Fry bacon until crisp. Remove bacon; drain on paper towel. Using bacon drippings, sauté onion, celery, and carrot. Sprinkle flour over cooking vegetables. Cook and stir the flour/vegetable mixture 1 minute. Add water and clam juice. Bring to a boil. Add cream and potato. Cook about 15 minutes or until potatoes are tender. Add fish and simmer 5 minutes. Garnish with bacon pieces and parsley.

Mrs. Sherri Myer – San Antonio, Texas
Wife of Lt. Colonel Greg Myer

Born February 13, 1923, in Myra, West Virginia, Charles Elwood "Chuck" Yeager enlisted as a private in the U.S. Army Air Forces (USAAF) on September 12, 1941, and became an aircraft mechanic at George Air Force Base, Victorville, California. Displaying natural talent as a pilot, Yeager received his wings and a promotion to Flight Officer on March 10, 1943, and became a P-51 fighter pilot. After WWII he became a test pilot of many kinds of aircraft and rocket planes. On October 14, 1947, Yeager became the first pilot (at age 24) to break the sound barrier, flying the experimental Bell X-1 (shown here) at Mach 1 at an altitude of 45,000 feet. He is now a retired Brigadier General in the United States Air Force.

Easy Crawfish Chowder

1 onion, chopped
1 stick butter
1 pound crawfish (frozen works
   great!)
1 (8-ounce) package cream
   cheese, diced
1 (15-ounce) can white corn
   with juice

1 pint half-and-half
1 (15-ounce) can yellow corn
   with juice
1 (10¾-ounce) can cream of
   mushroom soup
2 (10¾-ounce) cans cream of
   potato soup

In large pot, wilt onion in butter on medium heat. Add crawfish and cook 3–5 minutes. Add diced cream cheese and let melt. Add all other ingredients and cook on medium-low for one hour, stirring often. (To prevent it from sticking, you may need to cook on low heat, depending on your stove.)

Mrs. Billie Neese – New Orleans, Louisiana
Wife of Lt. Colonel (Ret.) Robert Neese

Potato, Cheese, and Corn Chowder

2 boxes Hungry Jack Au Gratin
   Potatoes
2 (15-ounce) cans yellow corn
1 (10-ounce) can Ro-Tel
   tomatoes

1 (14½-ounce) can diced
   tomatoes
1 tablespoon minced garlic
1 pint half-and-half
16 ounces Velveeta cheese

In a large stockpot, combine au gratin cheese package and potatoes with enough water to cover them. Cook on medium heat, covered, 20 minutes. Drain corn and add to potatoes. Add Ro-Tel tomatoes, diced tomatoes, and garlic. Bring to a boil. Turn heat to medium-low and add half-and-half and Velveeta. Stir often until cheese is melted.

Note: Velveeta will melt quicker if cubed.

Mrs. Cathy Harvey – Georgetown, South Carolina
Wife of Lt. Colonel Joe Harvey

Chicken and Sausage Gumbo

1 quart water
¾ cup oil
¾ cup all-purpose flour
1 cup diced onion
¾ cup diced green onions
½ cup diced bell pepper
½ cup diced celery
Minced garlic (fresh garlic is
  better)
Bouillon cubes, chicken stock,
  or just plain water

Cayenne pepper to taste
Salt, black pepper, and white
  pepper to taste
2 (10-ounce) cans Ro-Tel
  tomatoes, drained
1 (1-pound) package smoked
  sausage, cut into rounds
1 pound chicken, cut up
1 (16-ounce) can cut okra, drained
Gumbo filé to taste
Rice

ROUX:

Have quart of water measured and ready. Put oil and flour in pot on medium heat (it should bubble in the middle) and stir constantly until brown (like chocolate). Be careful not to burn. Should take about 30–45 minutes. (As an alternative, just microwave for 6 minutes then for 1-minute periods, stirring, until desired color—works just as well.) When done, add onions, bell pepper, celery, and garlic; stir. Add the quart of water when onions are clear.

GUMBO:

Add more water/stock and bring to a high boil for a few minutes. Bring to low boil and add seasonings except gumbo filé. Next add Ro-Tel tomatoes. Let boil for about 10 minutes and add raw chicken and sausage. Add more water/stock, if needed. Bring to high boil then progressively down to a simmer over a 10-minute period. Continue simmering and add okra, simmering another 15 minutes (prevents sliminess). Add gumbo filé just before serving. Serve over rice.

Tech Sergeant Jon Bourgeois – St. Amant, Louisiana

Major Mac's Chili

I decided to enter a chili cook-off my squadron was having as a fundraiser. I had never made chili before. I threw this recipe together at the last minute based on what I thought was supposed to be in chili. Amazingly, it won first prize! Since that time I have made this chili for several fundraisers. I am frequently asked for the recipe. At least one person I have given the recipe to has also won first place in the cook-off in which they entered it. It takes at the most 30 minutes to make and will feed 10–15 people, depending on how big their appetites are. Be sure to vary the pepper and hot sauce to suit your taste.

1 pound ground meat, ground
  turkey, or meat substitute
1 (15-ounce) can dark red
  kidney beans
1 (15-ounce) can light red
  kidney beans
1 (28-ounce) can baked beans
1 (14½-ounce) can diced
  tomatoes

1 (16-ounce) jar picante sauce
½ package chili seasoning
  (optional)
1 (8- to 10-ounce) jar nacho
  jalapeño slices or chopped
  habanera peppers
1 (5-ounce) jar favorite hot sauce

Brown meat. Drain liquid from kidney beans before you add them to the chili (unless you want your chili to be soupy). Add meat and all the rest of the ingredients into a 3-quart pot and heat up on the stove. Stir frequently until it starts boiling a little. Remove from heat. Serve.

Hint: (1.) To save time, you can heat up all the ingredients while you are browning the meat. Add the chili seasoning, peppers, and hot sauce in amounts to suit your palette for spicy chili.

(2.) Canned baked beans come in many varieties. Just pick the type you like best. Use your favorite mild, medium, or hot picante sauce, depending on how spicy you want the chili (the picante sauce is the secret for the unique flavor of this chili). For hot sauce, I have used Buffalo wing seasoning with great success.

Lt. Colonel Todd McCready – Junction City, Kansas

Southwest White Chili

2 tablespoons olive oil
2 pounds boneless, skinless
 chicken breasts, cut into
 small cubes
1 clove garlic, minced
½ onion, chopped
2 cups chicken broth

2 (4-ounce) cans chopped
 green chiles
3 (16-ounce) cans Great Northern
 beans, undrained
2 green onions, sliced
Shredded Monterey Jack cheese
 (optional)

Heat oil in large saucepan over medium-high heat. Add chicken, garlic, and onion; cook 4–5 minutes. Stir in broth, green chiles and Southwest Spice Blend; simmer 15 minutes. Mash 1 can of beans (use blender, food processor, or fork). Stir beans (mashed and whole) into broth mixture. Simmer 5–10 minutes. Top with green onions. Garnish with Monterey Jack cheese, if desired.

SOUTHWEST SPICE BLEND:
1 teaspoon oregano leaves
1 teaspoon cilantro leaves

2 teaspoons ground cumin
¼ teaspoon ground red pepper

Master Sergeant (Ret.) Lin Howe-Young – Fruitport, Michigan

On the evening of March 25, 1948, a tornado roared through Tinker Air Force Base, Oklahoma, causing considerable damage, a few injuries, but no fatalities. However, the destruction could have been much worse. A few hours earlier, Air Force Captain Robert C. Miller and Major Ernest J. Fawbush correctly predicted that atmospheric conditions were ripe for tornadoes in the vicinity of Tinker AFB. This first tornado forecast was instrumental in advancing the nation's commitment to protecting the American public and military resources from the dangers caused by natural hazards.

White Chicken Chili

Quick, easy, and very tasty! It was a big hit at this year's annual chili cook-off. Great for a squadron potluck lunch.

2 cups cooked, chopped chicken (approximately 4 large breasts)
3 (16-ounce) cans Great Northern beans, drained
1 (16-ounce) jar salsa
8 ounces shredded Monterey Jack cheese

2 teaspoons cumin (or more, to taste)
½ (14-ounce) can chicken broth (or more, if you like your chili soupy)

Mix together all ingredients, and simmer 30–60 minutes.

Mrs. Lisa Hook – Minot, North Dakota
Wife of Captain Patrick Hook

Peanut Butter Stew

1 large onion, chopped
1 green bell pepper, chopped
3 tablespoons butter, or ⅓ cup oil
1 pound lean beef, cubed or bite-size
1 (6-ounce) can tomato paste, divided

Water to cover
1 habanera pepper, chopped (for spicier flavor)
2 potatoes, peeled, cubed
3 heaping teaspoons peanut butter
Salt and pepper to taste
Cooked rice

Sauté onion and green pepper in oil or butter. Once onion is cooked, sear meat and add half the tomato paste. Add water (enough to cover everything), habanera, and potatoes. Bring to a boil then let simmer until meat and potatoes are tender. Add remaining tomato paste and peanut butter, incorporating into meat and potatoes. Season. Let sit for 2 minutes. Serve hot over rice.

Senior Airman Nabeel Razzak – Silver Spring, Maryland

Lower Alabama Brunswick Stew

2 medium onions, thinly sliced
½ teaspoon garlic powder
1 (10-ounce) package frozen
  whole-kernel corn
1 (10-ounce) package frozen
  lima beans
1 (10-ounce) package frozen
  English peas
3 pounds new potatoes

1 (2½- to 3-pound) broiler-fryer
  chicken, cooked, cut up
2 cups chicken stock
1 teaspoon salt
¼ teaspoon pepper
1 bay leaf
2 (14½-ounce) cans stewed
  tomatoes
½ cup vinegar

Sauté onions with garlic powder in stew pot or Dutch oven. Add remaining ingredients. Bring to a boil; lower heat, cover, and cook 1 hour, stirring occasionally. Remove bay leaf before serving.

Colonel (Ret.) Ronald G. Noland – Baton Rouge, Louisiana

Crockpot Ranger Beef Stew

2 pounds chuck roast, cut into
  cubes
2–3 tablespoons oil
6 cups water
6 beef bouillon cubes
½ cup red wine
1 tablespoon dried basil
1 tablespoon dried thyme

3 cloves garlic, minced
1 large onion, chopped
2 stalks celery, chopped
1 (6-ounce) can spicy V8 juice
3 carrots, peeled, sliced
4 potatoes, peeled, cut into
  bite-size pieces
1 envelope brown gravy mix

Brown roast in oil. Put browned meat into crockpot set on HIGH. Add water, bouillon, red wine, basil, thyme, garlic, onion, celery, and V8 juice. Cook about 3 hours. Add carrots, potatoes, and brown gravy mix. Turn crockpot down to LOW. Cook 2 more hours.

Mrs. Mary Ranger – St. Louis, Missouri
Wife of Colonel Kelly Ranger

Hopkins County Stew

5–6 pieces chicken (I use at least
 3 boned breasts, split and
 2 or 3 thighs)
1 (16-ounce) can tomatoes
 (add a little chicken broth or
 water to rinse out the can)
2 garlic pods, diced

2 onions, sliced
1 tablespoon chili powder
1 tablespoon sugar
Salt and pepper to taste
2–3 slices bacon, chopped
1 (16-ounce) can cream-style corn
1 or 2 potatoes, cubed

In stockpot or Dutch oven, combine chicken, tomatoes, garlic, onions, and seasonings. Simmer two hours, till chicken is tender.

Remove chicken; cool and debone. Return to pot. Add bacon, corn, and potatoes and cook at a simmer until done, about an hour. Serves 6–8.

Mrs. Paula Johnson – Texarkana, Texas
Wife of First Lt. Dr. William C. Johnson (deceased 1977)

Salute to Salads

An Air Force crew chief salutes a **KC-10 Extender** as it departs for a mission in support of Operation Enduring Freedom.

The KC-10 Extender can combine the tasks of a tanker and cargo aircraft by refueling fighters and simultaneously carrying the fighter support personnel and equipment on overseas deployments. The KC-10 can transport up to 75 people and nearly 170,000 pounds of cargo a distance of about 4,400 miles unrefueled. During boom refueling operations, fuel is transferred to the receiver at a maximum rate of 1,100 gallons per minute; the hose and drogue refueling maximum rate is 470 gallons per minute. Combined, the capacity of KC-10's six tanks carry more than 53,000 gallons (356,000 pounds) of fuel—almost twice as much as the KC-135 Stratotanker.

B. J.'s Vegetable Salad

1 cup sugar
¾ cup vinegar
½ cup vegetable oil
1 (15-ounce) can French-style
    green beans
1 (15-ounce) can shoepeg corn

1 (15-ounce) can tiny peas
1 cup finely diced celery
1 cup finely diced onion
1 cup finely diced bell pepper
½ cup pimento

Boil sugar, vinegar and oil for 1 minute. Cool. Drain and mix canned vegetables. Add celery, onion, bell pepper, and pimento. Pour sugar mixture over vegetables and marinate overnight. Mix frequently until ready to serve. This salad has the best flavor when served cold.

Mrs. Jacquie Hoggard – Denbigh, Virginia
Wife of Lt. Colonel (Ret.) Clarence "Klu" Hoggard

Gail Lay's Pea Salad

2 (10-ounce) boxes frozen
    English peas, thawed
½ cup Miracle Whip
½ cup chopped celery

1 cup chopped green onions
1 cup cocktail peanuts
Chopped green pepper (optional)
Water chestnuts (optional)

Mix all ingredients together. If desired, you can also add green pepper and water chestnuts. Chill at least an hour before serving.

Mrs. Jacquie Hoggard – Denbigh, Virginia
Wife of Lt. Colonel (Ret.) Clarence Hoggard

Snappy Green Bean Salad with Mint

Every time I make these beans, people clamor for the recipe. I first had them at a Bunko party while stationed at Ramstein AFB, Germany. The process of blanching the green beans makes them crunchy. The rest of the ingredients add even more snap. And the dressing with the hint of fresh mint makes you go, "Mmmmmm!" Before I tried this, I only used mint in tea.

1½ pounds fresh green beans	1 cup crumbled feta cheese
1 cup chopped toasted walnuts	½ cup (or more) crispy fried
1 cup diced red onion	bacon pieces

Clean and trim ends of beans and cut in half. Boil 4 quarts of water and cook beans 4 minutes. Strain beans and plunge into ice bath (large bowl of cold water and ice) till cool. Remove and pat dry. Arrange beans in a shallow dish and sprinkle with walnuts, onion, feta, and bacon.

DRESSING:

½ cup light olive oil	1 teaspoon (or more) minced
½ cup finely chopped	garlic
packed fresh mint	¾ teaspoon salt
¼ cup white wine vinegar	½ teaspoon pepper

Blend Dressing ingredients in a food processor or standard blender and pour over beans just before serving. Toss to coat.

Mrs. Melinda Smith – Monument, Colorado
Wife of Lt. Colonel (Ret.) Fred Smith

Corn and Black Bean Salad

Can be served as a salad, or with tortilla chips as a salsa dip.

DRESSING:

2 tablespoons oil	6 tablespoons lime juice
1 teaspoon salt	2 tablespoons cider vinegar
½ teaspoon cumin	Pepper to taste

Mix all above ingredients into a bowl. Set aside.

1 pound frozen sweet whole- kernel corn	4 plum tomatoes, chopped
	1 jalapeño, seeded, chopped
2 tablespoons oil	2 (16-ounce) cans black beans,
4 green onions, chopped	drained, rinsed
1 cup chopped cilantro	2 large avocados, chopped

Heat oven to 450°. Stir corn with oil on cookie sheet and bake for approximately 15 minutes, stirring twice. Let cool.

In large bowl, combine onions, cilantro, tomatoes, jalapeño, black beans, and avocados. Add Dressing and mix. Add cooled corn and mix well. Refrigerate.

Mrs. Marty Holcomb – Athens, Georgia
Wife of Lt. Colonel Pete Holcomb

In military traditions of various times and places, there have been numerous methods of performing salutes, using hand gestures, cannon or rifle shots, hoisting of flags, removal of headgear, flyovers, or other means of showing respect.

A common military hand salute consists of raising the right hand, held flat, to the right eyebrow. In the United States, the hand is slightly canted forward, as if shading the eyes so that the palm is not visible to the one being saluted. Saluting indoors is forbidden except when formally reporting to a superior officer or during an indoor ceremony.

Other salutes include a ceremonial aerial salute called a "flyover," which often accompanies a rendition of "The Star-Spangled Banner." Gun salute by aircraft, primarily displayed during funerals, is the missing man formation, where either a formation of aircraft is conspicuously missing an element, or where a single plane abruptly leaves a formation. A casual salute by an aircraft, somewhat akin to waving to a friend, is the custom of "waggling" the wings by partially rolling the aircraft first to one side, and then the other.

Broccoli Salad

2–3 bunches broccoli
1 pound bacon, cooked
  and crumbled
1/2 cup chopped purple onion
1 1/2 cups chopped lettuce
1/2 cup sunflower seeds

1/2 cup raisins
1 cup mayonnaise
1/2 cup sugar
1 tablespoon vinegar
1 tablespoon lemon juice

Wash broccoli and chop into bite-size pieces. In serving bowl, combine broccoli, bacon, onion, lettuce, sunflower seeds, and raisins. In another bowl, combine mayonnaise, sugar, vinegar, and lemon juice. Pour dressing over broccoli salad. Toss and chill at least one hour.

Mrs. Laurie Smith – Seattle, Washington
Wife of Lt. Colonel Bruce Smith

Spinach Salad and Honey Mustard Dressing

The dressing is the key to this delicious salad.

HONEY MUSTARD DRESSING:

1/2 cup honey
1/2 cup white vinegar
1 cup olive oil

8 teaspoons dried, minced onion
4 tablespoons Dijon mustard
1 1/3 cups mayonnaise

Mix ingredients together with wire whisk and refrigerate until onions are soft. Serve with Spinach Salad.

SPINACH SALAD:

1 large bag fresh spinach leaves,
  washed, stems removed
1 hard-boiled egg, chopped
Fresh mushrooms, sliced
Crumbled bacon

Fresh Parmesan cheese, grated
Mozzarella cheese, grated
  (enough to mix through salad)
Sunflower seeds, salted, roasted

Combine all ingredients in large bowl. Serve with Dressing.

Mrs. Marcia Vanderwood – Cullman, Alabama
Wife of Lt. Colonel Rex S. Vanderwood

Strawberry Romaine Salad

1 cup vegetable oil
¾ cup sugar
½ cup red wine vinegar

2 cloves garlic, crushed
½ teaspoon salt
¼ teaspoon pepper

Combine in jar the oil, sugar, vinegar, garlic, salt, and pepper; shake to combine.

1 head romaine lettuce
1 head Boston lettuce
1 pint sliced strawberries

1 cup shredded Monterrey Jack
    cheese
½ cup toasted chopped walnuts

Combine lettuces, strawberries, cheese, and walnuts. Toss gently with dressing at very last minute.

Mrs. Jenny Monroe – Chicago, Illinois
Wife of Captain Timothy Monroe

Greek Layered Salad

2 heads romaine lettuce
2 large tomatoes, chopped
1 cucumber, peeled, thinly sliced

1 red onion, thinly sliced
4 ounces feta cheese, crumbled
1 cup Greek black olives

Shred lettuce. Put into a large bowl. Layer tomatoes, cucumber, and red onion on top of lettuce. Spread crumbled feta cheese and black olives on top of salad.

DRESSING:
½ cup light olive oil
2 tablespoons red wine vinegar
1 teaspoon oregano

½ teaspoon salt
½ teaspoon pepper

Combine all ingredients together and pour over salad. You may increase amount of oregano to your desired taste.

Mrs. Alice Taylor – Bann / Rheinland-Pfalz-Germany
Wife of Lt. Colonel (Ret.) Kerry Taylor

Sensation Salad Dressing

1 (6-ounce) package grated
Romano cheese
3 cloves garlic, crushed

2 teaspoons salt
4 teaspoons fresh lemon juice
2 cups oil

Combine cheese, garlic, salt, lemon juice, and oil in jar. Shake well.
Refrigerate. Serve over iceberg and romaine lettuce.

Mrs. Frances Anderson – Pineville, Louisiana
Wife of Lt. Colonel (Ret.) Andy Anderson

General 'Hap' Arnold is one of the greatest American military figures of all time. After graduation from the United States Military Academy, Arnold was appointed a Second Lieutenant of Infantry in 1907. In 1911, he became an aviator, and was one of the first flyers taught by the Wright brothers. In June 1912, he established a new altitude record of 6,540 feet.

   In September 1938, Arnold was named Chief of Staff of the Air Corps. The Army Air Forces was established in 1941 and Major General Arnold became Chief of Staff for Air and Chief of the Army Air Forces. In 1942, General Arnold played a key role in the formation of the Women Air Force Service Pilots. Immediately prior to U.S. entry into World War II, Arnold directed the Army Air Force's expansion into the largest and most powerful air force in the world. An advocate of research and development, Arnold's tenure saw the development of the intercontinental bomber, the jet fighter, the extensive use of radar, global airlift, and atomic warfare as mainstays of modern air power.

   General Arnold retired from the service on June 30, 1946, with the ratings of Command Pilot and Combat Observer. His many accomplishments gained him the distinction of becoming the first five-star General of the United States Air Force on May 7, 1949, by an act of Congress.

Blue Cheese and Bacon Potato Salad

20 small red potatoes
2 tablespoons salt
1 cup mayonnaise
¼ cup heavy cream, lightly
  whipped

¼ cup blue cheese, crumbled
½ pound bacon, fried crisp,
  crumbled
¼ cup finely chopped fresh
  parsley

Boil potatoes in salted water until tender. Drain and allow potatoes to cool. Quarter potatoes and put into large bowl. Combine mayonnaise, heavy cream, blue cheese, and bacon. Pour sauce over potatoes and gently stir. Sprinkle with chopped parsley. Makes 8–10 servings.

Mrs. Brenda Burrows – Yorktown, Virginia
Wife of Major (Ret.) Chris Burrows

Caramel Apple Salad

1 (3-ounce) package butterscotch
  instant pudding
1 (8-ounce) carton Cool Whip
1 (8-ounce) can crushed
  pineapple and juice

3 cups chopped Red Delicious
  apples, unpeeled
1 cup miniature marshmallows
1 cup salted dry roasted peanuts

Mix together dry pudding mix, Cool Whip, pineapple and juice until well blended. Stir in apples, marshmallows, and peanuts. Refrigerate and enjoy!

Mrs. Jenny Monroe – Chicago, Illinois
Wife of Captain Timothy Monroe

Lenes Family Fruit Salad

Great with Christmas and Thanksgiving dinner.

2 oranges
2 apples
1 (5-ounce) bottle cherries
1 (8-ounce) can fruit cocktail
1 (8-ounce) can chopped
  pineapple

1 (11-ounce) can Mandarin
  oranges
3 cups sugar
1 (1-quart) carton whipping
  cream

Peel oranges and apples and cut up in large bowl. Open cherries, fruit cocktail, pineapple, and oranges; strain, discarding juice. Mix fruit in bowl; set aside. In separate bowl, mix sugar and whipping cream on low and let get thick. After thick, mix in with fruit, then set in refrigerator at least 30 minutes before serving.

Mrs. Cara Lenes – Dallas, Texas
Wife of Senior Airman Jared Lenes

Fruit Junk

2 eggs, beaten
2 tablespoons lemon juice
2 tablespoons sugar
1 (11-ounce) can Mandarin
  oranges, drained
1 (15-ounce) can pineapple
  chunks, drained

5 bananas, sliced
10 cherries
1 cup miniature marshmallows
1 (½-pint) carton whipping
  cream

Whip eggs with wire whisk. Add lemon juice and sugar. Cook over low heat until thickened. Cool. Mix all fruit and marshmallows in large bowl. Whip cream until thick peaks. Add to cooled egg mixture and blend well. Fold cream and egg mixture into fruit.

Mrs. Barbara McGee – Hampton, Virginia
Wife of Lt. Colonel (Ret.) Guy McGee

Cherry-Cinnamon Jell-O

Great for football parties or celebrations on a cool night. Spicy and delicious!

¼ cup red hots (cinnamon red
   imperils)
1 cup boiling water

1 (3-ounce) package cherry
   Jell-O (regular or sugar-free)
1 (15-ounce) can applesauce

Melt red hots in boiling water; add Jell-O and applesauce. Mix well and pour into 4-cup Jell-O mold; chill until set. Serves 4–5.

Mrs. Nancy Townsend – Colorado Springs, Colorado
Wife of Colonel Bruce Townsend

Cherries in the Snow

1 cup all-purpose flour
½ cup butter, softened
¼ cup brown sugar, firmly
   packed
½ cup chopped nuts
1 (8-ounce) package cream
   cheese, softened

2 cups confectioners' sugar
2 teaspoons vanilla extract
½ pint whipping cream, whipped
1 (21-ounce) can cherry pie filling

Preheat oven to 375°. Combine flour, butter, brown sugar, and nuts in bowl; mix well. Spread in 8-inch-square pan. Bake 15 minutes; cool. Crumble into a 9x13-inch serving dish or a 2-quart casserole dish. Blend cream cheese, confectioner's sugar, and vanilla together into a large bowl. Fold whipped cream into cheese mixture. Spoon over crust. Top with pie filling. Freeze overnight. Let thaw slightly before serving. Makes 12 servings.

Variation: Try other pie fillings such as blueberry, blackberry, raspberry, strawberry, or apple in place of the cherry pie filling.

Mrs. Lori Fluker – Reno, Nevada
Wife of Lt. Colonel Mark Fluker

Mother's Cranberry Salad

1 quart fresh cranberries
2 cups sugar
Mini marshmallows
2 cups halved red seedless grapes
  (or pineapple chunks)

1 cup toasted pecan pieces
Whipped cream or Cool Whip

At least 24 hours before serving time, grind cranberries and mix well with sugar, then add marshmallows. Refrigerate. Fold in grapes (or pineapple) and pecan pieces. Fold in whipped cream or Cool Whip. Refrigerate until ready to serve.

Mrs. Jacquie Hoggard – Denbigh, Virginia
Wife of Lt. Colonel (Ret.) Clarence "Klu" Hoggard

Salad of the Angels

1 (3-ounce) package cream
  cheese, softened
2 tablespoons sugar
2 tablespoons mayonnaise
1 package mini marshmallows

1 (20-ounce) can crushed
  pineapple
12 maraschino cherries, chopped
½ pint whipping cream, whipped
Chopped nuts (optional)

Combine cream cheese, sugar, and mayonnaise. Add marshmallows, pineapple, and cherries. Fold in whipped cream. Add nuts, if desired. Chill.

Master Sergeant Deb Marsh – Hubbard, Ohio

ABC Salad
(Apples and Blue Cheese)

1 head lettuce, torn
2 Red Delicious apples (or your choice), sliced thin

2 (3-ounce) packages blue cheese, crumbled
1 red onion, thinly sliced

Combine salad ingredients and set aside.

POPPY SEED DRESSING:

¾ cup sugar
1 teaspoon dry mustard
2 tablespoons ketchup
1 teaspoon salt

⅓ cup vinegar
1 cup oil
1 tablespoon poppy seeds

Mix sugar, mustard, ketchup, salt, and vinegar. Add oil slowly, beating constantly and continuing to beat until thick. Add poppy seeds and beat for a few minutes. Store in refrigerator. Toss salad gently with prepared dressing just before serving.

Note: This dressing is tasty over fruit, too.

Mrs. Beverly Martin – Bellevue, Nebraska
Wife of Chief Master Sergeant (Ret.) John R. Martin

Pistachio Pudding

1 (3-ounce) box pistachio instant pudding
1 (8-ounce) can crushed pineapple

1 (8-ounce) carton Cool Whip
½ cup chopped nuts

Mix pistachio pudding according to directions on box. Drain crushed pineapple; add to pudding. Let set in refrigerator until slightly firm (30–45 minutes). Fold in Cool Whip. Add chopped nuts.

Master Sergeant Deb Marsh – Hubbard, Ohio

Congealed Spinach Salad with Crabmeat Dressing

9 ounces lime gelatin
3 cups boiling water
½ cup cold water
6 tablespoons vinegar
1½ cups mayonnaise
3 cups cottage cheese

4 tablespoons minced onion
1 cup finely chopped celery
3 (10-ounce) packages frozen
spinach, thawed, drained,
squeezed dry

Dissolve gelatin in boiling water; add cold water and vinegar. Stir in mayonnaise, cottage cheese, onion, celery, and spinach. Mix well. Pour into a 9x13-inch pan that has been sprayed with cooking spray. Refrigerate until congealed. Cut into squares, and serve with Crabmeat Dressing. Serves 12.

CRABMEAT DRESSING:

3 cups mayonnaise
¾ cup chili sauce
6 tablespoons horseradish

½ large onion, finely chopped
Tabasco (optional)
2 cups crabmeat

Mix mayonnaise, chili sauce, horseradish, onion, and Tabasco, if desired, until well combined. Fold in crabmeat. Serve over congealed salad.

Mrs. Monetta Noland – Mobile, Alabama
Wife of Colonel (Ret.) Ronnie Noland

Greek Pasta Salad

1 (1-pound) package medium shell macaroni	1 red sweet bell pepper
1 package Good Seasons Garlic & Herb dry salad dressing mix	1 bunch green onions
	1 (8-ounce) package feta cheese
⅓ cup olive oil	1 (2- to 4-ounce) can chopped black olives

Boil macaroni according to package directions. Meanwhile, empty salad dressing package into an extra large mixing bowl. Add olive oil and mix thoroughly. Set aside.

Wash and drain bell pepper and green onions. Remove and discard stem, seeds, and roots. Dice bell pepper. Chop green onions crosswise into rings. Carefully dice feta cheese into small (¼-inch) cubes. Drain macaroni. While still hot, add macaroni to salad dressing and mix until well-coated. Add bell pepper, green onions, feta cheese, and black olives to macaroni and mix well. Refrigerate and serve cold.

Note: Best made a day ahead to allow flavors to mingle. Store in refrigerator for up to a week. To double recipe, double all ingredients except olive oil—increase to only ½ cup.

Mary Italiano Layman – Perrysburg, Ohio
Wife of Major Phillip A. Layman

Orzo Pasta Salad

I got this recipe from my sister-in-law when we were living at Edwards AFB, California. I have made it at gatherings in Germany, New Mexico, and now here in Hawaii. Everyone who tastes it loves it. The funny thing is, finding the ingredients wherever I live has been interesting. In Germany, I had trouble finding orzo noodles and ended up going to Luxembourg to find them. In New Mexico, I could find as many jalapeño peppers as I wanted for a small amount of money. Now here in Hawaii, not only do I have trouble finding jalapeños, but when they are in the stores, they are $6.99/lb. and up!

1 red bell pepper
1 yellow bell pepper
1 small purple onion
½ pound orzo pasta, cooked
   according to package
   directions, cooled
2 (15-ounce) cans black beans,
   rinsed well
2–3 fresh jalapeño peppers,
   seeds removed

2 cloves garlic, mashed with
   ½ teaspoon salt
3–6 tablespoons fresh lime juice
⅓ cup vinegar (red wine, rice,
   or a mixture)
⅔ cup olive oil
1½ teaspoons cumin
Cilantro, chopped
Avocado, peeled and cubed

Dice the red and yellow peppers and purple onion and mix with cooled pasta and beans. Process jalapeños, garlic, lime juice, vinegar, olive oil, and cumin in a food processor until smooth, then pour over pasta, beans, and peppers. Stir in fresh cilantro and cubed avocados just before serving.

Note: Orzo is rice-shaped pasta.

Mrs. Jackie Gaffner – Waimea, Hawaii
Wife of Master Sergeant (Ret.) Kevin Gaffner

Chicken Tortellini Salad

¼ cup red wine vinegar
4 shakes Tabasco
1 (10-ounce) package cooked
  seasoned chicken breast chunks
2 green onions, chopped
½ yellow bell pepper, chopped
½ red bell pepper, chopped
⅜ cup raisins
½ cup halved seedless green
  grapes
½ cup halved seedless red grapes

¾ tablespoon Italian seasoning
1½ teaspoons dill weed
1 clove garlic, minced
¾ teaspoon celery seed
⅛ teaspoon salt
⅛ teaspoon pepper
Juice of 1½ lemons
⅜ cup poppy seed dressing
1 (13½-ounce) package cheese
  and herb tortellini, cooked

Combine vinegar and Tabasco. Mix with chicken breasts, onions, bell peppers, raisins, grapes, Italian seasoning, dill, garlic, celery seed, salt, pepper, lemon juice, and poppy seed dressing. Add tortellini and toss. Refrigerate for several hours.

Mrs. Melanie Hostetler – Baton Rouge, Louisiana
Wife of First Lt. Jacob Hostetler

Chicken Caesar Pasta Salad

1 (8-ounce) package mini
  penne, cooked, drained
2 cups diced cooked chicken

1 cup creamy Caesar dressing
½ cup grated Parmesan cheese
Salt and pepper to taste

Mix all ingredients and chill until ready to serve.

Mrs. Laurie Smith – Seattle Washington
Wife of Lt. Colonel Bruce Smith

Garden Twist Macaroni Salad

1 (12-ounce) package spiral
  pasta
½ bunch green onions, chopped
1 small cucumber, sliced
  very thin

½ cup finely chopped celery
¼ cup finely chopped green
  bell pepper
¼ cup shredded carrots

Cook pasta according to package directions. Drain and cool. Add green onions, cucumber, celery, green pepper, and carrots.

DRESSING:
½ teaspoon salt
½ cup sugar
⅔ cup oil
½ teaspoon celery seed

⅛ teaspoon black pepper
2 teaspoons prepared mustard
2 tablespoons mayonnaise

Mix all Dressing ingredients in blender. Pour over pasta salad mixture. Stir well. Refrigerate overnight.

Mrs. Tara Hansen – Fort Worth, Texas
Wife of Captain Eydin Hansen

Japanese Chicken Salad

¼ cup soy sauce
¼ cup sugar
4 chicken breasts
2 packages won ton wrappers,
  cut into halves
1 (2-ounce) package rice noodles

Peanut oil
4 green onions, chopped
2 tablespoons toasted sesame
  seeds
2 tablespoons chopped or sliced
  almonds

Combine soy sauce and sugar. Marinate chicken breasts in mixture about an hour.

Preheat oven to 350°. Bake chicken in marinade for 1 hour, covered. Dice chicken. Fry won ton pieces in peanut oil. Fry rice noodles in peanut oil. Drain on paper towels. Combine chicken, won tons, rice noodles, green onions, sesame seeds, and almonds in bowl.

DRESSING:

2 tablespoons sugar
1 teaspoon Ac'cent
½ teaspoon pepper
¼ teaspoon oil

1 tablespoon sesame seed oil
3–4 tablespoons Japanese rice
  wine vinegar

Combine sugar, Ac'cent, pepper, oil, sesame seed oil, and rice wine vinegar. Pour over salad and stir well. Serves 6–8.

Mrs. Cathy Harvey – Georgetown, South Carolina
Wife of Lt. Colonel Joe Harvey

Oriental Salad

2 packages ramen noodles
¼ cup butter
1 (4-ounce) package sliced
   almonds

2 tablespoons sesame seeds
1 head Chinese (Napa) cabbage
1 bunch green onions, chopped

Break noodles into small pieces; discard seasoning package. Melt butter in saucepan. Brown noodles, almonds, and sesame seeds in butter. Cool. Slice cabbage into small pieces. Add chopped green onions. Pour Dressing over cabbage mixture. Toss and serve.

DRESSING:
½ cup sugar
¾ cup oil

¼ cup white vinegar
2 tablespoons soy sauce

Boil sugar, oil, vinegar, and soy sauce together for 1 minute. Cool.

Mrs. Beverly Martin – Bellevue, Nebraska
Wife of Chief Master Sergeant (Ret.) John R. Martin

The United States Forces Japan (USFJ) refers to the various divisions of the United States Armed Forces that are stationed in Japan. Under the Treaty of Mutual Cooperation and Security between the United States and Japan, the USAF is obliged to defend Japan in close cooperation with the Japan Self-Defense Forces.

After the Japanese surrendered in World War II, the United States Armed Forces acquired the overall administrative authority in Japan. The Japanese Imperial Army and Navy were decommissioned and all of their military bases were taken over by the United States. After the Korean War began in 1950, Douglas MacArthur, the Supreme Commander of the Allied Powers in Japan, ordered the Japanese government to establish the paramilitary "Reserved Police," which was later developed into the Japan Self-Defense Forces. The Treaty of Mutual Cooperation and Security was signed between the United States and Japan in 1960, and is still in effect. As of 2007 there are 33,453 U.S. military personnel stationed in Japan, and another 5,500 American civilians employed there by the United States Department of Defense. The United States Seventh Fleet is based in Yokosuka. One hundred thirty USAF fighters are stationed in the Misawa Air Base and Kadena Air Base.

Sara's Hot Chicken Salad

3 cups cubed cooked chicken
½ cup slivered almonds
2 cups minced celery
1 cup mayonnaise
2 tablespoons lemon juice
1 cup small mushrooms

2 teaspoons grated onion
1 cup sliced water chestnuts
2 tablespoons pimento
½ cup minced bell pepper
½ cup grated Cheddar cheese
1 cup crushed potato chips

Combine chicken, almonds, celery, mayonnaise, lemon juice, mushrooms, onion, water chestnuts, pimento, and bell pepper, and pour into a 2-quart casserole dish. Mix cheese and potato chips and sprinkle on top. Bake at 375° for 25 minutes.

Mrs. Sara Tosten – Alexandria, Louisiana
Wife of Lt. Colonel (Ret.) Charles T. Tosten, Jr.

Hot Chicken Salad

2 cups chopped cooked chicken
2 cups chopped celery
⅓ cup chopped bell pepper
3 tablespoons pimento strips
1 teaspoon lemon juice
1 teaspoon salt

2 tablespoons chopped onion
½ cup mayonnaise
½ cup slivered almonds
⅓ cup grated mild Cheddar
Crushed potato chips

Preheat oven to 350°. Blend chicken, celery, bell pepper, pimento strips, lemon juice, salt, onion, and mayonnaise. Pour into an 8x8-inch pan. Top with slivered almonds, cheese, and crushed potato chips. Bake 25–30 minutes.

Staff Sergeant Christy M. Hardy – Douglas, Georgia
Wife of Staff Sergeant Christopher Hardy

Crowd-Pleasing Cornbread Salad

DRESSING:

1 cup sugar
⅔ cup vegetable oil
⅔ cup ketchup
⅔ cup vinegar

2 teaspoons minced onion
1 teaspoon salt
1 teaspoon pepper

Whisk ingredients together in a bowl. Refrigerate, covered, 8–12 hours.

4 (6-ounce) packages yellow
cornbread mix
1 (10-ounce) can green chiles,
drained, chopped
2 (15-ounce) cans pinto beans,
rinsed, drained
2 (15-ounce) cans whole-kernel
corn, drained

2 green bell peppers, finely
chopped
4 large tomatoes, chopped
1 red onion, chopped
1 (16-ounce) package shredded
Cheddar cheese

Prepare cornbread using package directions, stirring chiles into batter before baking. Cool completely, and cut into 2-inch squares. Place cornbread squares in a large salad bowl. Layer with beans, corn, bell peppers, tomatoes, and onion. Sprinkle with cheese. Toss before serving. Serve with Dressing. Yields 20 servings.

Mrs. Connie Leetsch – Abilene, Texas
Wife of Chief Master Sergeant (Ret.) Cecil H. Leetsch
Mrs. Leetsch also served in the Women's Air Force from 1951–1954.

Insignia of the United States Air Force

The standard USAF uniform is decorated with an insignia to designate rank. USAF rank is divided between enlisted airmen, noncommissioned officers, and commissioned officers, and ranges from "airman basic" to the commissioned rank of general. Promotions are granted based on a combination of test scores, years of experience, and selection board approval. Among enlisted men and noncommissioned officers, rankings are generally designated by increasing numbers of insignia chevrons. Commissioned officer rank is designated by bars, oak leaves, a silver eagle, and anywhere from one to five stars. (Five stars are awarded only in war-time or as honorary.)

Commissioned Officers

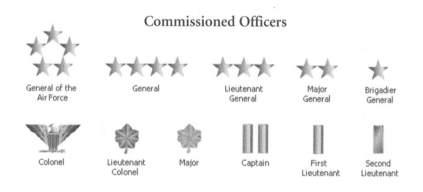

General of the Air Force	General	Lieutenant General	Major General	Brigadier General

Colonel	Lieutenant Colonel	Major	Captain	First Lieutenant	Second Lieutenant

Enlisted and Non-Commissioned Offers

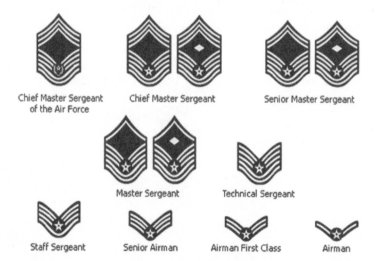

Chief Master Sergeant of the Air Force   Chief Master Sergeant   Senior Master Sergeant

Master Sergeant   Technical Sergeant

Staff Sergeant   Senior Airman   Airman First Class   Airman

Victorious Vegetables

The **F-15E Strike Eagle** is a modern American all-weather strike fighter, designed for long-range interdiction of enemy ground targets deep behind enemy lines. A derivative of the F-15 Eagle air superiority fighter, the Strike Eagle proved its worth in Desert Storm, carrying out deep strikes against high-value targets, performing "Wild Weasel" patrols and providing close air support for coalition troops. The F-15E Strike Eagle can be distinguished from other U.S. Eagle variants by its darker camouflage and the conformal fuel tanks mounted along the engine intakes.

Patacones

Green plantains
Oil for frying

Salt to taste

The green plantains are salty. Slice into ½-inch pieces. Fry them lightly in vegetable oil until golden–a few at a time is easier. Drain on paper towels. Press them down until flattened. Deep-fry again until golden. Salt to taste. May serve them with Mojo. You may shave plantain into thin long slices and deep-fry until golden brown. They are a lot like potato chips.

MOJO:

Olive oil, infused with minced garlic and chopped yellow onion
1 cup oil

6 cloves garlic, minced
1 whole onion, minced
Juice from 1 lemon

Combine ingredients. Let sit for a couple of days prior to using. Use for dipping or seasoning meats or chicken.

Mrs. Irene Morgan – Fort Lauderdale, Florida
Wife of Captain Clifford W. Morgan

Yucca Fingers

Frozen yucca (casaba)
Bacon bits
Salt and pepper

Oil for frying
Ranch Dressing

Cook yucca in water with salt until tender. Drain and mash, taking out thick fibers. Add bacon bits and salt and pepper; mix well. Wait until mass has cooled off and then roll into size of fingers. Place them in a sheet of wax paper to avoid sticking to anything. Deep-fry in vegetable oil until lightly golden. Serve with ranch dressing for dipping or Mojo (recipe above).

Mrs. Irene Morgan – Fort Lauderdale, Florida
Wife of Captain Clifford W. Morgan

Blue Ribbon Baked Onions

While visiting my parents in Prescott, Arizona, I decided to enter the local county fair baking contest in the vegetable category. This recipe won a blue ribbon!

2 tablespoons butter	Bread crumbs, buttered to
2 tablespoons white wine	cover top
1 tablespoon Worcestershire	1 teaspoon oregano
6 or 7 large onions, sliced	½ cup grated Parmesan cheese
¼ pound sharp cheese,	
shredded	

Preheat oven to 350°. Add butter, wine, and Worcestershire to sliced onions, and pour into buttered pie plate. Add a layer of shredded cheese, then cover with crumbled and buttered bread crumbs. Sprinkle with a little oregano and Parmesan cheese. Bake 20 minutes.

Mrs. Linda Rufi – Tucson, Arizona
Wife of Chief Master Sergeant (Ret.) Tony Rufi

Classic Sweet Potato Casserole

3 cups cooked sweet potatoes	2 eggs, beaten
½ cup sugar	½ cup butter, melted
½ teaspoon salt	½ teaspoon vanilla

Preheat oven to 350°. Combine potatoes, sugar, salt, eggs, butter, and vanilla in mixer. Pour into 2-quart casserole dish. Sprinkle with Topping and bake 30 minutes.

TOPPING:

⅔ cup brown sugar	⅓ cup flour
1 cup chopped pecans	⅓ cup butter, melted

Mix all ingredients together. Sprinkle over sweet potato casserole.

Mrs. Cathy Harvey – Georgetown, South Carolina
Wife of Lt. Colonel Joe Harvey

Really Creamy Potatoes

2–3 pounds small new red
  potatoes, cut to 1½-inch
  cubes
1 stick butter or margarine
½–¾ cup heavy whipping
  cream (or half-and-half or milk)

3 tablespoons cornstarch
¼ teaspoon black pepper
¼ teaspoon celery seed
Salt to taste

Boil potatoes in water to cover till just before tender; remove from heat and pour out half the water. Add butter and allow it to melt. Add cream. Mix cornstarch with just enough hot water to make a slushy paste. Return potatoes to heat and slowly bring to a simmer. Gradually add cornstarch paste while stirring. Add pepper and celery seed. Add salt to taste, remove from heat, and allow to sit 5 minutes.

Staff Sergeant Christy M. Hardy – Douglas, Georgia
Wife of Staff Sergeant Christopher Hardy

Super Yum Potatoes

1 stick plus 6 tablespoons
  butter, melted, divided
6–8 potatoes, cooked, peeled,
  and shredded
1 (10¾-ounce) can cream of
  chicken soup

1 (16-ounce) carton sour cream
⅓ cup chopped onion
1 cup shredded Cheddar cheese
1 teaspoon salt
2 cup crushed cornflakes

In casserole dish, pour 1 stick melted butter over potatoes. Combine soup, sour cream, onion, cheese, and salt; pour over potatoes and mix. Combine remaining 6 tablespoons butter with cornflakes and sprinkle on top of potatoes. Bake at 350° for 30–45 minutes.

Mrs. Cathy Harvey – Georgetown, South Carolina
Wife of Lt. Colonel Joe Harvey

Potatoes Charlotte

10 medium potatoes, peeled,
diced
6 tablespoons butter, divided
⅓ cup chopped chives, or 3 green
onions, chopped
1 teaspoon salt
½ teaspoon pepper
1 cup sour cream
1 (8-ounce) package cream
cheese, room temperature
Paprika

Preheat oven to 350°. Boil potatoes in water to cover until tender; drain and mash; add 4 tablespoons butter, chives, salt, and pepper. Combine sour cream and cream cheese. Mix together with potatoes.

Pour into well-greased 2-quart casserole dish. Dot with remaining 2 tablespoons butter and sprinkle with paprika. Bake approximately 25 minutes.

Mrs. Samantha Laidlaw – Ft. Walton Beach, Florida
Wife of Captain Brian Laidlaw

Cheese Potatoes

This recipe is one of our family favorites, and I consider it to be my mother's "specialty." It was the dish that had to be made each Easter, Thanksgiving, and Christmas when I was growing up. It always goes over well. I have brought this dish to many holidays that we have shared with our Air Force friends.

2 pounds frozen, cubed hash
browns
2 (10¾-ounce) cans cream of
potato soup
2 cups shredded Cheddar cheese
(or more, to taste)
1 stick butter, melted
1 (16-ounce) carton sour cream
Salt and pepper to taste

Preheat oven to 350°. Mix all ingredients together and put into a buttered 9x13-inch pan. Bake 2 hours, stirring every half hour.

Mrs. Lisa Hook – Minot, North Dakota
Wife of Captain Patrick Hook

Libby's Make-Ahead Mashed Potatoes

5 pounds potatoes, cooked, mashed
2 cups sour cream

1 (8-ounce) package cream cheese
Salt and pepper to taste
½ stick butter

Mix together mashed potatoes, sour cream, cream cheese, salt and pepper. Place in bowl with cover. Refrigerate until ready to use.

Preheat oven to 350°. Top with pats of butter and bake until heated through, about 45 minutes.

Senior Master Sergeant (Ret.) Ray Graber – Panama City, Florida

Copper Pennies

2 pounds carrots, sliced
1 small green bell pepper, thinly sliced
1 medium onion, sliced
1 (10¾-ounce) can condensed tomato soup

¾ cup apple cider vinegar
½ cup oil
1 cup sugar
1 teaspoon mustard
1 teaspoon Worcestershire
Salt and pepper to taste

Cook carrots in salted water until tender. Rinse; arrange in layers of carrots, green pepper, and onion in dish or bowl. Combine remaining ingredients in a saucepan. Bring to a boil, stirring thoroughly until blended. Pour marinade over carrot mixture and refrigerate overnight.

Mrs. Duchess Sicay – Union, South Carolina
Wife of Major (Ret.) George Sicay

Roasted Winter Vegetables

1–2 pounds small red potatoes
(or frozen whole red potatoes)
1–2 pounds small whole beets
(or canned whole beets,
rinsed, drained)

1 small bag baby carrots
1 pound Brussels sprouts
3–4 teaspoons olive oil
Salt and pepper to taste

Preheat oven to 425°. Clean and trim all vegetables. Combine all above and mix well on a jellyroll pan. Bake 20–30 minutes.

Mrs. Nancy Townsend – Colorado Springs, Colorado
Wife of Colonel Bruce Townsend

Broccoli Puff

1 (10-ounce) package frozen
chopped broccoli
1 (10¾-ounce) can cream of
mushroom soup (or cream
of chicken)
3 ounces sharp or medium
Cheddar cheese, shredded

¼ cup milk
¼ cup mayonnaise
1 egg, beaten
¼ cup fine dry bread crumbs
1 tablespoon butter, melted

Preheat oven to 350°. Cook broccoli according to package directions, omitting salt. Drain thoroughly. Place broccoli in greased 6x10x1½-inch buttered baking dish. Stir together condensed soup and shredded cheese. Gradually add milk, mayonnaise, and beaten egg to soup mixture; stirring until well blended. Pour over broccoli in baking dish. Combine bread crumbs and melted butter in a separate dish. Sprinkle evenly over soup mixture. Bake 45 minutes. Serves 8–10.

Major Odette Perkins – Sacramento, California

Super Special Baked Cauliflower

2 (10-ounce) packages frozen
cauliflower
1 pound bacon, fried crisp,
crumbled
1 (10¾-ounce) can cream of
mushroom soup

½ cup plain dry bread crumbs
½ cup sour cream
1 tablespoon chopped pimento
¼ cup shredded Cheddar cheese

Preheat oven to 350°. Cook cauliflower according to package directions. Drain and place in a greased 8x8-inch baking dish. Combine bacon, soup, bread crumbs, sour cream, and pimento together. Pour over cauliflower. Sprinkle with shredded cheese. Bake 20 minutes. Serves 6–8.

Mrs. Brenda Burrows – Yorktown, Virginia
Wife of Major (Ret.) Chris Burrows

Fried Cabbage

1 large head cabbage
Cooking oil
1 (2-pound) tin cooked ham,
or 2–3 cups chopped ham

Lemon pepper
Seasoned salt

Cut up cabbage and rinse. Heat enough oil to cover bottom of a large pot. Put cabbage in—be careful, it may splatter. Stir until cabbage is saturated. Pour in ham and stir again. Shake in some lemon pepper and seasoned salt to taste. Cook, stirring occasionally, till cabbage is wilted.

Master Sergeant (Ret.) Catherine "Cat" Hardy
– Baltimore, Maryland

Grandma's Cabbage Casserole

3 tablespoons butter
2 tablespoons flour
1 teaspoon salt
⅛ teaspoon pepper
1 teaspoon prepared mustard
1⅓ cups milk
1 egg yolk, beaten

2 cups shredded cabbage, divided
1 small onion, thinly sliced, divided
1 cup shredded Cheddar cheese, divided
1 cup Ritz Cracker crumbs, divided

Preheat oven to 375°. Melt butter in saucepan. Add flour, salt, pepper, and mustard. Stir constantly until bubbly. Slowly pour in milk. Stir until thickened. Add egg yolk and stir well. Place 1 cup shredded cabbage in an 8x8-inch baking dish. Layer cabbage with half of onion, cheese, and cracker crumbs. Repeat with remaining cabbage and onions, cheese and cracker crumbs. Pour sauce over top. Cover and bake 20 minutes. Remove cover and bake additional 5 minutes. Serves 6–8.

Mrs. Brenda Burrows – Yorktown, Virginia
Wife of Major (Ret.) Chris Burrows

Mexican-Style Corn-Cheese Casserole

2 (15-ounce) cans cream-style corn
1 onion, minced, sautéed in 1 stick butter
1 (6-ounce) package Mexican-style cornbread mix

1 cup grated sharp Cheddar cheese
1 egg, beaten

Preheat oven to 325°. Mix cream corn, onion-butter mixture, cornbread mix, cheese, and egg, and pour into greased casserole. Bake 25 minutes.

Colonel (Ret.) Ronald G. Noland – Baton Rouge, Louisiana

Corn Scallop

1 (8-ounce) can cream-style corn
1 (8-ounce) can whole-kernel
  corn, undrained
1 (8-ounce) package corn
  muffin mix
1 stick butter, melted

1 cup sour cream
2 eggs, slightly beaten
1 (4-ounce) can green chiles,
  chopped
Tabasco (optional)

Preheat oven to 350°. Mix both cans of corn, muffin mix, butter, sour cream, eggs, and green chiles together well. Add Tabasco, if desired. Pour into 7x11-inch greased baking dish. Bake 40 minutes. Serves 8.

Mrs. Barbara McGee – Hampton, Virginia
Wife of Lt. Colonel (Ret.) Guy McGee

Faye's Escalloped Corn

2 eggs
1 (15-ounce) can whole-kernel
  corn, drained
½ cup milk

1 cup bread or cracker crumbs
1 teaspoon salt
¼ teaspoon pepper
2 tablespoon melted butter

Preheat oven to 350°. Beat eggs well and add corn, milk, crumbs, seasonings, and melted butter. Bake in buttered pan for about 1 hour, or until no milk runs out when pierced with knife.

Karel Huether – Glendive, Montana
Wife of Master Sergeant (Ret.) Ernie Huether

In 1995, the following core values for the United States Air Force were approved:
    1. Integrity First
    2. Service Before Self
    3. Excellence in All We Do
The Air Education and Training Command along with the USAF Academy are responsible for teaching these principles throughout the Air Force.

Corn Pudding

1 tablespoon cornstarch
2 cups milk
2 cups canned or frozen corn

3 tablespoons butter, melted
1 teaspoon salt
2–3 eggs, slightly beaten

Preheat oven to 325°. Combine cornstarch and milk. Mix corn (drained, if canned), butter, salt, and beaten eggs with the milk/cornstarch mixture. Pour into oiled 8- or 9-inch baking pan. Bake 45–60 minutes until set and slightly golden.

Mrs. Nancy Townsend – Colorado Springs, Colorado
Wife of Colonel Bruce Townsend

Sugar's Butternut Squash Casserole

1 butternut squash
1 cup white sugar
1½ cups milk
1 teaspoon vanilla extract
Pinch of salt

2 tablespoons all-purpose flour
3 eggs
¼ teaspoon ginger
¼ cup margarine, melted

Microwave squash on HIGH 2–3 minutes. Cut in half, scoop out seeds, and cube. Bring large pot of water to a boil. Add squash and cook until tender, approximately 15 minutes.

Preheat oven to 425°. Combine the squash with remaining ingredients. Bake in 9x13-inch baking dish 45 minutes.

TOPPING:
16 ounces gingersnap cookies, crushed

4 tablespoons margarine, softened
1 cup brown sugar

In a medium bowl, combine Topping ingredients. Crumble over top of squash mixture; return to oven and cook until browned.

Mrs. Frances Anderson – Pineville, Louisiana
Wife of Lt. Colonel (Ret.) Andy Anderson

Zucchini and Squash Casserole

3 zucchini, peeled, sliced
3 yellow squash, peeled, sliced
1 large onion, sliced
1 cup cooked rice
1 (14½-ounce) can diced
   tomatoes (reserve juice)
½ stick butter
1 teaspoon minced garlic
1 teaspoon oregano
Salt and pepper to taste
½ cup mozzarella cheese
½ cup grated Parmesan cheese

Preheat oven to 350°. In two layers, place ½ the zucchini, squash, and onion in 9x13-inch baking dish. Spread all rice and tomatoes over zucchini and squash. Pinch pieces of butter off and place all on top of rice and tomato layer; season with half the spices. Repeat with layer of zucchini and squash; season again. Cover and bake 50 minutes. Remove from oven and top with mozzarella and Parmesan cheese. Bake 10 more minutes or until cheese melts.

Mrs. Barbara McGee – Hampton, Virginia
Wife of Lt. Colonel (Ret.) Guy McGee

Squash Casserole

8–10 medium squash, sliced
   into rounds
1 teaspoon salt
1 (10¾-ounce) can cream of
   mushroom soup
¼ stick butter or margarine,
   melted
1 cup sour cream
2 cups Pepperidge Farm herb
   stuffing mix
1 cup shredded Cheddar cheese

Boil squash in water to cover with salt until tender. Drain.
Preheat oven to 350°. Combine soup, butter, and sour cream. Combine squash, soup mixture, and stuffing. Pour into greased 2-quart casserole dish. Top with cheese. Bake 30–40 minutes.

Mrs. Cathy Harvey – Georgetown, South Carolina
Wife of Lt. Colonel Joe Harvey

Creamed Spinach

2 (10-ounce) packages frozen
 spinach
1 (8-ounce) package cream cheese

1 teaspoon lemon juice
Salt and pepper to taste

Cook spinach as directed on package. Drain very well. Add cream cheese and lemon juice. Cook over low heat until cheese is melted. Add salt and pepper to taste.

Major Rhonda Donze – Melbourne, Florida
Wife of Lt. Colonel (Ret.) Robert Donze

Spinach and Artichoke Casserole

2 (10-ounce) boxes frozen
 chopped spinach
1 (8-ounce) package cream
 cheese
1 (15-ounce) can small
 artichoke hearts, chopped
 and drained

1 onion, chopped
½ stick butter
1 cup grated mozzarella cheese
½ cup grated Parmesan cheese

Boil spinach in a small amount of water; squeeze dry, then return to pan. Add block of cream cheese to pan and stir until melted. In another pan, sauté artichokes and onion in butter. Add to spinach. Add mozzarella and Parmesan (reserve some of each for topping) and pour into a casserole dish. Top with small amount of remaining mozzarella and Parmesan. Eat right now, or heat later at 350° for 10–15 minutes.

Colonel (Ret.) Ronald G. Noland – Baton Rouge, Louisiana

Roasted Asparagus

1–2 bunches fresh asparagus
Fresh ground pepper to taste
1 teaspoon salt

1–2 teaspoons olive oil
1 teaspoon dill or rosemary
(optional)

Preheat oven to 425°. Combine all ingredients on a jellyroll pan, mix well with your hands, and bake 20–25 minutes. Serves 2–4.

Note: My favorite way is to wrap the asparagus with a little piece of Italian ham, and roast as above—minus the salt.

Mrs. Nancy Townsend – Colorado Springs, Colorado
Wife of Colonel Bruce Townsend

Almond Mushroom Asparagus

1 pound fresh asparagus, or
  2 (10-ounce) packages frozen
  asparagus, cooked, drained
¼ cup fresh mushrooms, sliced
2 tablespoons butter
2 tablespoons flour

½ teaspoon salt
⅛ teaspoon pepper
1 cup half-and-half
½ cup almonds, chopped, toasted
½ cup grated Parmesan cheese

Preheat oven to 450°. Arrange asparagus in a 1½-quart baking dish. In saucepan, sauté mushrooms in butter. Sprinkle flour over sautéed mushrooms and stir well 1 minute. Add salt and pepper. Slowly pour in half-and-half; stir until thickened. Pour over asparagus. Sprinkle with almonds and Parmesan cheese. Bake 5 minutes or until cheese melts. Serves 4.

Mrs. Brenda Burrows – Yorktown, Virginia
Wife of Major (Ret.) Chris Burrows

World's Best Baked Beans

1 pound dry navy beans
1 pound ground sausage
   (or bacon)
1½ teaspoons salt
¼ teaspoon pepper

½ cup brown sugar
¼ cup molasses
2 medium onions, chopped
1 cup ketchup
Water to cover

Soak beans in water overnight. Drain and rinse beans. Brown sausage. Combine beans, sausage, salt, pepper, brown sugar, molasses, onions, and ketchup in heavy pan. Add enough water to just cover beans. Boil 1 hour or until beans are soft. Make sure you stir frequently and check for water amount. You don't want the water to run low, or beans will dry out and burn. Once softened, pour bean mixture into a baking dish.

Preheat oven to 300°. Bake about 6 hours. This can also be done in a crockpot.

Mrs. Denise Hoyt – Oxford, Nebraska
Wife of Lt. Colonel (Ret.) Jeff Hoyt

Baked Lima Beans

1 pound dry lima beans
1 teaspoon salt
1 green bell pepper, finely
   chopped
1 medium onion, finely chopped
5 stalks celery, finely chopped

2 tablespoons brown sugar
Salt and pepper to taste
1 (10¾-ounce) can tomato soup
⅓ cup ketchup
1 tablespoon mustard
6 slices bacon

Soak lima beans in water overnight. Boil 30 minutes with salt. Drain the beans. Add green pepper, onion, celery, brown sugar, salt and pepper, tomato soup, ketchup, and mustard. Stir well. Pour into baking dish. Cover with sliced bacon. Bake 1 hour in 325° oven.

Mrs. Brenda Burrows – Yorktown, Virginia
Wife of Major (Ret.) Chris Burrows

Home Sweet Beans

My husband Tommy Foil and I were good friends in the Air Force with Ray and Aileen Deselms and did a lot of camping together. This was Aileen's recipe that was a favorite to take along.

Many years after retirement, Ray and I lost our spouses. When Hurricane Katrina hit, Ray in Colorado called me in Baton Rouge to see if I was okay. We talked often, and were soon taking trips to visit each other.

One Thursday about a year later, we decided . . . we're 75 and 89 . . . we might as well get married while we're still young! My family was having a big reunion that Saturday, so why not surprise everybody and get married with family there? Having begged city clerks to wave the 72-hour clause, we were joined in marriage by minister cousin Kevin, while the rest of the cousins and some of Ray's family witnessed on benches and tables under a park pavilion. "These two have 110 years of married life between them," Kevin acknowledged, "so I think they know what they're doing." Through tears of joy, everyone agreed it was a privilege and a delight to witness our wonderfully happy spontaneous wedding. We honeymoon all the time now in Ray's big RV!

1 (15-ounce) can green beans	½ cup chopped celery
1 (15-ounce) can wax beans	½ cup oil
1 (15-ounce) can red kidney	½ cup vinegar
beans	¾ cup sugar
½ cup chopped green bell	1 teaspoon salt
pepper	½ teaspoon pepper
½ cup chopped onion	

Drain all beans. Mix all ingredients together. Let marinate at least 12 hours.

Mrs. Elizabeth Foil Deselms – Donna, Texas
Wife of Master Sergeant (Ret.) Tommy Foil (deceased)
and now Lt. Colonel (Ret.) Ray Deselms

JP's Famous Seabee Baked Beans

JP was a Seabee in the Navy in World War II. This recipe is named in honor of the man who taught me how to make the best baked beans I've ever eaten.

1 onion, chopped
¼ pound uncooked bacon,
  chopped
1 (28-ounce) can baked beans

1 cup tomato ketchup
½ cup honey or brown sugar
1 tablespoon garlic powder
1 tablespoon onion powder

Sauté onions and bacon together until the onions are clear and bacon is browned. Add beans, ketchup, honey or brown sugar, garlic powder, and onion powder. Stir together and let simmer over low heat 30–45 minutes.

Master Sergeant (Ret.) Thomas Melvin – Minot, North Dakota

Eggplant Parmigiana

1 eggplant
1 onion, finely chopped
¼ cup plus 1 teaspoon oil
2 (16-ounce) cans tomato sauce
1 tablespoon sugar
3 eggs

½ teaspoon salt
½ teaspoon pepper
2 cups Italian bread crumbs
Oil for frying
2 cups shredded mozzarella
  cheese, divided

Peel and slice eggplant into rounds. Sauté onion in oil until transparent. Add tomato sauce and sugar. Let simmer 30 minutes over medium-low heat. Stir frequently. In a medium-size bowl, beat eggs with salt and pepper. Dip eggplant into eggs and then bread crumbs. Pan-fry in hot oil. Drain on paper towels.

Preheat oven to 350°. Layer half of fried eggplant in bottom of 9x13-inch casserole dish. Spread half of tomato sauce over eggplant. Sprinkle with half of cheese. Repeat layers ending with sauce and cheese. Bake 30 minutes. Allow to rest 5 minutes before serving. Serves 4.

Mrs. Cathy Harvey – Georgetown, South Carolina
Wife of Lt. Colonel Joe Harvey

Fried Green Tomatoes

Vegetable oil for frying
⅔ cups all-purpose flour
2 teaspoons salt

⅛ teaspoon pepper
3 pounds green tomatoes, cut
into ½-inch slices

Heat oil. Mix flour, salt and pepper. Coat tomato slices in flour mixture; fry in hot oil until golden brown. Drain on paper towels.

Mrs. Sara Tosten – Alexandria, Louisiana
Wife of Lt. Colonel (Ret.) Charles T. Tosten, Jr.

Pineapple Casserole

Great with ham.

2 sticks butter, softened
2 cups sugar
6 eggs, beaten
10–12 slices white bread

2 (15-ounce) cans crushed
pineapple, undrained
Dash of salt

Preheat oven to 400°. Cream butter and sugar. Add eggs. Stir well. Cut bread into small cubes (electric knife works great); add to mixture with pineapple, and stir well. Place in greased 9x13-inch baking pan, and bake 45 minutes.

Mrs. Barbara McGee – Hampton, Virginia
Wife of Lt. Colonel (Ret.) Guy McGee

Presidential
Pasta & Rice

The mission of the **VC-25** aircraft—*Air Force One*—is to provide air transport for the president of the United States. The presidential air transport fleet consists of two specially configured Boeing 747-200B's—tail numbers 28000 and 29000—with the Air Force designation VC-25. While these planes are referred to as *"Air Force One"* only while the president is onboard, the term is commonly used to describe either of the two aircraft normally used and maintained by the U.S. Air Force solely for the president. These aircraft are flown by the presidential aircrew, maintained by the presidential maintenance branch, and are assigned to Air Mobility Command's 89th Airlift Wing at Andrews Air Force Base in Maryland.

Baked Ziti

1 (16-ounce) package ziti
1 pound ground beef
1 (15-ounce) carton ricotta
   cheese
½ cup grated Parmesan
1 egg, slightly beaten

¾ teaspoon salt
¼ teaspoon pepper
1 (29-ounce) jar spaghetti sauce,
   divided
1 (8-ounce) package shredded
   mozzarella cheese

Cook ziti as package directs; drain. Set aside. Cook ground beef until well browned; drain. Add ricotta, Parmesan cheese, egg, salt, pepper, and ⅓ of spaghetti sauce. Add ziti and gently toss. Spoon into 9x13-inch pan; add mozzarella and remaining sauce. Bake in preheated 350° oven for 20 minutes. Serves 8.

Mrs. Heather Frederick – Fort Wayne, Indiana
Wife of Captain Rory Frederick

Baked Ziti with Italian Sausage

1 pound Italian sausage
Olive oil
2 cloves garlic, minced (to taste)
1 (1-pound) box ziti, cooked
   (or penne)
1 cup small-curd cottage cheese

1 cup ricotta cheese
1 (26-ounce) jar pasta sauce
1 teaspoon oregano
1 cup shredded mozzarella
   cheese, divided
½ cup grated Parmesan cheese

Preheat oven to 350°. Remove sausage from casings; crumble and brown in oven-proof skillet over low heat with a small amount of olive oil. Add minced garlic. Drain excess oil; set aside. Cook and drain ziti; set aside–do not rinse! Mix cottage cheese, ricotta cheese, pasta sauce, oregano, and sausage; simmer on low heat until hot. Continue to stir. Gently fold in cooked ziti and some of the mozzarella cheese. Mix well and sprinkle top with more mozzarella and Parmesan cheese. This will form a nice golden cheesy crust. Bake 20 minutes or until golden brown.

Mrs. Irene Morgan – Fort Lauderdale, Florida
Wife of Captain Cliff Morgan

Chicken Tetrazzini

1 large chicken	6 tablespoons butter, divided
1 onion, quartered	1 tablespoon lemon juice
2 carrots	2 tablespoons flour
2 ribs celery	⅛ teaspoon nutmeg
8 ounces spaghetti noodles	¼ teaspoon pepper
2 (4-ounce) cans mushrooms,	1 cup heavy cream
drained	⅔ cup grated Parmesan cheese

Boil chicken in water to cover with onion, carrots, and celery. Cool and remove meat from bones. Strain chicken broth. Cook noodles in broth, reserving ¼ cup.

Sauté mushrooms in 3 tablespoons butter. Add lemon juice. Melt remaining 3 tablespoons butter. Add flour and stir, cooking about 1 minute. Add nutmeg and pepper; slowly stir in reserved broth. Cook until thick.

Add cream, then spaghetti noodles, and chicken. Pour sauce over noodles. Mix well. Pour into a 9x13-inch baking dish. Top with Parmesan cheese. Bake 25 minutes at 400°.

Mrs. De Edra Farley – Alpine, Texas
Wife of Captain Rich Farley

Air Force One is a prominent symbol of the American presidency and its power. Along with the White House and the presidential seal, it is one of the most familiar presidential symbols of the United States. *Air Force One* has often appeared in popular culture and fiction, most notably as the setting of the 1997 action movie *Air Force One.*

Everybody Loves Spaghetti Pie

1 pound ground beef
½ cup minced onion
1 (26-ounce) jar spaghetti sauce
5 tablespoons butter, melted
2 eggs, beaten

½ cup grated Parmesan cheese
6 ounces spaghetti, cooked,
  rinsed, and drained
1 cup ricotta or cottage cheese
1 cup grated mozzarella cheese

Brown ground beef with onion; drain. Add spaghetti sauce. Set aside.
Preheat oven to 350°. Add melted butter, eggs, and Parmesan cheese to cooked spaghetti, then transfer to deep-dish pie pan, forming a crust. Spread ricotta or cottage cheese in center of spaghetti crust. Pour sauce/meat mixture over; top with mozzarella cheese. Bake 30–35 minutes and serve.

Note: Mushrooms, olives, and peppers may be added to the meat mixture for added flavor, if desired.

Mrs. Tanya Harencak – Hartley, Iowa
Wife of Colonel Gary Harencak

COURTESY RONALD REAGAN LIBRARY

In 1937, Ronald Reagan enlisted in the Army Reserves as a private but was quickly promoted to second lieutenant in the Officers Reserve Corps of the Calvary. In 1942, Reagan went into active duty in the United States Army Air Force. It was there that the Army assigned Reagan to the first Motion Picture Unit in Culver City, California, where he made over 400 training films. Reagan was promoted to captain in 1943 and was discharged in 1945. Reagan became the 33rd governor of California (1967–1975) and was the 40th president of the United States (1981–1989).

Spaghetti Carbonara

During my Air Force career, I have had the pleasure of living overseas on several occasions. The most recent was a three-year tour to Italy. I can honestly say, our Italian tour was the highlight of my military career, and leaving was tough on the entire family.

1 heaping tablespoon salt	½ pound bacon (preferably
1 pound spaghetti	thick cut)
3 eggs	⅓ cup olive oil
1 pint heavy whipping cream	1 small to medium onion,
¼ teaspoon salt	finely chopped
¼ teaspoon pepper	Parmesan cheese, freshly grated

Fill a large pot with water; once water is boiling, add a heaping tablespoon of salt. Cook spaghetti according to package directions. In a bowl, whip eggs. Add whipping cream to eggs. Add salt and pepper to cream/egg mixture. Mix well. Cut bacon into small pieces and fry in olive oil. Add diced onion to bacon and cook until translucent. Remove from heat and drain on paper towels. Add bacon and onion to cream and egg mixture. Stir well. Add enough cream mixture to coat hot spaghetti. Top with fresh Parmesan; serve with the Lombard Family Garlic Bread.

LOMBARD FAMILY GARLIC BREAD:

Butter mixed with crushed	Parmesan cheese
fresh garlic	Paprika (lightly sprinkled)
Italian or French loaf, split	
lengthwise	

Spread garlic butter on bread halves. Sprinkle with Parmesan cheese and paprika. Bake at 350° for 5 minutes until lightly browned.

Master Sergeant Thomas Lombard – Union City, California

Taco Pasta Casserole

I received this recipe from a young Airman when I was stationed at Incirlik Air Base, Turkey. It's a great casserole to take to other people's homes. I've also cooked it in a crockpot at work for lunchtime potlucks when I couldn't go home.

½ cup dry small shell pasta
4 teaspoons garlic salt, divided
2 tablespoons dried chives
1 pound ground beef
1 teaspoon onion salt
2 teaspoons garlic pepper
1 tablespoon dried parsley
1½ tablespoons chili powder
1–3 shots white tequila
  (do not use 180 proof)

1 container onion and chive
  cream cheese
1 cup salsa
Crushed taco chips
Shredded cheese (amount to
  personal taste)
Black olives (optional)
Sour cream

Bring water to boil for pasta. Add pasta, 2 teaspoons garlic salt, and dried chives to water. Cook until done. Drain, leaving the chives (garlic soaks into the shells). Brown meat, then drain excess fat; add remaining 2 teaspoons garlic salt, onion salt, garlic pepper, parsley, chives, chili powder, and tequila. Cook until the tequila has been absorbed. Add cream cheese. Once blended, add salsa, then shells.

Preheat oven to 350°. Place crushed taco chips in the bottom of an 8x8-inch pan as a crust. Add a layer of cheese, half of meat mixture, black olives, and more cheese; repeat with last layer being cheese and olives. Bake 25 minutes and serve with sour cream. The recipe makes enough for 2–4 people. It can be easily doubled.

Major Dani Johnson – Maxwell, Nebraska

Easy-Breezy Anytime Pasta

1 (12-ounce) box thick
  spaghetti
1 tablespoon salt
6–8 tablespoons extra virgin
  olive oil
One whole garlic head (about
  14–18 cloves)

¼ teaspoon crushed red pepper
2 tablespoons fresh chopped
  parsley
1½ cups shredded fresh
  Parmesan cheese
Salt to taste

Cook pasta according to package directions with salt. In a large non-stick frying pan, heat olive oil. Peel garlic cloves and fry them in oil at medium-low heat. Keep turning garlic until soft and light to medium brown on all sides. (Do not burn garlic as it will taste bitter.) When garlic is nice and soft, "crush" garlic so that it is in little stringy pieces. For garlic lovers, leave the garlic in larger pieces. Turn off heat; add crushed red pepper and more salt to taste, and let sit about 3 minutes. Drain pasta and empty it into a large bowl. Add parsley to garlic mix and pour whole mix over pasta. Add Parmesan cheese. Mix well. Serve immediately.

Mrs. Corinna Thomas – Eugene, Oregon
Wife of Master Sergeant Roger Thomas

An Air Force aircraft carrying the vice president is designated as *Air Force Two.* Occasionally, the vice president, when traveling long distances will travel in one of the VC-25A's and the plane will fly as *"Air Force Two."*

Aircraft that have formerly served as *Air Force One* are on display in the presidential hangar of the National Museum of the United States Air Force at Wright-Patterson AFB, Ohio, as well as at the Museum of Flight in Seattle, Washington. The Boeing 707 that served as *Air Force One* from the Nixon years to the current administration (SAM 27000) is on display in Simi Valley, California, at the Ronald Reagan Presidential Library. A VC-118A Liftmaster used by John F. Kennedy is on display at the Pima Air & Space Museum in Tucson, Arizona.

Spinach-Artichoke Lasagna with Feta

I've spent my life traveling, having lived in eight different states and three countries, taking advantage of the surrounding areas as much as possible. My wife and I are both first generation Americans with roots in Mexico (Mexico City and Nayarit). Here is a recipe we compiled ourselves . . . it's one of our favorites.

1 (16-ounce) package lasagna
1 (26-ounce) jar pasta sauce
1 (1-pound) carton cottage
 cheese
1½ teaspoons olive oil
1 tablespoon rosemary
2 cloves garlic, finely chopped
1 onion, finely chopped
1 (14-ounce) can vegetable broth
1 (14-ounce) can artichoke
 hearts, drained, finely chopped

1 (10-ounce) package frozen
 chopped spinach, thawed
 and drained
2 cups shredded mozzarella
 cheese
2 cups shredded Cheddar cheese
1 cup Parmesan and ricotta
 cheese mix
4 ounces crumbled feta

In a large pot, bring water to a boil; add lasagna noodles and cook 10 minutes or until al dente; drain. Lay pasta on paper towels and place to the side. Blend pasta sauce and cottage cheese until smooth; set aside.

Heat olive oil and rosemary in saucepan on medium. Add garlic and onion; sauté until tender. Stir in broth and bring to a boil. Stir in artichokes and spinach; mix well. Reduce heat, cover, and simmer 5 minutes. Mix in cottage cheese mixture and stir.

Preheat oven to 350°. Spray 9x13-inch dish with cooking spray. Spread ¼ cottage cheese mixture in bottom of dish. Top with 3

(continued)

(Spinach-Artichoke Lasagna with Feta continued)

noodles. Then top with another 1/4 cottage cheese mixture and half the cheeses (excluding feta). Next add 3 more noodles. Again, top with one more 1/4 cottage cheese mixture and second half of cheeses (excluding feta). Repeat step with 3 noodles. Top lasagna with last 1/4 cottage cheese mixture and sprinkle feta cheese over all. Cover with foil and bake 35 minutes, then remove foil, and bake 15 minutes more. Remove from oven, let stand 10 minutes, and serve.

Captain Juan Jose Guzman – Killeen, Texas, and
Lt. Sandra Martinez-Guzman – Alexandria, Virginia

Lt. Sandra Martinez-Guzman

Captain Juan Guzman

Teresa's Lasagna

This recipe was originally used by my mother as a young Air Force wife. It has been used now by three generations of Air Force wives (my daughter included) to entertain Air Force families and neighbors based in Newfoundland, Canada (now closed), Maine (Dow AFB, now closed), New Hampshire (Pease AFB, now closed), Massachusetts (Otis AFB, then Hanscom Field), Virginia (Langley AFB), Florida (Eglin AFB), North Carolina (Seymour-Johnson AFB), Washington (McChord AFB), California (George AFB), Illinois (Scott AFB), New Mexico (Cannon AFB), Texas (Dyess AFB), and Germany (Spangdahlem AFB and Zweibrucken AFB).

1 pound ground beef
2 tablespoons oil
1 clove garlic, minced
1 medium onion, chopped
2 teaspoons salt
½ teaspoon rosemary
2 (6-ounce) cans tomato paste

3–4 cups hot water
1½ pounds lasagna noodles,
  cooked and drained
½ pound shredded Parmesan and
  mozzarella, mixed
Additional cheese for top

Brown beef in oil with, garlic, onion, and seasonings; drain. Mix in tomato paste and hot water. Simmer for 5 minutes.

Preheat oven to 350°. Layer a thin layer of sauce into a 9x13-inch pan. Next layer half the noodles, then all the cheese mixture. Repeat meat and sauce layer again. Top with additional cheese. Bake 30 minutes.

Mrs. Teresa Margaret Cossaboom – Brunswick, Maine
Wife of Senior Master Sergeant (Ret.) George Cossaboom

Mrs. Rowanne Cossaboom Tryon – Brunswick, Maine
Wife of Chief Alvin Tryon

Chicken and Cheese Lasagna

½ cup butter
2 cloves garlic, minced
½ cup flour
1 teaspoon salt
2 cups milk
2 cups chicken broth
2 cups shredded mozzarella
1 cup grated Parmesan cheese, divided

1 onion, chopped
½ teaspoon dried oregano
½ teaspoon pepper
1 (8-ounce) package uncooked lasagna noodles
1 (8-ounce) carton cottage cheese, divided
2 cups cut-up cooked chicken

Heat butter in 2-quart saucepan over low heat until melted; add garlic. Stir in flour and salt. Cook, stirring constantly, until bubbly. Remove from heat; stir in milk and broth. Heat to boiling, stirring constantly. Boil and stir for 1 minute. Stir in mozzarella cheese and ½ cup Parmesan cheese, the onion, oregano, and pepper. Over low heat, stir constantly until mozzarella cheese is melted.

Preheat oven to 350°. Spread ¼ of the cheese sauce (about 1½ cups) into an ungreased 9x13-inch pan. Top with 3–4 uncooked lasagna noodles, overlapping if necessary. Spread half the cottage cheese over noodles. Add a layer of cooked chicken. Repeat layers. Sprinkle remaining ½ cup Parmesan cheese on top. Bake uncovered 35–40 minutes until noodles are done. Let stand 15 minutes before cutting.

Mrs. Marty Miracky – Omaha, Nebraska
Wife of Tech Sergeant Danny Miracky

Marvelous Baked Manicotti

1 (1-pound) box manicotti shells
1 cup cottage cheese
1 cup ricotta cheese
2 cups shredded mozzarella
  cheese
½ cup grated Parmesan cheese

2 teaspoons Italian seasoning
1 teaspoon garlic salt
1 teaspoon oregano
⅛ teaspoon pepper
4 cups spaghetti sauce

Cook manicotti shells according to package directions. Drain and lay out on a piece of wax paper to cool enough to handle. Preheat oven to 350°. In a bowl, combine cottage cheese, ricotta cheese, mozzarella, Parmesan, Italian seasoning, garlic salt, oregano, and pepper. Put cheese mixture into a pastry bag and fill manicotti shells. Lay shells in a 9x13-inch baking dish. Cover with spaghetti sauce and bake 45 minutes. Allow to stand 5 minutes before serving.

Mrs. Marty Holcomb – Athens, Georgia
Wife of Lt. Colonel Pete Holcomb

Penne Pasta with Vodka Sauce

1 (1-pound) package penne pasta
1 onion, diced
4 tablespoons olive oil
1 (14¼-ounce) can tomatoes,
  drained
1 (8-ounce) can tomato sauce

⅔ cup vodka
1 cup heavy cream
1 cup cooked chopped ham
1 cup frozen baby peas, thawed
¼ teaspoon cayenne pepper
Parmesan cheese, grated

Cook penne pasta according to package directions and drain. Sauté onion in olive oil until tender. Add tomatoes, tomato sauce, and vodka. Cook 5 minutes. Add cream and stir well; bring to very slight boil. Reduce heat and stir in ham, peas, and cayenne pepper. Add cooked pasta; stir well. Serve with grated Parmesan cheese. Serves 6–8.

Mrs. Billie Borders – Poquoson, Virginia
Wife of Major (Ret.) Jerry Borders

Parmesan Penne Pasta

½ (16-ounce) box penne pasta
1 yellow bell pepper, seeded,
  sliced
1 red bell pepper, seeded, sliced
1 tablespoon olive oil
1 (1-pound) package Italian
  sausage

1 (8-ounce) package sliced
  mushrooms
2 tablespoons Italian seasoning
1 (8-ounce) package grated
  Parmesan cheese

Cook pasta according to directions on box. Save some pasta water when draining.

Preheat oven to 375°. Lay sliced peppers on cookie sheet and drizzle oil evenly over peppers. Place in oven. Bake until soft, and peppers are beginning to blacken on edges; set aside. Crumble and brown Italian sausage in large saucepan until no longer pink in center. Remove sausage from pan, and leave as much grease from meat as possible. Add mushrooms, and sauté in sausage grease. After mushrooms are sautéed, add meat and stir. Stir in baked peppers, Italian seasoning, and cooked pasta. Poor cheese evenly over and let melt. Add water to the edge for moisture, if needed. Serves 4.

Mrs. Cara Lenes – Dallas, Texas
Wife of Senior Airman Jared Lenes

Fabulous Fettuccini Alfredo

Great with grilled chicken or crabmeat.

1 (8-ounce) package fettuccini noodles	5 ounces freshly grated Parmesan cheese
1 stick real butter	Dash of nutmeg
1 (1-pint) carton heavy whipping cream	

Cook noodles according to package. Melt butter in saucepan; add heavy cream. When small bubbles begin around the sides of the pan, add Parmesan cheese; stir until melted. Do not boil. Add nutmeg. Pour over noodles.

Miss Elizabeth Tosten – Birmingham, Alabama
Daughter of Major (Ret.) William Tosten

Rigatoni with Creamy Tomato Sauce

1 (11- to 16-ounce) package rigatoni noodles	2 tomatoes, chopped (can use canned tomatoes)
¼ pound ground Italian sausage	½ cup white wine
1 small onion, finely chopped	¼ teaspoon salt
2 tablespoons butter	¼ cup frozen peas
2 cloves garlic, minced	½ cup whipping cream
½ cup tomato sauce	Parmesan cheese, grated

Cook pasta according to package directions; drain and set aside. Sauté sausage and onion in butter. Add garlic, tomato sauce, tomatoes, wine, salt, and peas. Simmer 30 minutes. Add whipping cream and Parmesan cheese. Simmer 10 minutes. Add cooked pasta, and stir well while heating through. Serves 6–8.

Mrs. Tara Hansen – Fort Worth, Texas
Wife of Captain Eydin Hansen

Spicy Shrimp Pasta

2 tablespoons olive oil
1 teaspoon crushed red pepper
  flakes
2 garlic cloves, minced
½ teaspoon salt
½ teaspoon pepper

12 ounces fresh shrimp, peeled
  and deveined
2 cups chopped tomatoes
8 ounces linguini noodles,
  cooked, drained
Parmesan cheese, grated

Heat olive oil in a large skillet over medium heat. Add crushed red pepper flakes, garlic, salt, and pepper. Sauté 1 minute. Add shrimp and sauté 3 minutes or until shrimp are opaque. Stir in tomatoes and heat through. Toss shrimp mixture with linguini. Sprinkle with Parmesan cheese.

Mrs. Connie Leetsch – Abilene, Texas
Wife of Chief (Ret.) Cecil H. Leetsch
Mrs. Leetsch also served in the Women's Air Force from 1951–1954.

In the early 1950s, Connie was a radio and radar tech at Kelly AFB, Texas, where she met Cecil Leetsch. They were married in 1954.

Crockpot Red Beans and Rice

1 (8-ounce) bag small red beans
½ cup small black beans
1 pound turkey or beef sausage
½ bell pepper, finely chopped
1 cup chopped ham
1 large onion, chopped
5 stalks celery, finely chopped

2 tablespoons garlic powder
2 tablespoons onion powder
2 teaspoons celery salt
2 tablespoons Creole seasoning
2 teaspoons black pepper
6 cups rice, cooked

Soak red and black beans overnight. Drain and wash. Place beans in crockpot with all ingredients except rice. Add enough water to cover beans. Place crockpot setting on LOW. Cook 4 hours then turn the setting to HIGH for 2 more hours. Serve over rice.

Note: Make sure to check beans throughout the day to be sure they have enough water, as they soak it up during the cooking process.

Lt. Colonel (Ret.) Deanna Paulk – Panama City, Florida
Wife of Lt. Colonel (Ret.) William Paulk

Quick Fix Sausage and Rice Casserole

1 pound bulk pork sausage
1 cup uncooked rice
2 cups finely chopped, peeled
   carrots
1 large onion, chopped

1 cup finely chopped celery
½ cup chopped green bell pepper
1 (14-ounce) can chicken broth
¼ cup water
½ cup sliced mushrooms

Brown sausage and drain fat. Preheat oven to 350°. Spread uncooked rice evenly over bottom of lightly greased 3-quart baking dish. Spoon vegetables over rice. Pour chicken broth and water over vegetables. Spoon sausage over vegetables. Top with mushrooms. Cover and bake 30 minutes. Stir and continue to bake another 30 minutes. Serves 8–10.

Mrs. Cathy Harvey – Georgetown, South Carolina
Wife of Lt. Colonel Joe Harvey

Jamie's Cajun Dirty Rice

1 (16-ounce) package hot
  ground sausage
¼ pound ground beef
2 cups rice
1 (14-ounce) can chicken broth
¼ cup water
1 onion, chopped
1 green bell pepper, chopped
5 stalks celery, chopped
1 (4-ounce) can mushrooms

4 tablespoons butter
1 teaspoon cumin
1 teaspoon curry powder
2 tablespoons seasoned salt
1 tablespoon black pepper
1 tablespoon garlic powder
1 tablespoon Creole seasoning
1 (10¾-ounce) can cream of
  chicken soup

Preheat oven to 350°. Brown sausage and ground beef; drain. Cook rice in chicken broth and water. Sauté onion, green pepper, celery, and mushrooms in butter with all seasoning/spices until tender. In a large pot, add ingredients together with soup, and blend well. Place in greased casserole dish and bake 20 minutes. Serves 8.

Note: You can adjust spiciness by using milder sausage and cutting back on pepper and Creole seasoning. If you want it even hotter, use spicy seasoned salt.

Master Sergeant (Ret.) Lin Howe-Young – Fruitport, Michigan

Mexican Sour Cream Rice

1 cup long-grain white rice
1 (14-ounce) can chicken broth
1 cup sour cream
1 (4-ounce) can green chile
  peppers
1 cup shredded Monterey Jack
  cheese, divided

1 (15-ounce) can whole-kernel
  corn, drained
Salt and pepper to taste
Cilantro (optional)

In a large pot, bring rice and chicken broth to a boil. Reduce heat to low, cover, and simmer 20 minutes. To the cooked rice, add sour cream, chile peppers, ½ cup cheese, and corn; mix. Season with salt and pepper to taste.

Preheat oven to 350°. Transfer mixture to a lightly greased 1½-quart casserole dish and top with remaining ½ cup cheese. Bake uncovered 30 minutes until cheese is bubbly and lightly browned. Top with chopped cilantro, if desired.

Tech Sergeant (Ret.) Carolyn Staley – South Orange, New Jersey

Top Secret Sauces & Marinades

The **B-2 Spirit**, also known as the **Stealth Bomber**, is a multi-role bomber capable of delivering both conventional and nuclear munitions. A dramatic leap forward in technology, the bomber represents a major milestone in the U.S. bomber modernization program. The B-2 brings massive firepower to bear, in a short time, anywhere on the globe through previously impenetrable defenses.

The B-2's low observability is derived from a combination of reduced infrared, acoustic, electromagnetic, visual, and radar signatures. These signatures make it difficult for the sophisticated defensive systems to detect, track, and engage the B-2. The B-2's composite materials, special coatings, and flying-wing design all contribute to its "stealthiness." The B-2 has a crew of two pilots—a pilot in the left seat and mission commander in the right.

Prickly Pear Bar-B-Q Sauce

1 tablespoon oil
1 medium onion, cut small dice
4 large cloves (or more) garlic, crushed
2–4 jalapeños diced (leave seeds in for HOT)
2 teaspoons chili powder
2 teaspoons cayenne pepper (or more)
1 teaspoon salt
1 teaspoon pepper
2 teaspoons basil
½ cup packed brown sugar
⅛ cup tomato paste
Juice from 1 lemon
2 teaspoons Worcestershire
2 tablespoons hot pepper sauce (or more)
1 (28-ounce) can tomato sauce
2 cups Prickly Pear juice
⅓ cup vinegar

In a preheated saucepan, put in oil, then add onion and garlic; stir and cook 2–3 minutes, or until onion is soft and clear. Add peppers and sauté. Add spices and sauté, then add remaining ingredients. Cook over medium heat until desired consistency. Use on beef, poultry, or pork. Refrigerate leftovers.

Master Sergeant Richard F. Rexin – Ovid, Michigan

Andy's Barbeque Sauce

2 cups ketchup
1 cup vinegar
4 tablespoons Worcestershire
1 cup butter
Juice of 2 lemons
½ cup molasses
1 cup brown sugar
Garlic powder to taste
1 tablespoon chili powder
4 tablespoons mustard
1 tablespoon salt
1 tablespoon pepper
Paprika

Mix all ingredients together and cook until thick, about 1 hour.

Lt. Colonel (Ret.) Andy Anderson – Pineville, Louisiana

Marvelous Marinara Sauce

2 cloves garlic, chopped
1 onion, chopped
1 tablespoon butter
1 tablespoon olive oil
3 anchovy fillets, chopped
2 tablespoons tomato paste
2 (28-ounce) cans Italian whole
   tomatoes in purée

1 cup water
2 tablespoons finely chopped fresh
   parsley
2 tablespoons finely chopped fresh
   oregano
½ teaspoon salt
¼ teaspoon pepper

Sauté garlic and onion in butter and oil over medium heat until soft. Stir in anchovies until dissolved. Add tomato paste. Stir and cook for 1 minute. Add canned tomatoes with purée, water, herbs, and seasonings. Bring to a boil. Reduce heat to low and simmer uncovered for 30 minutes.

Mrs. Marty Holcomb – Athens, Georgia
Wife of Lt. Colonel Pete Holcomb

Second Lt. Pete Holcomb and wife Marty in front of an F-4 Phantom II aircraft at a 1987 airshow. The F-4 aircraft, which still flies in defense of eight nations, was retired in 1996 from U.S. military forces, ending a record-studded 38-year career.

Spoleto Spaghetti Sauce

4 tablespoons olive oil, divided
1 pound sweet Italian sausage,
cut into 12 pieces
⅔ pound hot Italian sausage,
cut into 8 pieces
1 pound spare ribs, cut into
2-inch lengths
½ pound ground beef
½ pound ground pork
1½ cups diced onions
5 cloves garlic, minced, divided
3 (35-ounce) cans Italian plum
tomatoes

¾ cup tomato paste
½ cup red wine
1 cup chopped Italian parsley,
divided
1 tablespoon oregano
1½ teaspoons black pepper
Salt to taste
Pinch of hot red pepper flakes
Pinch of granulated sugar
Grated zest of 2 lemons, divided

Heat 2 tablespoons olive oil in skillet. Brown sausages and spare ribs in oil. Remove to a large heavy stockpot. Drain all but 3 tablespoons grease. Brown ground beef and pork; remove to stockpot. Add onions and half the garlic to skillet. Cook over medium heat 5 minutes, stirring; add to meat in stockpot. Add tomatoes (with juice), tomato paste, wine, ½ cup parsley, remaining olive oil, oregano, pepper, salt, pepper flakes, sugar, and half the lemon zest. Bring to a boil and reduce heat. Simmer, partially covered, over low heat 2½ hours, stirring occasionally so sauce won't stick. After 2½ hours, add remaining garlic, parsley, and lemon zest. Stir well and cook, uncovered, an additional hour, stirring occasionally.

Master Sergeant Deb Marsh – Hubbard, Ohio

Parma Rosa Sauce

3 cloves garlic, minced
3 tablespoons extra virgin
  olive oil
16–20 ounces canned tomato
  paste
½ teaspoon chopped fresh
  oregano
1 teaspoon chopped fresh basil
½ teaspoon sugar

Salt and pepper to taste
16–20 ounces tomato sauce
16–20 ounces beef, chicken or
  vegetable broth
1 cup red wine
16–20 ounces ricotta cheese
½ cup grated Romano or
  Parmesan cheese
Cooked noodles

In a large saucepan, lightly sauté minced garlic in olive oil. Add tomato paste and cook over medium heat, stirring continuously 5–10 minutes until tomato paste turns deeper red and becomes more fragrant—don't allow sauce to scorch. Add herbs and spices. Stir and simmer 3–5 more minutes. Then add tomato sauce, broth, wine and ricotta cheese. Simmer uncovered 30–60 minutes, stirring occasionally to prevent scorching. Add Romano or Parmesan cheese during last 15 minutes of cooking time, stirring frequently. Serve over noodles.

Lt. Colonel Marie C. Elliott – Helotes, Texas

Enchilada Sauce

1 onion, diced
2 tablespoons oil
Flour
Chili powder, to taste

Cumin powder, to taste
1 (8-ounce) can tomato sauce
Salt to taste

Sauté onion in oil until tender. Add enough flour to make a paste. Add chili powder and cumin powder and stir. Add enough tomato sauce to desired thickness. Salt to taste.

Major Rhonda Donze – Melbourne, Florida
Wife of Lt. Colonel (Ret.) Robert Donze

Sour Cream Horseradish Sauce

1 cup sour cream
2 teaspoons prepared
  horseradish

1 onion, thinly sliced
⅛ teaspoon salt
¼ teaspoon paprika

Mix sour cream, horseradish, and onion in blender. Blend until smooth. Add salt and paprika. Blend well.

Mrs. Billie Borders – Poquoson, Virginia
Wife of Major (Ret.) Jerry Borders

Blender Hollandaise Sauce

6 egg yolks
2 tablespoons lemon juice
2 sticks butter, melted,
  slightly cooled

Red pepper to taste

Drop egg yolks and lemon juice into blender. Blend on HIGH. Slowly pour melted butter into eggs. Blend 30 seconds. Add red pepper to taste.

Mrs. Karen Tosten – Hattiesburg, Mississippi
Wife of Major (Ret.) William Tosten

Béarnaise Sauce Par Excellence

Great on meats and vegetables.

1–2 shallots, chopped
½ teaspoon black peppercorns,
  ground
½ cup dry white wine

3 tablespoons white wine vinegar
Coarse salt to taste
3–4 sprigs tarragon, chopped
1¼ cups mayonnaise

Combine all ingredients well. Keep refrigerated.

Mrs. Frances Anderson – Pineville, Louisiana
Wife of Lt. Colonel (Ret.) Andy Anderson

Sweet and Sour Sauce

¼ cup ketchup
⅔ cup brown sugar
⅓ cup pineapple juice
½ cup cider vinegar
2 tablespoons soy sauce

1 tablespoon cooking oil
2 tablespoons cornstarch
⅓ cup water
1 cup pineapple chunks

Mix ketchup, brown sugar, pineapple juice, vinegar, soy sauce, and oil. Dissolve cornstarch in water. Add to ketchup mixture. Bring to a boil, stirring constantly. When thickened, add pineapple.

Mrs. Brenda Burrows – Yorktown, Virginia
Wife of Major (Ret.) Chris Burrows

Sassy Rémoulade Sauce

½ medium onion
4 green onions
1 small bunch parsley
½ medium green bell pepper
3 stalks celery
1 quart mayonnaise
½ cup Creole mustard
⅓ cup white vinegar

¼ cup red wine vinegar
¼ cup Worcestershire
1 teaspoon salt
1 tablespoon red pepper
¼ teaspoon black pepper
¼ cup sugar
1½ teaspoons garlic powder
Hot sauce to taste

Process onions, parsley, bell pepper, and celery in food processor to a finely chopped stage. Set aside. Mix mayonnaise, mustard, white vinegar, red wine vinegar, and Worcestershire in large bowl. Whisk until smooth. Add vegetable mix to sauce. Mix well and season with salt, pepper, sugar, and garlic powder. Add hot sauce to taste. Refrigerate overnight. Will keep in jar for up to one month.

Mrs. Karen Tosten – Hattiesburg, Mississippi
Wife of Major (Ret.) William Tosten

Homemade Hot Fudge Sauce

1 cup sugar
2 blocks unsweetened chocolate
¼ cup butter

1 (12-ounce) can evaporated
  skim milk
1 teaspoon vanilla

Put sugar in heavy saucepan over medium heat with chocolate and butter, stirring till melted; add evaporated milk. Stir constantly 25 minutes over medium heat with wooden spoon. Turn off heat, then add vanilla; stir. Store leftovers in refrigerator; to thin, add milk and stir. Great over ice cream.

Mrs. Barbara McGee – Hampton, Virginia
Wife of Lt. Colonel (Ret.) Guy McGee

Caramel Apple Dipping Sauce

1 (8-ounce) package cream
  cheese, softened
1 teaspoon vanilla

½ cup brown sugar
3 tablespoons caramel ice cream
  sauce

Beat cream cheese with mixer until fluffy. Add vanilla, brown sugar, and caramel sauce. Pour into bowl. Serve with sliced apples.

Mrs. Melinda Smith – Monument, Colorado
Wife of Lt. Colonel (Ret.) Fred Smith

A base exchange (BX), also referred to as a post exchange (PX) on Army installations, is a large department store-like shop that operates on United States military installations worldwide. A typical exchange is similar to a department store, but other services such as barber shops, hair care, beauty, gas stations, fast food outlets, convenience stores ("Shoppettes"), beer and wine sales, liquor stores ("Class Six"), and even vehicle maintenance and repair services are commonly available. Most (but not all) sales by exchanges are free of local sales or VAT taxes, as the sales take place on military reservations (exceptions may include gasoline sales in the United States and sales by concessionaires licensed by the exchange).

Berry Topping

This topping is wonderful for Belgian waffles or cheesecake.

1 (12-ounce) bag frozen
raspberries, partially thawed
1 (12-ounce) bag frozen
blackberries, partially thawed

1⅓ cups water, divided
1 cup sugar
3 tablespoons cornstarch

Combine 1 cup mashed berries (some from each kind) with 1 cup water in saucepan. Boil 5 minutes. Add sugar and cornstarch which has been dissolved in small amount of water. Boil until mixture turns clear, approximately 5 minutes, stirring constantly. Cool glaze. Add remaining berries to glaze and toss gently to coat. If blackberries are very large, cut in half before adding to glaze.

Mrs. Gail Teigeler – Riverside, California
Wife of Lt. Colonel (Ret.) Thomas Teigeler

Lemon Curd

1 stick butter
1 cup fine sugar

2 large lemons, zest and juice
2 large eggs

Cook butter, sugar, lemon zest and juice in double boiler until butter has melted. Temper some of the eggs with the hot mixture, then add the rest. Cook until mixture coats back of wooden spoon. Pour into a jar and store in the refrigerator.

Mrs. Frances Anderson – Pineville, Louisiana
Wife of Lt. Colonel (Ret.) Andy Anderson

Cranberry Wine Sauce

This sauce is good served hot or cold. Wonderful with Thanksgiving turkey.

3 tablespoons sugar
1 teaspoon cinnamon
⅛ teaspoon nutmeg
⅛ teaspoon cloves

1 lemon rind, grated
½ cup port wine
1 (1-pound) can whole berry
    cranberry sauce

In a saucepan, combine sugar, cinnamon, nutmeg, cloves, lemon rind, and wine. Simmer 5 minutes. Add cranberry sauce; mix well.

Mrs. Billie Borders – Poquoson, Virginia
Wife of Major (Ret.) Jerry Borders

Honey Mustard Marinade

1 cup dry white wine
3 tablespoons honey
2 cloves garlic, minced

3 tablespoons Dijon mustard
1 tablespoon oil
⅛ teaspoon pepper

Combine all ingredients in small mixing bowl. Great marinade for beef, lamb, chicken, or pork.

Mrs. Marty Holcomb – Athens, Georgia
Wife of Lt. Colonel Pete Holcomb

Marinade for Any Kind of Meat

Naturally, the amount I use depends on how much meat I am cooking. This mixture is a great marinade, as it doesn't take long to soak in and it is not as hot as one would think.

½ cup Worcestershire
⅛ cup soy sauce
Approximately 1 tablespoon
    black pepper
Approximately ½ teaspoon
    chili powder

Approximately ¼ teaspoon
    cayenne pepper
2 quick shakes garlic salt

I often use this as a marinade and then put the meat straight on the grill or in the dehydrator to make jerky.

The completion of this recipe is this: Take an appropriate amount of jalapeños for the amount of meat you have. Slice the peppers in half and be sure to get all the seeds out. Soak peppers in cold water and change water about every 30 minutes. Do this as many times as you want, depending on how hot you want your peppers. This really takes the heat out of them. Then slice meat in appropriate slices. Place meat in pepper, wrap with bacon, secure with a toothpick, and you are ready to grill. You may also put cheese, cream cheese, or another filling between pepper and meat. With all wild game, you must be sure to not overcook, but with beef and others, you can cook to your desired taste. Also, if using any dark meat besides beef, you should soak meat in cold salt water overnight or as long as the day allows.

Senior Airman Dusty Easton – Minot AFB, North Dakota

Ten Major Commands
of the United States Air Force

- **Air Combat Command**—headquartered in Langley AFB, Virginia. ACC operates fighter, bomber, reconnaissance, battle-management, and electronic-combat aircraft. ACC also provides command, control, communications and intelligence systems, and conducts global information operations.

- **Air Educational and Training Command**—headquartered in Randolph AFB, Texas. AETC recruits, trains, and educates Airmen.

- **Air Force Material Command**—headquartered in Wright-Patterson AFB, Ohio. AFMC conducts research, development, test, and evaluation, and provides the support necessary to keep Air Force weapon systems ready for war.

- **Air Force Space Command**—headquartered in Peterson AFB, Colorado. AFSPC contributes to United States deterrence through its intercontinental ballistic missile force and plays a vital role tying together the U.S. military worldwide through the use of satellites and other space operations.

- **Air Force Special Operations Command**—headquartered in Hurlburt Field, Florida. The AFSOC is composed of highly trained, rapidly deployable Airmen equipped with specialized aircraft. They conduct global missions ranging from precision application of firepower, to infiltration, aviation foreign internal defense, exfiltration, and resupply and refueling.

- **Air Mobility Command**—headquartered in Scott AFB, Illinois. AMC provides airlift, special missions, aerial refueling, and aeromedical evacuation for U.S. troops. AMC also operates VIP flights such as Air Force One.

- **Pacific Air Force**—headquartered in Hickam AFB, Hawaii. PACAF provides ready air and space power to promote U.S. interests in the Asia-Pacific region during peacetime, crisis, and in war.

- **United States Air Force in Europe**—headquartered in Ramstein AFB, Germany. USAFE trains and equips USAF units pledged to NATO, maintaining combat-ready wings spanning three continents, covering more than 20 million square miles in 91 countries, from Great Britain to Turkey.

- **Air Force Reserve Command**—headquartered in Robins AFB, Georgia. AFRC provides combat-ready units and individuals for active duty whenever there are not enough trained units and people in the regular component of the Air Force to perform any national security mission.

- **Air Force Cyber Command**—is the newest major command whose development was announced on November 2, 2006. A Cyber Innovation Center will be built on a 58-acre site, near Barksdale AFB, Louisiana.

Mission Essential Meats

U.S. AIR FORCE PHOTO BY MASTER SGT. LANCE CHEUNG

The **B-1B Lancer** holds almost fifty world records for speed, payload, range, and time of climb in its class. Carrying the largest payload of both guided and unguided weapons in the Air Force inventory, the multimission B-1B is the backbone of America's long-range bomber force.

The B-1B's blended wing/body configuration, variable-geometry wings, and turbofan afterburning engines combine to provide long-range maneuverability and high speed while enhancing survivability. Forward wing settings are used for takeoff, landings, air refueling, and occasionally, high-altitude weapons employment scenarios. Aft wing sweep settings—the main combat configuration—are typically used during high subsonic and supersonic flight, enhancing the B-1B's maneuverability in the low-altitude and high-altitude regimes.

Charlie Tango's Brisket

1 (3- to 4-pound) brisket, trimmed of excess fat
1 tablespoon celery powder (not celery salt)

1 tablespoon garlic powder
1 tablespoon onion powder
⅛ cup liquid smoke
¼ cup Worcestershire

Preheat oven to 275°. Line pan with foil and make a jacket, large enough to completely encase brisket. Rinse brisket and place in pan in jacket.

Mix celery, garlic, and onion powders in small bowl. Mix liquid smoke and Worcestershire in another bowl. Pour liquid mixture over brisket. Sprinkle dry seasonings over brisket. Close brisket tightly in aluminum foil so that no steam can escape. Bake 6–7 hours. Remove from oven.

Pour juices from brisket into container to be used later. Turn oven off and replace brisket with foil opened back into the oven; allow brisket to cool. You may refrigerate if you like. When ready to serve, place back into pan; use saved juices to pour over brisket. Heat and serve.

Lt. Colonel (Ret.) Charles "Charlie Tango" Tosten, Jr.
– Alexandria, Louisiana

Officers Club, Nellis AFB. William Tosten finds his father's nickname— Charlie Tango—on the famous wall (an old bar top).

Shaun's Texas Brisket

1 large beef brisket	1 bottle liquid smoke
3 tablespoons olive oil	3 beef bouillon cubes
Lawry's Seasoned Salt, red label	3 cups water
1 teaspoon garlic salt	Salt and pepper to taste
1 teaspoon onion salt	2 tablespoons Worcestershire
1 teaspoon celery salt	

Preheat oven to 325°. In a Dutch oven brown both sides of brisket in olive oil. Sprinkle meat with Lawry's Seasoned Salt, garlic salt, onion salt, and celery salt. Saturate with liquid smoke. Dissolve beef bouillon cubes in at least 3 cups water and add salt, pepper, and Worcestershire. Pour into Dutch oven. Bake until tender, 3–4½ hours or until meat falls apart.

Lt. Colonel Mark Fluker – Houston, Texas

Commando Crockpot Roast

1 (5½-ounce) can vegetable juice	1 (14½-ounce) can petite diced tomatoes
1 pound baby cut carrots	2–4 garlic cloves
1 (2-pound) beef roast	
1 envelope Good Seasons Italian dry salad dressing mix	

Pour can of vegetable juice into slow cooker. Add carrots. Place roast atop carrots. Sprinkle roast with salad dressing mix. Cover with tomatoes and garlic cloves. Cover and cook on LOW 8–9 hours.

Mrs. Anne Ratta – Tucson, Arizona
Wife of Master Sergeant Glenn Ratta

Bulgogi

Bulgogi is one of Korea's most popular meat dishes. It means "fire meat" in Korean.

1½ pounds top round or
   tenderloin
3 tablespoons sugar
2 tablespoons rice wine
6 tablespoons soy sauce
2 tablespoons chopped garlic

1 tablespoon salt
2 tablespoons sesame oil
5 tablespoons chopped green
   onion
Black pepper to taste

Slice beef thinly and score lightly with a knife to make it more tender. Cut into bite-size pieces and marinate in sugar and rice wine 2 hours. Mix beef with soy sauce, garlic, salt, and oil. Broil over hot charcoal on a grill, or in a frying pan. It is delicious served with lettuce leaves, sesame leaves, garland chrysanthemum, and garlic. Bulgogi is generally broiled over a charcoal grill at the table. You may use an oven broiler heated to 570° for 10 minutes.

Chief Deborah Moran – Mariton, New Jersey

Mission Essential: Military materials and equipment authorized and available to combat, combat support, combat service support, and combat readiness training forces in order to accomplish their assigned missions.

Rinder-Rouladen

This German dish is a good meal to have the second day, too, especially the red cabbage, as the flavor only gets better!

Large roast, butcher-sliced for
  beef jerky
Mustard
Salt and pepper to taste
1 large onion, chopped fine
1 pound bacon, fried and
  crumbled
Pickles, cut lengthwise

1 large head red cabbage
¾ cup sugar
½ cup white vinegar
3–4 bay leaves
8–10 whole cloves
1 apple, sliced
1 beef gravy packet

Spread slices of meat with mustard, then season with salt and pepper. Layer each piece with bits of onion, bacon, and pickles. Then roll the meat from one end to the other with the goodies inside; tie with thread, wrapping string around entire piece of meat, securing it well. Do this until meat is gone. Brown the meat in pan. Save all drippings to make gravy.

While meat is browning, shred cabbage thinly. Put in large pot and add to taste, sugar, vinegar, bay leaves, cloves, and apples slices. The taste you are going for is sweeter but has a sour tang to it. Cook on low till tender, 1–2 hours (you may have to add more sugar or vinegar until desired favor is reached). Check liquids often. When meat is done, make gravy from drippings and gravy mix. Remove string from meat. Serve with mashed potatoes. Preparation time is consuming—but worth it.

Mrs. Tammy Swanson – Chico, California
Mother of Airman Shayna Swanson

Beef Stroganoff

1 medium onion, chopped
1 stick butter
1 (4-ounce) can sliced mushrooms
1 large sirloin steak
Salt and pepper to taste
Flour
1 cup bouillon

1 cup white wine
2 tablespoons tomato paste
3 shakes garlic powder
3 shakes Worcestershire
1 cup sour cream
Rice or noodles, cooked

Sauté onion in butter; add mushrooms after onion is translucent, then remove from pan. Cut steak in strips; salt and pepper and dredge in flour; brown in butter that is left in the pan. After browning steak, put onions and mushrooms in with meat strips. Add bouillon, white wine, tomato paste, garlic powder, and Worcestershire. Allow to cook over low heat until meat is tender, 30–45 minutes. Continue to add liquid so that it doesn't become too thick. Add sour cream; stir to incorporate, then cook just long enough to heat through. Serve over rice or noodles.

Mrs. Tara Hansen – Ft. Worth, Texas
Wife of Captain Eydin Hansen

Steak au Poivre

4 (6- to 8-ounce) tenderloin
steaks, no more than 1½
inches thick
Kosher salt
2 tablespoons whole peppercorns

1 tablespoon unsalted butter
1 teaspoon olive oil
⅓ cup Cognac, plus 1 teaspoon,
divided
1 cup heavy cream

Remove steaks from refrigerator at least 30–60 minutes prior to cooking—best if cooked at room temperature. Sprinkle all sides with salt. Place cracked black pepper on a plate. Press fillets on both sides into pepper until it coats the surface. Set aside.

In a medium skillet over medium heat, melt butter and olive oil. As soon as the butter and oil begin to turn golden and smoke, gently place steaks in pan. For medium-rare, cook 4 minutes on each side. Once done, remove steaks to a plate, tent with foil, and set aside. Pour off excess fat, but do not wipe or scrape the pan clean. Turn off; add ⅓ cup Cognac to pan and carefully ignite alcohol with a long match or lighter. Gently shake pan until flames die. Return pan to medium heat and add cream. Bring mixture to a boil and whisk until sauce coats back of a spoon, approximately 5–6 minutes. Add remaining teaspoon of Cognac, and season to taste with salt. Add steaks back to pan, spoon sauce over, and serve.

Major (Ret.) William Tosten – Alexandria, Louisiana

*Karen and William Tosten at
B-1 Bomber "Bag" Party, 1996.
28 FTU, Dyess AFB, Abilene, Texas*

Veggie Stuffed Steak

1½ pounds boneless top
  sirloin steak
Salt and pepper to taste
2 tablespoons horseradish
6 slices provolone cheese,
  divided

2–3 handfuls fresh spinach
  leaves
½ cup sliced mushrooms
½ cup roasted red pepper
1 tablespoon cooking oil

Butterfly steak and pound to about ¼ inch; season with salt and pepper. Spread with horseradish. Layer steak with 3 slices cheese, spinach, mushrooms, red pepper, and remaining cheese. Roll up and secure with toothpicks (it will be big, but everything shrinks while cooking). Season outside with salt and pepper. Put in refrigerator for at least 2 hours.

Preheat oven to 350°. Heat oil in pan over high heat and sear all sides of meat. Then transfer to oven for 35–40 minutes to finish cooking.

Mrs. Jessica Martin – La Plata, Maryland
Wife of Staff Sergeant Jeffery Martin

Chile Relleno Casserole

Great for brunch or dinner.

1 pound lean ground beef
½ cup chopped onion
½ teaspoon salt
¼ teaspoon pepper
2 (4-ounce) cans green chiles,
  divided

1½ cups grated Cheddar cheese
1½ cups milk
¼ cup all-purpose flour
½ teaspoon salt
Dash of pepper
4 eggs, beaten

Sauté beef and onion until browned. Drain. Add salt and pepper. Spread 1 can green chiles in 8x10-inch baking dish. Layer cheese, meat, and remaining can of chiles. Combine milk, flour, salt, and pepper with eggs. Beat until smooth. Pour over meat and chili layers. Bake at 350° for 45–60 minutes.

Mrs. Cathy Harvey – Georgetown, South Carolina
Wife of Lt. Colonel Joe Harvey

Shepherd's Pie

An England-acquired recipe.

7 tablespoons butter, divided
1 onion, chopped
1 pound lean ground beef
3 tablespoons garlic, minced
1 cup beef broth, divided
1 tablespoon flour
1 tablespoon ketchup

1 tablespoon Worcestershire
½ teaspoon dried thyme
¼ teaspoon red pepper
2 pounds red potatoes, peeled,
   boiled
¾ cup milk

Melt 3 tablespoons butter in frying pan and cook onion until soft. Add meat and garlic, cooking until meat is browned. Pour off excess fat. Add about ⅓ cup beef broth; simmer 5 minutes. Add remaining broth, flour, ketchup, Worcestershire, thyme, and pepper.

Preheat oven to 400°. Prepare hot mashed potatoes with milk and remaining butter. Spread meat mixture into an 8x8-inch baking dish. Spread potatoes over top and bake uncovered until potatoes turn golden brown, about 20 minutes.

Mrs. Linda Slater – Long Island, New York
Wife of Chief Master Sergeant Kevin G. Slater

Beeble's Golabki

These cabbage rolls originated in Russia.

1 head cabbage
1 pound ground beef, browned
½ pound ground pork,
  browned
¼ cup chopped onion

2 tablespoons chopped green
  bell pepper
1 egg
Salt and pepper to taste
1 cup cooked rice

Steam cabbage leaves until limp. Brown meats with onion, green pepper, and egg; season with salt and pepper. Add rice. Put a scoop of meat mixture into center of cabbage leaf. Roll meat in leaves, turning ends under. Place in Dutch oven and add remaining cabbage. Cover with Sauce. Simmer covered 1 hour.

SAUCE:

½ pound bacon, cut in pieces
3 tablespoons flour
1 (14½-ounce) can tomatoes,
  undrained

1 tablespoon vinegar

Brown bacon. Sprinkle flour over bacon and grease. Stir and add tomatoes with juice and vinegar.

Mrs. Frances Anderson – Pineville, Louisiana
Wife of Lt. Colonel (Ret.) Andy Anderson

Natchitoches Meat Pies

1½ pounds ground chuck
1½ pounds ground pork
1 cup chopped green onions, tops and bottoms
1 tablespoon salt

1 teaspoon coarsely ground black pepper
1 teaspoon coarsely ground red pepper
⅓ cup all-purpose flour

Combine ground chuck, pork, green onions, salt, black pepper, and red pepper. Cook over medium heat until meat loses its red color. Sift flour over mixture, stirring often, until well combined in meat. Remove from heat and drain excess grease and juice in large colander.

CRUST:
2 cups self-rising flour
⅓ heaping cup Crisco

1 egg, beaten
¾ cup milk

Combine ingredients; roll out, and cut into 5-inch circles. Assemble by placing a heaping tablespoon of filling on one side of each circle; fold over and crimp edges. Prick with fork twice on top. Fry at 350° until golden.

Mrs. Frances Anderson – Pineville, Louisiana
Wife of Lt. Colonel (Ret.) Andy Anderson

*Andy and Frances Anderson on their wedding day (April 18, 1959)
and in September 2005*

Cajun-Style Jambalaya

1 pound pork or beef, cut into
  2-inch cubes
3 pounds smoked sausage,
  sliced
2 bell peppers, chopped
3 large onions, chopped
2 large ribs celery, chopped
3 bunches green onions,
  chopped

3 cloves garlic, minced
½ stick butter or margarine
2 tablespoons salt
1 tablespoon red pepper flakes
1 (10-ounce) can Ro-Tel tomatoes,
  drained
4½ cups chicken stock
3 cups long-grain rice

In a pot, brown meat and remove. Brown sausage in same pot and remove; drain grease. Add all chopped vegetables into pot and cook to a golden brown. All liquid should be cooked out. Add meat, sausage, butter, salt, and pepper. Add tomatoes and chicken stock. Simmer on medium heat 20–25 minutes with lid on. Remove lid and bring to a boil. Add rice and mix well. Lower heat, put lid on and let simmer 25 minutes. Do not remove lid. After 25 minutes, remove lid and stir. Feeds 10–20.

Colonel (Ret.) Ronald G. Noland – *Baton Rouge, Louisiana*

Sauerbraten

This Sauerbraten recipe is a special recipe that my grandmother brought with her from Germany. She was born around 1900 and lived in Bavaria until she and my grandfather moved to the United States around the 1920's. We used to have this every Easter instead of ham. My grandmother passed it down to my mother and she passed it down to me. This is one of my children's favorite dinners. We complete the meal with red cabbage, potato pancakes with applesauce, or hot potato salad, and pumpernickel bread.

2 cups red wine vinegar
2 cups water
2 medium onions, sliced
1 lemon, sliced
4 bay leaves
6 peppercorns
2 tablespoons salt

10 whole cloves
3 tablespoons sugar, divided
4 pounds beef rump or sirloin tip
6 tablespoons flour
6 tablespoons butter
10 gingersnaps, crushed

Combine red wine vinegar, water, onions, lemon, bay leaves, peppercorns, salt, cloves, and 2 tablespoons sugar. Place meat in large deep non-metal bowl; pour vinegar mixture over meat. Refrigerate 72 hours, turning meat once or twice a day.

Remove meat, pat dry, and rub lightly with a little flour; brown well on all sides in 1 tablespoon butter or margarine. Strain vinegar mixture; add 2 cups of the liquid to meat. Cover and simmer 3 hours.

Melt remaining butter or margarine; blend in remaining flour and sugar; stir until rich brown. Add remaining strained vinegar mixture. Add to simmering meat mixture; simmer 1 hour longer or until meat is tender. Remove meat; stir crushed gingersnaps into gravy. Stir until thickened.

Ms. Corrine Osborn, Operations Support – Elmendorf AFB, Alaska

Tacoritos

1 pound ground beef, cooked
3 (10¾-ounce) cans cream of
  chicken soup
2 cans water
3 tablespoons chili powder
1 teaspoon garlic powder
1 teaspoon onion powder
1 teaspoon sage
1 teaspoon cumin

Dash of red pepper flakes
Dash of cayenne pepper
2 cups shredded Cheddar cheese,
  divided
Flour tortillas
Shredded lettuce, black olives,
  chopped tomatoes, sour cream,
  salsa, for garnish

Brown ground beef; drain. Combine soup, water, chili, garlic powder, onion powder, sage, cumin, red pepper flakes, and cayenne pepper. Add 1 cup Cheddar cheese. Stir over low heat until cheese is melted.

Place about ½ cup ground beef and ¼ cup sauce in middle of flour tortillas and roll up. Place seam side down in 9x13-inch casserole dish. Once all flour tortillas are filled, pour remaining sauce over tortillas. Bake 20 minutes at 350° or until bubbly. Serve with remaining 1 cup shredded cheese, shredded lettuce, black olives, chopped tomatoes, sour cream, and salsa, if desired.

Mrs. Nancy Townsend – Colorado Springs, Colorado
Wife of Colonel Bruce Townsend

Picadillo

A decidedly Cuban dish.

1 pound ground beef
1 cup water
2 (6-ounce) cans tomato paste, divided
Bay leaves to taste (start with 4)

4 cloves garlic, minced
2 tablespoons minced onion
Salt and pepper to taste
Stuffed green olives, to taste

Combine ground beef, water, and 1 can tomato paste in medium pot set at medium heat. Stir frequently, making sure that there are no big clumps of beef. Add bay leaves, minced garlic cloves, and minced onion. Salt and pepper to taste. Let simmer over low heat; add stuffed olives along with some of their juice and remaining tomato paste. Make sure it warms up again. Serve over white rice, alongside Goya black bean soup, found in the Latin section of the grocery store.

Mrs. Irene Morgan – Fort Lauderdale, Florida
Wife of Captain Clifford W. Morgan

The United States Air Force Academy (USAFA) is located north of Colorado Springs, Colorado. It is an institution for the undergraduate education of officers for the United States Air Force. Graduates of the four-year program receive a Bachelor of Science degree and most are commissioned as second lieutenants in the United States Air Force. The Air Force Academy is among the most selective colleges in the United States. Candidates are judged based on their academic achievement, demonstrated leadership, athletics and character. To gain admission, candidates must also pass a fitness test, undergo a thorough medical examination, and secure a nomination, which usually comes from one of the candidate's members of Congress. Recent incoming classes have usually consisted of about 1,400 cadets; just under 1,000 of those usually make it through to graduation. Cadets pay no tuition, but incur a commitment to serve a number of years in the military service after graduation.

Easy Tex-Mex Casserole

1 pound ground beef
1 package taco seasoning mix
1 (15-ounce) can refried beans
1 (8-ounce) package tortilla
  chips, crushed, divided

1 (15-ounce) can chili
4 ounces (1 cup) shredded cheese
Optional extras*

Brown meat with taco seasoning mix. While this cooks, spray casserole dish with cooking spray.

Preheat oven to 350°. Layer bottom of dish with refried beans. Top with half of crushed tortilla chips. Next layer in chili. Top chili with remaining crushed tortilla chips. Then, place taco meat mixture on top of second layer of chips. Cook, covered, about 30 minutes or until heated through. You might want to remove the lid after about 20 minutes to firm up the top a little. After removing casserole from oven, layer shredded cheese on top of taco meat, and let sit for a few minutes to melt cheese. Serve hot.

*Some optional extras: green chiles, onions, jalapeños, black olives, sour cream, Pepper Jack cheese, hot sauce, and salsa.

Lt. Colonel Steve Harris – St. Louis, Missouri

The buildings in the Cadet Area of the United States Air Force Academy were designed by Walter Netsch in a distinct, modernist style, and make extensive use of aluminum on building exteriors, suggesting the outer skin of aircraft and some spacecraft. The most recognizable building in the Cadet Area is the seventeen-spired Cadet Chapel (shown at right), and is often used as a symbol of the Academy itself. The subject of controversy when it was first built in 1956, it is now considered among the most beautiful examples of modern American academic architecture. It was named a National Historic Landmark in 2004. The academy is also one of the largest tourist attractions in Colorado, attracting more than a million visitors each year.

Super-Good Enchilada Casserole

1 pound ground beef or 1 large
  package chicken breasts
½ onion, chopped
1 (4-ounce) can mild green
  chiles, chopped
¼ teaspoon garlic powder

½ teaspoon MSG
Salt and pepper to taste
2 cups shredded Jack cheese
1 cup sour cream
Flour tortillas
Additional cheese for top

Preheat oven to 350°. Brown beef or bake chicken and chop. Sauté onion, chiles, and spices. Add meat and 2 cups cheese. Mix in sour cream. Heat tortillas till soft. Roll 2½ tablespoons meat mix in each tortilla and place in shallow baking dish. Cover with Sauce and top with additional shredded Jack cheese. Bake 30 minutes.

SAUCE:

1 (15-ounce) can chili (no beans)
1 (10-ounce) can mild enchilada
  sauce
2 tablespoons mild taco sauce

6 shots Tabasco
¼ teaspoon garlic powder
1 (10¾-ounce) can golden
  mushroom soup

Mix all ingredients together and serve over enchiladas.

Mrs. Samantha Laidlaw – Ft. Walton Beach, Florida
Wife of Captain Brian Laidlaw

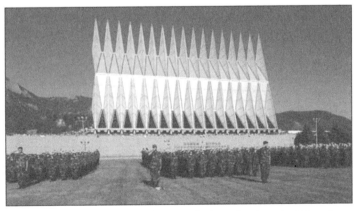

Cadet Chapel at the United States Air Force Academy in Colorado

Easy Enchiladas

1 (16-ounce) carton sour cream
1 (10¾-ounce) can cream of
  chicken (mushroom or beef)
  soup
1 (15-ounce) can enchilada sauce

2–3 cups cut-up, cooked chicken
  or beef
Flour tortillas (about 10)
1 (16-ounce) package shredded
  Monterey Jack cheese

Preheat oven to 350°. Mix sour cream, soup, and enchilada sauce together. Put chicken or beef in tortillas with some cheese and some sauce. Roll up and place in lightly greased pan. Put extra sauce and cheese on top of rolled-up tortillas. Cover and bake about 30 minutes.

Mrs. Laurie Smith – Seattle, Washington
Wife of Lt. Colonel Bruce Smith

Easy Beef Bourguignon-Crockpot Style

1 (10¾-ounce) can cream of
  mushroom soup
½ cup dry red wine
1 envelope Lipton Onion Soup
  Mix
½ teaspoon thyme

2 pounds lean beef chunks for
  stewing
2 cups fresh carrot pieces
2 cups sliced mushrooms
  (optional)

Whisk mushroom soup, wine, soup mix, and thyme in slow cooker until well blended. Add remaining ingredients and stir until coated. Cover and cook on HIGH 4 hours or on LOW 8–10 hours, or until meat is very tender. Serve over noodles or mashed potatoes.

Mrs. Laurie Smith – Seattle, Washington
Wife of Lt. Colonel Bruce Smith

Savory Pot Roast

This pot roast strays from the traditional with a blend of savory herbs and coffee. It is a jazzy way to add a new twist on an old favorite. After hours of cooking, the pot roast falls apart and the sauce reduces to almost a burgundy-wine taste. Serve with baked small red potatoes, grilled asparagus, and crusty sourdough rolls. OOOOh-la-la!

2 bay leaves, crumbled
1 cup coffee
¼ cup soy sauce
2 cloves garlic (or more),
   minced

½ teaspoon oregano
2 onions, sliced, divided
1 (3-pound) pot roast (any cut
   you like)
3 tablespoons oil

Preheat oven to 300°. Combine bay leaves, coffee, soy sauce, garlic, oregano, and 1 of the sliced onions, and place in a roasting pan. In a heavy skillet, brown all sides of meat in hot oil. Transfer meat to roasting pan and lay on top of seasonings. Place remaining onion on top of roast; cover. Bake 3½–4 hours. Baste each hour with pan juices. The sauce is best left as a juice that is poured over meat when served.

Mrs. Melinda Smith – Monument, Colorado
Wife of Lt. Colonel (Ret.) Fred Smith

Beef and Green Beans

This recipe has been tasted and tested by my family since we were stationed at Kadena AFB, Japan, in the 1960s.

MEAT:
½ pound beef (eye of round
  or round steak), shredded

MARINADE:

1½ tablespoons soy sauce	Dash of black pepper
2 teaspoons cornstarch	1 teaspoon finely chopped ginger
1 tablespoon wine	1 clove garlic, crushed
1 tablespoon sesame seed oil	

Mix Marinade ingredients and marinate beef at least 1 hour before frying.

VEGETABLE MIXTURE:

5 tablespoons oil for frying, divided	1 cup sliced water chestnuts
1 cup green beans (can use green pepper or snow peas)	¼ teaspoon salt
	Soy sauce to taste

Heat 2 tablespoons oil on high heat on stove. Sauté vegetables. Sprinkle on salt and soy sauce, and fry 2 minutes. Remove to platter.

Heat 3 tablespoons oil in same skillet and fry meat until medium-rare (2–3 minutes). Add vegetables and mix well.

GLAZE:

2 teaspoons soy sauce	1 teaspoon cornstarch
⅓ cup water	

Add water and soy sauce to cornstarch. Pour over beef and vegetable mixture in skillet, and stir until thick.

Mrs. Tana Moran – Cincinnati, Ohio
Wife of Colonel (Ret.) Jack Moran

Seaway Sukiyaki

1 (4- to 6-count) package frozen
  hamburger patties, quartered
1 teaspoon oil
2 tablespoons sugar
2 teaspoons cornstarch

3 tablespoons soy sauce
5 tablespoons water
½ green bell pepper
1 medium onion
1 cup celery cubes, including tops

Place meat in skillet with oil, and brown while still frozen. Combine sugar and cornstarch, and slowly add soy sauce and water. Blend well. Slice green pepper in thick strips, the onion in thick rings. When meat has browned on each side, arrange vegetables on top. Pour sauce mixture over all. Place lid on skillet. Reduce heat and cook until vegetables are fork-tender. Serve over rice or with chow mein noodles.

Master Sergeant Deb Marsh – Hubbard, Ohio

Sausage and Pepper Stir Fry

3 cups long-grain white rice
1 (1-pound) package Hillshire
  Farms smoked sausage (hot
  or mild)

2 yellow bell peppers
2 red bell peppers
2 green bell peppers
1 medium or large onion

Cook rice according to directions. Slice sausage lengthwise, then cut into bite-size pieces. Put cut-up sausage into deep frying pan. Fry sausage until cooked thoroughly, stirring often. Chop bell peppers and onion into bite-size pieces and add to sausage in frying pan. Sauté until tender. Finally, add cooked rice to mixture while cooking for a few more minutes. Serves 4.

Mrs. Cynthia Shaner – West Newton, Pennsylvania
Wife of Senior Master Sergeant (Ret.) Rick L. Shaner

Beef Jerky

1–2 pounds thinly sliced
  (¼ inch) beef
¼ cup soy sauce
1 tablespoon Worcestershire

1 teaspoon garlic salt
1 teaspoon pepper
¼ teaspoon red chili powder
  for an extra "kick" (optional)

Trim fat from meat and marinate in remaining ingredients 1 hour. Drain and place in dehydrator trays. Dry on HIGH until properly dried and chewy, 6–12 hours.

Master Sergeant Joel Bertrand – Tucson, Arizona

Apple-Glazed Pork Tenderloin

¾ cup apple jelly
2 tablespoons lemon juice
½ teaspoon pumpkin pie spice

1 pound pork tenderloin
2 tart red cooking apples

Preheat oven to 375°. In small bowl, combine apple jelly, lemon juice, and pumpkin pie spice; blend well. For easy clean-up, spray roasting rack with nonstick cooking spray; place in shallow pan lined with foil. Place pork tenderloin on prepared rack, and brush with apple jelly mixture. Roast at 375° for 45 minutes, or until meat thermometer indicates just short of 160°. Remove from oven and let stand 5 minutes.

Leave skin on apples, but core and slice thinly. Place apple slices on broiler pan lined with foil and sprayed with cooking spray so that apples won't stick, and brush with remaining apple jelly mixture. Broil 5–6 inches from heat about 5 minutes, or until apple slices are tender. Slice pork tenderloin and serve with cooked apple slices.

Master Sergeant (Ret.) Michael Chapman – Las Vegas, Nevada

Really Good Baby Back Ribs

DRY RUB:

8 tablespoons light brown sugar
3 tablespoons kosher salt
1 tablespoon chili powder
½ teaspoon black pepper
½ teaspoon cayenne

½ teaspoon jalapeño seasoning
½ teaspoon Old Bay Seasoning
½ teaspoon rubbed thyme
½ teaspoon onion powder

Mix all ingredients together; set aside or store in airtight container.

2 slabs baby back ribs

Preheat oven to 250°. Using a sharp knife, cut just about halfway through the slab between every other rib bone. Rub Dry Rub mixture generously on to both sides of slab. The more the better, and the spicier, too. Wrap slab in aluminum foil, place in a shallow pan, and bake for 1½ hours. While slabs are baking, prepare Braising Liquid.

BRAISING LIQUID:

1 cup white wine
2 tablespoons white wine vinegar
2 tablespoons Worcestershire

1 tablespoon honey
2 cloves garlic, chopped fine

After baking 1½ hours, remove ribs from oven. They can stay wrapped in the foil until you are ready to put them on the grill. When grill is ready, unwrap rib slabs and place over either direct or indirect heat, but not too hot. You don't want them to burn. Frequently baste them with Braising Liquid, turning slabs every 5–10 minutes, until done, probably about 20–25 minutes. You can add mesquite smoking wood during the grilling phase if you like, for an added delicious flavor. No other sauces or coatings are needed with this recipe.

Master Sergeant (Ret.) Michael Chapman – Las Vegas, Nevada

Schnitzel Pfanne
(German Pork Steak)

This is an excellent dish to make ahead for dinner guests when you don't want to spend all day in the kitchen. This will be the hit of your party!

8 (1-inch-thick) medium large
   pork tenderloin steaks
Salt and pepper to taste
3 eggs, beaten
Plain or Italian style bread
   crumbs
Olive oil for frying plus
   2 tablespoons, divided

¼ cup water
2 large onions, diced
1 pound cooked ham, diced
3–5 (4-ounce) cans sliced
   mushrooms, drained
1 cup dry white wine
2 cups heavy whipping cream
2 cups milk

Tenderize, salt and pepper tenderloin steaks. Dip in beaten eggs, then bread crumbs. Fry in olive oil on both sides until golden brown. When all tenderloins are fried, put all together into frying pan, add ¼ cup of water, cover pan, and simmer 5–10 minutes. Arrange in large deep baking dish and set aside.

Meanwhile, heat 2 tablespoons olive oil and cook onions to golden brown, then add ham; cook and brown ham a few minutes, then add mushrooms. Cook and brown mixture together another few minutes, then add dry white wine. Close pan and let mixture simmer at least 15 minutes. Pour onion/ham/mushroom mixture over arranged pork tenderloins, covering all the meat.

Mix heavy whipping cream and milk together and pour over entire mixture in baking dish. Cover completely with foil and set into refrigerator at least 6–8 hours before serving. (Best done the day before.) Reheat in 325° oven 30–40 minutes. Serve with French bread and mixed salad; kids like French fries. Guten Appetit!

Mrs. Alice Taylor – Bann / Rheinland-Pfalz-Germany
Wife of Lt. Colonel (Ret.) Kerry Taylor

Pork Tenderloin à la Crème

This is a beautiful dinner entrée to serve to company. Delicious!

8 strips bacon
8 slices pork tenderloin (2 inches thick, butterflied)
½ cup brandy
2–3 teaspoons dry mustard
Dash of salt
½ teaspoon pepper
¼ teaspoon thyme

¼ teaspoon rosemary
¼ teaspoon garlic
½ cup dry white wine
3 tablespoons beef bouillon
2 cups heavy cream
3 tablespoons all-purpose flour
¼ pound sliced mushrooms

Preheat oven to 350°. Fry bacon until limp, then wrap bacon around outside edge of tenderloin slices; secure with toothpick. Place tenderloin pieces in ungreased roasting pan or glass dish. Drizzle brandy over meat, then sprinkle mustard and other spices over tenderloin. Bake uncovered for 20–30 minutes. Pour the drippings into a skillet. Add wine and bouillon and whisk until it bubbles, 1–2 minutes. Whisk cream and flour together and add to skillet. Stir and boil until thickened and smooth, 3–4 minutes. Pour sauce over meat and sprinkle mushrooms on top. Bake another 10–15 minutes or until sauce is thickened.

Lt. Colonel Deborah McMurtrey – Cape Carteret, North Carolina

Sweet and Sour Pork

This comes from Taipei, Taiwan.

1 (1-pound) pork tenderloin
2 tablespoons vinegar
2 tablespoons sugar
2 tablespoons ketchup
½ cup water

1 tablespoon soy sauce
Dash of salt and pepper
1½ tablespoons cornstarch
Oil for frying

Cut pork into bite-size pieces. Mix together vinegar, sugar, ketchup, water, soy sauce, salt and pepper, and marinate pork 3 hours, mixing occasionally. Drain pork of most of the liquid, then roll in cornstarch and fry until brown and crisp. Keep warm while making Sauce.

SAUCE:
¼ cup vinegar
¼ cup sugar
Dash of salt
¼ cup water
3 tablespoons Worcestershire

¼ cup ketchup
2 teaspoons cornstarch
Grated gingerroot or small
amount crystallized ginger

Mix all ingredients thoroughly and cook slowly for a few minutes. Pour over pork just before serving.

Mrs. Frances Anderson – Pineville, Louisiana
Wife of Lt. Colonel (Ret.) Andy Anderson

Hot Tamales

2 pounds lean boneless pork loin
4 tablespoons chili powder
4 tablespoons paprika
2 teaspoons ground cumin
1 teaspoon oregano
1 teaspoon cayenne pepper

2 teaspoons black pepper
1 teaspoon salt
4 cloves garlic, minced
1 cup stock
50–60 dried corn shucks

Cut pork in large 3- to 4-inch chunks. Boil in 2 quarts water 45 minutes. Put through meat grinder. Reserve all stock. Add all the seasoning, and 1 cup stock to ground pork mixture.

PASTE MIXTURE:
½ pound softened lard
1 pound Tamalina*

4 teaspoons salt
2⅔ cups warm stock

Work lard mixture well into tamalina by hand or mixer. Add salt, then add stock, using electric mixer. This will make a thick paste which is called masa.

Soak corn husks for several hours in hot water. Trim to about 4x6 inches. Apply paste to lower left corner of husk with a butter knife about ⅛ inch thick. Apply about 1 tablespoon pork mixture to center of masa. Roll up like a cigarette, folding the end. This empty end will allow for swelling during cooking. Put tamales into a steamer side by side as to hold in place. Steam for 1 hour. Serve with enchilada sauce.

*Tamalina is the brand name for dehydrated corn flour that is used to make masa.

Major Rhonda Donze – Melbourne, Florida
Wife of Lt. Colonel (Ret.) Robert Donze

The Military Wife

The good Lord was creating a model for military wives and was into his sixth day of overtime when an angel appeared. She said "Lord, you seem to be having a lot of trouble with this one. What's wrong with the standard model?"

The Lord replied, "Have you seen the specs on this order? She has to be completely independent, possess the qualities of both father and mother, be a perfect hostess to four or forty with an hour's notice, run on black coffee, handle every emergency imaginable without a manual, be able to carry on cheerfully, even if she is pregnant and has the flu, and she must be willing to move to a new location ten times in seventeen years. And oh, yes, she must have six pairs of hands."

The angel shook her head. "Six pairs of hands? No way."

The Lord continued. "Don't worry; we will make other military wives to help her. And we will give her an unusually strong heart so it can swell with pride in her husband's achievements, sustain the pain of separation, beat soundly when it is overworked and tired, and be large enough to say, "I understand," when she doesn't, and say "I love you," regardless.

"Lord," said the angel, touching his arm gently, "Go to bed and get some rest. You can finish this tomorrow."

"I can't stop now," said the Lord. "I am so close to creating something unique. Already this model heals herself when she is sick, can put up six unexpected guests for the weekend, wave good-bye to her husband from a pier, a runway, or a depot, and understand why it's important that he leave."

The angel circled the model of the military wife, looked at it closely and sighed. "It looks fine, but it's too soft."

"She might look soft," replied the Lord, "but she has the strength of a lion. You would not believe what she can endure."

Finally, the angel bent over and ran her finger across the cheek of the Lord's creation. "There's a leak," she announced. "Something is wrong with the construction. I am not surprised that it has cracked. You are trying to put too much into this model."

The Lord appeared offended at the angel's lack of confidence. "What you see is not a leak," he said. "It's a tear."

"A tear? What is it there for?" asked the angel.

The Lord replied, "It's for joy, sadness, pain, disappointment, loneliness, pride, and a dedication to all the values that she and her husband hold dear."

"You are a genius!" exclaimed the angel.

The Lord looked puzzled and replied, "I didn't put it there."

Author Unknown

Wings & Things: Poultry

U.S. AIR FORCE PHOTO

The **C-17 Globemaster III** is the newest, most flexible cargo aircraft to enter the airlift force. The C-17 was designed to meet the changing requirements of U.S.-mechanized firepower and equipment, which have grown in response to improved capabilities of potential adversaries. The C-17 is capable of rapid strategic delivery of troops and cargo. It is also able to perform tactical airlift and airdrop missions.

Here a C-17 releases flares during a training mission.

Mediterranean Chicken Sandwich

2–3 cooked chicken breasts,
cubed
1 (15-ounce) carton ricotta
cheese
½ cup shredded mozzarella
cheese
¼ cup grated Parmesan cheese
½ (10-ounce) package frozen
chopped spinach, thawed,
drained

1 cup tomato purée
1 loaf French bread
4 tablespoons rosemary-flavored
olive oil (or regular olive oil
with added rosemary)

Preheat oven to 350°. Mix chicken, cheeses, spinach, and tomato purée in a medium bowl. Slice bread in half and brush with olive oil. Spread chicken mixture on bread and toast open face on a cookie sheet 10–12 minutes at 350°.

First Lt. Kelly Russell – Buffalo, NY
Wife of First Lt. Patrick Applegate

"Wing" is a term used for a unit of command. In the USAF, a wing is a relatively large formation, comprising six or more squadrons. USAF wings are structured to fulfill a mission from a specific base, and contain a headquarters and four groups: an operations group, a maintenance group, a medical group, and a mission support group. Such a wing is referred to as a Combat Wing Organization. Other wings, such as Air Expeditionary Wings, exist for various other purposes, and their scope may extend to one base, one theater, or worldwide. Hierarchical Structure of the USAF: Major Commands, Numbered Air Forces, Operational Commands (now inactive), Wings, Groups, Squadrons.

Chicken Squares

4 cups cooked, cubed chicken
1 (8-ounce) package cream
  cheese, softened
4 tablespoons soft margarine
¼ teaspoon garlic salt
¼ teaspoon pepper

4 tablespoons milk
2 teaspoons finely chopped onion
2 (8-ounce) packages crescent rolls
2 tablespoons margarine, melted
¾ cup croutons, crushed

Preheat oven to 325°. Cut chicken into ½-inch cubes. Set aside. Mix softened cream cheese and margarine together. Add garlic salt, pepper, milk, and onion. Add chicken and mix together. Combine 2 crescent rolls to make a square. Spread ½ cup chicken mixture in center of dough. Pull 4 corners of dough to center of mix and twist firmly. Pinch to seal. Place on cookie sheet. Brush top with melted margarine and crushed croutons. Bake 25–30 minutes, until tops are brown.

Mrs. Jenny Monroe – Morton Grove (Chicago), Illinois
Wife of Captain Timothy Monroe

Poppy Seed Chicken

2 boxes Rice-A-Roni (fried rice
  with almonds)
2 pounds chicken, cooked,
  chopped
1 (16-ounce) carton light sour
  cream

2 (10¾-ounce) cans low-fat
  cream of chicken soup
½ cup margarine, melted
3 cups crumbled Ritz Crackers
  (2 sleeves)
¼ cup poppy seeds

Cook rice according to package instructions.
  Preheat oven to 350°. Spread rice in bottom of 9x13-inch dish. Combine chicken, sour cream, and soup. Spread on top. Mix melted butter and crackers. Spread over chicken mixture. Top with poppy seeds. Bake 30 minutes uncovered.

Mrs. Laurie Smith – Seattle, Washington
Wife of Lt. Colonel Bruce Smith

Apricot Chicken

6 boneless and skinless chicken
  breasts
1 cup apricot jam

1 cup Russian salad dressing
1 package onion soup mix

Preheat oven to 350°. Place chicken in 9x13-inch baking dish. Combine jam, salad dressing, and soup mix. Pour over chicken. Bake uncovered 30 minutes. Serve over rice.

Mrs. Cathy Harvey – Georgetown, South Carolina
Wife of Lt. Colonel Joe Harvey

Marlene's Chicken Adobo

4–6 whole chicken legs (2–3
  pounds), cut into drumstick
  and thigh sections
¾ cup soy sauce
½ cup distilled white vinegar
3 garlic cloves, crushed

2 bay leaves
1 large yellow onion, chopped
½ tablespoon crushed black
  pepper
2 cups water
Cooked white rice

In a large kettle, combine chicken, soy sauce, vinegar, garlic, bay leaves, onion, pepper, and 2 cups water. Bring to a boil, then let simmer, covered, 60 minutes. Transfer chicken with tongs to a plate, and boil the liquid another 10 minutes, or until it is reduced to about 1 cup. Let sauce cool, then remove bay leaves and skim fat from surface. Transfer chicken to a large rimmed platter, pour heated sauce over it, and serve with rice.

Mrs. Marlene Goldie – Minot, North Dakota
Wife of Chief Master Sergeant David Goldie

Chicken Enchiladas

1 (16-ounce) carton sour cream
1 (10¾-ounce) can cream of
  mushroom soup
1 (4-ounce) can mushroom
  pieces, drained
2 cups shredded cooked chicken

1 medium onion, chopped
1 (8- to 10-count) bag flour
  tortillas, divided
1 pound shredded Cheddar cheese,
  divided

Preheat oven to 350°. Mix sour cream, mushroom soup, mushrooms, chicken, and onion in a bowl. Spray bottom of 9x13-inch dish with cooking spray. Put first layer of tortilla shells down, just enough to cover bottom of dish. Pour sour cream mixture on tortillas to cover; sprinkle with ⅓ of cheese. Do the same thing on next layer: tortilla shells, sour cream mixture, then cheese. Top last layer with cheese. Bake 30 minutes. Let cool about 10 minutes; cut and serve. Serves 10.

Mrs. Jennifer Willand – Northwood, Iowa
Wife of Master Sergeant Dan Willand

Badges of the United States Air Force are military awards that signify aeronautical ratings or qualification in several career fields, and also serve as identification for personnel in certain assignments. The Air Force currently authorizes 51 separate rating and occupational badges. Badges include: Aviation, Occupational, Medical Service, Religious Service, Air and Space Warfare, Restricted Warfare, and Service.

 An Aviator Badge, also known as Pilot Wings, is the most widely recognized badge by civilians, and designates those who have received training and qualification in military aviation. Pilot Wings are issued in three ratings: Basic (shown here), Senior, and Command/Master/Chief. The higher degrees are denoted by a star or star with wreath above the badge. The basic rating denotes completion of specified training; advanced ratings denote experience levels.

Green Chile Enchilada Casserole

2–3 pounds chicken breasts
20–24 corn tortillas
1 (14-ounce) can chicken broth
1 (16-ounce) carton sour cream
½ cup chopped onion
1 (10¾-ounce) can cream of
  chicken soup

½ cup (hot or mild) roasted
  green Anaheim chile sauce
2 pounds Cheddar cheese,
  divided
2 tablespoons garlic powder

Boil chicken breasts in water to cover 1 hour; drain and let cool. Shred chicken by hand.

Preheat oven to 350°. Tear corn tortillas into small pieces in a large mixing bowl; add chicken broth, sour cream, chopped onion, soup, green chili sauce, chicken, ½ the cheese, and garlic powder. Mix ingredients. Pour into 9x13-inch pan and spread evenly. Spread remaining cheese on top, cover with foil, and bake 30 minutes.

Note: If made ahead and refrigerated overnight, increase baking time to 1 hour at 300°.

Master Sergeant Joel Bertrand – Tucson, Arizona

Arnie's Chicken Enchilada Casserole

2 (10¾-ounce) cans cream of
   chicken soup
1 (14-ounce) can chicken broth
1 (4-ounce) can chopped green
   chiles

Shredded cheese
1 chicken, boiled (3 cups cooked)
1–2 packages corn tortillas

Preheat oven to 350°. In medium pan, mix soup, broth, chiles, ½ cup shredded cheese, and chicken. Cook until hot. In greased 9x13x2-inch pan, layer corn tortillas, chicken mixture, and cheese. Repeat, ending with cheese on top. Bake 20–30 minutes.

Mrs. Diana Donnelly – Enterprise, Alabama
Wife of Lt. Colonel (Ret.) Robert Donnelly

Mexican Chicken

1 medium onion, chopped
1 green bell pepper, chopped
Garlic salt to taste
1 (10-ounce) can Ro-Tel
   tomatoes
1 (10¾-ounce) can cream of
   mushroom soup
1 (10¾-ounce) can cream of
   chicken soup

1 (10-count) package 10-inch
   tortillas
2 chickens, boiled and diced
   (reserve broth)
½ pound sharp Cheddar
   cheese, grated

Sauté onion, pepper, and garlic salt. Mix with canned ingredients. Tear tortillas into pieces and dip in warm reserved chicken broth. Preheat oven to 350°. In buttered 9x13-inch pan, place a layer of tortillas, soup mixture, chicken, and cheese. Repeat. Bake 35–45 minutes, uncovering last 15 minutes of baking time.

Mrs. Billie Neese – New Orleans, Louisiana
Wife of Lt. Colonel (Ret.) Robert Neese

Tex-Mex Chicken Meatloaf

This is one of my favorite comfort foods that my mom taught me how to make. It's a great meal to make tons of and freeze and cook on those nights you just don't have time to cook an entire meal from scratch. Pull out the frozen casserole in the morning, cook it when you get home, and serve with a nice salad—you have a great meal in a hurry.

1 (4-ounce) can chopped green chiles, drained
½ cup regular oats, uncooked
1 egg
2 tablespoons chopped onion
½ teaspoon chili powder
½ teaspoon salt
⅓ cup chili sauce (or ketchup)
1 pound ground chicken or turkey
1 (15-ounce) can Great Northern beans, drained

Preheat oven to 375°. Combine green chiles, oats, egg, onion, chili powder, salt, and chili sauce; mix well. Add ground chicken or turkey and mix gently. Fold in beans. Shape into loaf and place in a greased baking dish. Bake 40–50 minutes, until internal temperature reaches 190°.

Slice and serve with rice. Top slice of meat with salsa and grated Cheddar cheese.

OPTIONAL TOPPING:
⅓ cup ketchup
1 tablespoon chopped chiles
1 teaspoon chopped onion
Dash of garlic powder

Combine and spread over cooked meatloaf. Bake 3–5 more minutes.

Mrs. Billie Borders – Poquoson, Virginia
Wife of Major (Ret.) Jerry Borders

Chicken Casserole

4–6 chicken thighs
1 (12-ounce) package macaroni
  noodles
2 cups reserved chicken broth
½ cup cubed Velveeta cheese

1 (4-ounce) can mushrooms
1–2 (10¾-ounce) cans golden
  mushroom soup, divided
Pepper to taste
½ cup saltine cracker crumbs

Boil chicken in 5 cups water until done. Remove chicken from broth. Cook macaroni in chicken broth till tender. Drain macaroni, reserving 2 cups liquid; put macaroni back in pan. Debone and skin chicken. Cut meat into bite-size pieces. Add chicken, cheese, mushrooms, and 1 can mushroom soup to macaroni. Stir till well blended; add reserved 2 cups liquid to moisten, second can of mushroom soup (to thicken if necessary), and pepper to taste.

Preheat oven to 350°. Pour mixture into greased 9x13-inch baking dish. Sprinkle with cracker crumbs. Bake 45–60 minutes.

Note: This dish freezes well; just don't add the cracker crumbs until ready to bake.

Staff Sergeant Tara M. Borton – Fayetteville, North Carolina
Wife of Tech Sergeant Randy Borton

The Department of the Air Force is headed by the civilian Secretary of the Air Force (Michael W. Wynne) who heads administrative affairs. The office is appointed by the president and generally must be confirmed by the Senate. The Department of the Air Force is a division of the United States Department of Defense, which is headed by the United States Secretary of Defense (Robert M. Gates). The highest ranking military officer in the department is the Chief of Staff of the Air Force (General T. Michael Moseley). The Chief of Staff of the USAF serves as the senior uniformed United States Air Force officer responsible for the organization, training, and equipping of active-duty, National Guard, Reserve, and civilian forces serving in the United States and overseas.

Chicken Cordon Bleu

2 eggs	2 chicken breasts
½ cup milk	3 ounces ham slices
2 cups seasoned bread crumbs	2 ounces Swiss cheese slices
1 cup flour	About 2 tablespoons olive oil
About 1 teaspoon each: salt, pepper, and garlic powder	

Preheat oven to 350°. Mix eggs and milk in bowl. Place bread crumbs in separate bowl. Place flour mixed with seasonings in third bowl. Butterfly chicken and stuff with ham and Swiss cheese. Dredge with flour, then egg mixture, then bread crumbs. Sauté chicken in olive oil until it is golden brown on each side. Place in oven; bake 30 minutes.

Mrs. Carolyn Staley – San Carlos, California
Wife of Staff Sergeant Chad Staley

Chicken and Rice Bake

1 cup rice, uncooked	1 package dry onion soup mix
1 (10¾-ounce) can cream of chicken soup	4–6 pieces uncooked chicken
1½ cans water	Poultry seasoning (optional)

Preheat oven to 375°. Grease a 9x13-inch pan; pour in the rice. Mix chicken soup, water, and soup mix. Pour carefully over rice and stir together. Place chicken on top. Sprinkle with poultry seasoning. Bake covered with foil 1 hour. Remove foil and bake an additional 15 minutes to brown chicken.

Mrs. Gail Teigeler – Riverside, California
Wife of Lt. Colonel (Ret.) Thomas Teigeler

Chicken and Broccoli Casserole

1 (20-ounce) package frozen
broccoli, cooked
1 (10¾-ounce) can cream of
mushroom soup
1 cup Miracle Whip
1 onion, chopped

1½ cups shredded Cheddar cheese
3 eggs, beaten
5 chicken breasts, cooked, cut
into bite-size pieces
2 tablespoons butter
½ cup crushed Ritz Crackers

Preheat oven to 350°. Mix broccoli, soup, Miracle Whip, onion, cheese, eggs, and chicken together. Melt butter and add to crushed crackers. Sprinkle over top of casserole. Bake 45 minutes.

Mrs. Eleanor Eells – Rowlett, Texas
Wife of Tech Sergeant (Ret.) Robert Eells

Chicken Divan

1 pound chicken breasts, cooked,
cubed
1 (10-ounce) package frozen
broccoli or fresh, cooked
1 (10¾-ounce) can cream of
chicken soup

1 cup mayonnaise
1 teaspoon curry powder
½ cup shredded Cheddar cheese
½ cup crushed saltine crackers
¼ cup butter, melted

Preheat oven to 350°. Place cooked, cubed chicken on bottom of a greased 9x9-inch casserole dish. Next place cooked broccoli on top. Combine soup, mayonnaise, and curry powder, and layer on top of chicken and broccoli. Sprinkle with shredded cheese, then crushed saltines. Pour melted butter on top. Bake 20 minutes.

Mrs. Jessica Romeo – Clarksdale, Arizona
Wife of Second Lt. Pierre Romeo

Easy Orange Barbeque Chicken

4 tablespoons orange drink mix
(such as Kool-Aid)
1½ cups barbeque sauce
(any flavor)

2–3 pounds boneless, skinless
chicken breasts

Preheat oven to 350°. Mix orange drink mix into the barbeque sauce; stir well to blend. Place chicken in an oven-safe dish. Pour barbeque mixture onto chicken, coating all pieces well. Bake 40 minutes, or until chicken is done.

Staff Sergeant Christy M. Hardy – Douglas, Georgia
Wife of Staff Sergeant Christopher Hardy

Chicken Simon and Garfunkle

6 boneless, skinless chicken
breast halves
1 stick butter, divided
Salt and pepper to taste
6 slices mozzarella cheese
Flour
1 egg, beaten

Bread crumbs
2 tablespoons parsley
½ teaspoon sage
½ teaspoon rosemary
½ teaspoon thyme
½ cup white wine

Preheat oven to 350°. Pound chicken until it is an even thickness, spread with butter, and season with salt and pepper. Put one piece of cheese on each piece of chicken. Roll and tuck ends, securing with toothpicks. Coat lightly with flour, dip in egg, and roll in bread crumbs. Place in baking dish. Melt remaining butter and add herbs. Pour over chicken. Bake 30 minutes, then baste. Add wine and continue cooking another 20 minutes.

Mrs. Diana Donnelly – Enterprise, Alabama
Wife of Lt. Colonel (Ret.) Robert Donnelly

Louisiana Jambalaya

1 (3- to 4-pound) chicken,
1½ pounds pork, cut into
    cubes
1 pound Hillshire Farm smoked
    sausage, cut into rounds
3 large onions, chopped

1 bunch green onions, chopped,
    divided
4 cloves garlic, minced
½ (12-ounce) can beer
4 cups Uncle Ben's Converted Rice
    (be sure to use Uncle Ben's)

Boil chicken in water (that has been seasoned with salt and pepper) until falling off bone. Reserve chicken broth. When cooled, debone and cut into chunks.

Brown pork and sausage. Remove from pan and set aside. Brown the onions, bottoms of green onions (save green tops), and garlic. When onions are transparent, add meat along with beer, stirring to remove brown from bottom of skillet; add rice and stir very well. Add chicken. Put in enough reserved chicken broth to cover mixture. Cover and cook over low heat, stirring gently. Occasionally stir but not too much—you don't want it to gum up. When rice is tender, turn off heat and stir in chopped green onion tops.

Mrs. Frances Anderson – Pineville, Louisiana
Wife of Lt. Colonel (Ret.) Andy Anderson

Chicken and Smoked Sausage Gumbo

1 cup vegetable oil
1 cup flour
1½ cups chopped onions
1 cup chopped celery
1 cup chopped bell peppers
3 cloves garlic, chopped
1 pound smoked sausage
  (andouille or kielbasa),
  sliced, cooked
1½ teaspoons salt

¼ teaspoon cayenne pepper
3 bay leaves
6 cups chicken stock
1 pound boneless chicken, cooked,
  cut into chunks
1 teaspoon seasoned salt
2 tablespoons chopped parsley
3 green onions, sliced
1 tablespoon filé powder
  (optional)

Combine oil and flour in large pot over medium heat. Stir slowly and constantly 20–25 minutes to make dark brown roux. Add onions, celery, bell peppers, and garlic; stir 4–5 minutes until wilted. Add sausage, salt, cayenne, and bay leaves. Stir 3–4 minutes. Add chicken stock and stir until all is evenly combined. Bring to a boil, then reduce heat to medium-low. Cook 1 hour uncovered, stirring occasionally. Season chicken and add to pot. Simmer until chicken is heated through. Skim off any fat on surface. Remove from heat. Stir in parsley, green onions, and filé powder. Remove bay leaves and serve over cooked rice.

Colonel (Ret.) Ronald G. Noland – Baton Rouge, Louisiana

Poor Man's Lobster

This uses an oven baking bag.

Chicken breasts, cut into
2- to 3-inch pieces (1 breast
per person, plus one extra)
Orange juice, enough to cover
chicken

Paprika
American cheese slices
Butter, melted

Preheat oven to 300°. Place chicken breast pieces into an oven bag and cover with orange juice. Place in a baking dish; cook 1 hour. Place chicken pieces on a cookie sheet and lightly sprinkle with paprika. Take pieces of cheese and lay over pieces of chicken and place under broiler until cheese melts. Brush with butter and serve.

Note: I like to add a dash of Old Bay Seasoning or a little cayenne pepper to the melted butter before brushing the chicken.

Mrs. Nancy Townsend – Colorado Springs, Colorado
Wife of Colonel Bruce Townsend

COURTESY OF FRANCES M. TONG
& ALAN H. ROSENBERG

Hazel Ying Lee, the first Chinese-American woman aviator, was also the first Chinese-American woman to fly for the United States military. Lee was born in Portland, Oregon, in 1912. In 1932, she took her first airplane ride, and fell in love with flying. At a time when less than one percent of pilots in the United States were women, she joined the Chinese Flying Club of Portland and took flying lessons to earn her pilot's license. She joined the Women Airforce Service Pilots and was trained to ferry aircraft and pilot fighter planes. Hazel Ying Lee was killed in the line of duty ferrying the P-63, the last WASP to die in service to her country. An effort is currently underway to honor Hazel with a U.S. postage stamp.

U.S. Air Force Bases

A partial list of U.S. Air Force bases and airfields, past and present.

Alabama
• Maxwell AFB

Alaska
• Eielson AFB
• Elmendorf AFB

Arizona
• Davis-Monthan AFB
• Luke AFB

Arkansas
• Little Rock AFB

California
• Beale AFB
• Edwards AFB
• Los Angeles AFB
• Travis AFB
• Vandenberg AFB

Colorado
• Buckley AFB
• Schriever AFB
• Peterson AFB
• United States Air Force Academy

Delaware
• Dover AFB

District of Columbia
• Bolling AFB

Florida
• Eglin AFB
• Hurlburt Field
• MacDill AFB
• Patrick AFB
• Tyndall AFB

Georgia
• Moody AFB
• Robins AFB

Hawaii
• Hickam AFB

Idaho
• Mountain Home AFB

Illinois
• Scott AFB

Kansas
• McConnell AFB

Louisiana
• Barksdale AFB

Maryland
• Andrews AFB

Massachusetts
• Otis AFB
• Hanscom AFB

Mississippi
• Columbus AFB
• Keesler AFB

Missouri
• Whiteman AFB

Montana
• Malmstrom AFB

Nevada
• Creech AFB
• Nellis AFB

Nebraska
• Offutt AFB

New Jersey
• McGuire AFB

New Mexico
• Cannon AFB
• Holloman AFB
• Kirtland AFB

North Carolina
• Pope AFB
• Seymour Johnson AFB

North Dakota
• Grand Forks AFB
• Minot AFB

Ohio
• Wright-Patterson AFB

Oklahoma
• Altus AFB
• Tinker AFB
• Vance AFB

South Carolina
• Charleston AFB
• Shaw AFB

South Dakota
• Ellsworth AFB

Tennessee
• Arnold AFB

Texas
• Brooks City-Base
• Dyess AFB
• Goodfellow AFB
• Lackland AFB
• Laughlin AFB
• Randolph AFB
• Sheppard AFB

Utah
• Hill AFB

Virginia
• Langley AFB

Washington
• Fairchild AFB
• McChord AFB

Wyoming
• F.E. Warren AFB

Guam
• Andersen AFB

Search & Rescue
Seafood

U.S. AIR FORCE PHOTO BY SENIOR AIRMAN RICHARD KAMINSKY

The primary mission of the **HH-60G Pave Hawk** helicopter is to conduct day or night combat search and rescue (CSAR) operations into hostile environments to recover downed aircrew or other isolated personnel during war. Because of its versatility, the HH-60G is also tasked to perform non-combat operations such as civil search and rescue, emergency aeromedical evacuation, disaster relief, and counterdrug activities.

An HH-60G Pave Hawk performs a rescue of a simulated downed airman off the coast of Iceland. During the rescue, a pararescueman jumps from the helicopter to help the survivor into the stretcher so he may be hoisted up.

Salmon with Gravlax Sauce

2 tablespoons dry mustard
2 tablespoons cold water
½ cup mayonnaise
⅛ teaspoon plus ½ teaspoon
   salt, divided
⅛ teaspoon plus ½ teaspoon
   dill, divided

1 tablespoon honey, plus
   additional for drizzling
2 pounds salmon fillets, center
   cut (4 pieces)
1 tablespoon cooking oil
¼ teaspoon fresh black pepper

In small glass or stainless steel bowl, whisk together mustard and water, and let stand 10 minutes. Whisk in mayonnaise, honey, ⅛ teaspoon salt, and ⅛ teaspoon dill. Heat broiler. Rub salmon on both sides with oil and put on broiler pan or baking sheet, skin side down, about 2 inches apart. Sprinkle with remaining ½ teaspoon salt, remaining ½ teaspoon dill (I usually put some fresh dill on top as well), and pepper, then drizzle with honey. Broil until golden brown and just barely done (salmon should still be translucent in center), 6–8 minutes for a 1-inch fillet. Serve salmon with sauce on the side. Other thick fillets like grouper, sturgeon, or halibut can be substituted for salmon.

Lt. Colonel (Ret.) Gloria Lewis – Hampton, Virginia
Wife of Colonel (Ret.) Howard J. Lewis

Air Force Special Operations Command's pararescuemen, also known as PJs, are the only Department of Defense specialty specifically trained and equipped to conduct conventional or unconventional rescue operations. Pararescuemen are among the most highly trained emergency trauma specialists in the United States military. They must maintain an emergency medical technician-paramedic qualification throughout their careers. With this medical and rescue expertise, along with their deployment capabilities, PJs are able to perform life-saving missions in the world's most remote areas. Their motto "That Others May Live" reaffirms the pararescueman's commitment to saving lives and self-sacrifice.

Honey Mustard Glazed Salmon with Sweet and Sour Relish

RELISH:

1 tablespoon white wine vinegar
1 tablespoon water
2 teaspoons sugar
¼ teaspoon salt

½ cup chopped red onion
1 tablespoon minced fresh mint
½ cup chopped yellow squash

Combine white wine vinegar, water, sugar and salt. Microwave on HIGH 30 seconds or until sugar dissolves. Cool. Stir in onion, mint and squash. Cover and refrigerate 1–2 hours.

SALMON:

¼ teaspoon salt
6 (6-ounce) salmon fillets, 1 inch thick, skin on

2 tablespoons Dijon mustard
2 tablespoons honey

Sprinkle salt over salmon fillets. Spray grill rack with cooking spray. Heat should be about 350°. Place fillets skin side down on grill rack. Cover and cook 9 minutes. Combine mustard and honey in bowl. Brush over fillets. Cover and cook 2 more minutes or until fish flakes with a fork. Remove from grill. Serve with Relish. Serves 6.

Mrs. Melinda Smith – Monument, Colorado
Wife of Lt. Colonel (Ret.) Fred Smith

Home Smoked Salmon, Step-By-Step

There are dozens of recipes for smoked fish. The following one has worked for me for many years and has provided a product with good consistent flavor. As always, you want to get the freshest salmon possible. You will need a brining container to hold the amount of fish you want to smoke. I have several different sizes ranging from 4 quarts all the way to a 48-quart cooler for large batches.

For the brine: 5 quarts water, 1 pound salt, ½ pound sugar (you can vary the amount of brine for the batch size). Add other ingredients to meet your taste that may include: bay leaves, thyme, black pepper, etc. The brine and salmon should be placed in a refrigerator and maintained between 38°–40°. For salmon that is 1–1¼ inches thick (thickest part), I normally leave in the brine for 12–13 hours. For pieces that are 1½ inches thick, I'll brine approximately 14 hours (experiment to fit your taste).

Take salmon out of brine and rinse with cold water; place on smoking rack, and gently pat dry with paper towels. Let salmon air-dry for at least 2 hours (this causes a "pellicle"—a tacky glaze on the fish—to form, indicating that it is ready for the smoking process).

Place in a preheated smoker at 130°, applying a heavy smoke. When fish start to turn brown, increase smoker temperature to 165°–170°. Hold this temperature until salmon is a golden brown. For softer salmon, look for an internal temperature of 125°–130°. For a firmer consistency, 131°–135° (you be the judge). Depending on fish size, type smoker, and how well you control the smoker temperature, it could take anywhere from 5–8 hours to smoke. However, I only apply smoke 3–4 hours. Again, adjust to meet your tastes.

When smoking is done, fish should be cooled for 2–3 hours. Then, wrap in wax paper and put in refrigerator. Remember, smoked salmon is perishable, I vacuum seal my smoked salmon and put it into the freezer for up to a year.

Lt. Colonel (Ret.) Bob Tom – Phillips, Wisconsin

Sea Bass in Foil with Pesto

4 (4-ounces) sea bass fillets
¾ teaspoon salt, divided
½ teaspoon ground pepper, divided
¼ cup pesto

3 carrots, grated
1 zucchini, grated
2 tablespoons olive oil
¼ cup dry white wine

Heat oven to 450°. Put 4 (12-inch) squares of aluminum foil on work surface and brush lightly with oil. Put fish fillet in center of each square. Sprinkle fillets with ¼ teaspoon salt and pepper. Spread fish with pesto. Cover pesto with carrots and zucchini. Sprinkle with remaining salt and pepper. Gather foil around fish and drizzle with oil and wine. Fold edges of foil to make a sealed package. Put on baking sheet and bake until just done, 12-15 minutes. Open and transfer to plates. Pour juices over to include vegetable toppings.

Fish alternatives: You can use other small, flat, white fish with or without skin, such as red snapper, pompano, or striped bass.

Lt. Colonel (Ret.) Gloria Lewis – Hampton, Virginia
Wife of Colonel (Ret.) Howard J. Lewis

As the United States' inland search and rescue coordinator, the Air Force Rescue Coordination Center serves as the single agency responsible for coordinating on-land federal search and rescue (SAR) activities in the forty-eight contiguous United States, Mexico, and Canada. The AFRCC operates twenty-four hours a day, seven days a week. The center ties directly into the Federal Aviation Administration's alerting system and the U.S. Mission Control Center. In addition to the Search and Rescue Satellite Aided Tracking information, the AFRCC computer system contains resource files that list federal and state organizations, which can conduct or assist in SAR efforts throughout North America. Since the center opened in May 1974, missions have resulted in more than 13,900 lives saved. (The United States Coast Guard is responsible for Search and Rescue missions over water and operates similar Rescue Coordination Centers in each of its districts.)

Tilapia and Spinach Casserole

1 (10¾-ounce) can cream of
mushroom with garlic soup
¾ can water
2 eggs
¼ teaspoon paprika
⅛ cup dried, chopped parsley
½ teaspoon ground fennel seeds
Juice of 1 lemon
1 (10-ounce) package frozen,
chopped spinach, thawed

Pam Olive Oil Spray
4 large tilapia fish fillets
1 cup (or to taste) freshly grated
Romano or Parmesan cheese,
divided
1 cup whole-wheat bread crumbs,
divided
Paprika

Preheat oven 350°. Place soup, water, eggs, paprika, parsley flakes, fennel seeds, and lemon juice in large mixing bowl; mix. Add thawed spinach to above, and mix well. Grease casserole dish with Pam Olive Oil Spray. Sprinkle with some bread crumbs. Sprinkle with some grated cheese. Place spinach mixture on top. Place fish fillets on top of spinach mixture. Spread remaining bread crumbs, then remaining cheese on top. Dust with paprika. Spray with Pam Olive Oil. Bake, uncovered, about 40 minutes or until done.

Variation: This same recipe can be used substituting fish with 4 chicken breast fillets, cream of chicken soup, 2 cloves garlic, crushed, ½ teaspoon thyme, rosemary, poultry seasoning; eliminate fennel seeds. Bake, uncovered at 375° for 40 minutes or until done.

Mrs. Alberta S. Yager – Bellevue, Nebraska
Wife of Chief Master Sergeant (Ret.) Donald A. Yager

Lemon Butter Pan-Fried Flounder

4 skinless flounder fillets
Salt and pepper to taste
Flour, for dredging
3 tablespoons butter, divided

2 tablespoons vegetable oil
1 lemon, juiced
1 small bottle capers

Wash fillets in cold water and pat dry. Season with salt and pepper. Dredge fillets in flour. Melt 2 tablespoons butter and oil in large heavy-bottomed skillet on medium-high heat. Fry fish on one side about 3 minutes. Turn fish and cook second side until golden brown. Remove fish to serving platter. Turn off heat. Into hot skillet, whisk remaining 1 tablespoon butter. Pour in lemon juice and capers with their liquid. Serve sauce over fish at once.

Mrs. Marty Holcomb – Athens, Georgia
Wife of Lt. Colonel Pete Holcomb

Whitby Crispy Crab Cakes

This recipe comes from Whitby, England.

8 ounces mixed prepared
  crabmeat
2 ounces fresh white bread
  crumbs
1 small egg, beaten
1 teaspoon Worcestershire

½ teaspoon dry English mustard
2 spring onions, finely chopped
1 tablespoon lemon juice
Grated rind of 1 lemon
2 tablespoons oil for frying

Combine all ingredients except oil in a large bowl until well mixed. Divide mixture into 8 little cakes shaped roughly with floured hands, and place on a baking tray. Chill in refrigerator 2–3 hours.

Heat oil in a shallow frying pan; place crab cakes in oil. Fry 3 minutes on each side until golden brown. Drain on paper towels, and serve immediately.

Master Sergeant Deb Marsh – Hubbard, Ohio

Classic Crab Cakes

1 large egg yolk
1 tablespoon Old Bay Seasoning
1 tablespoon Dijon mustard
½ teaspoon grated lemon zest
and juice
1½ teaspoons cider vinegar
½ cup peanut or canola oil
¼ teaspoon kosher salt
¼ teaspoon freshly ground
black pepper

1 tablespoon minced scallions,
both white and green parts
1 pound lump crabmeat, picked
clean of shell
4 cups fresh bread crumbs
¼ cup chopped parsley
4 tablespoons unsalted butter,
divided

Put egg yolk, Old Bay, mustard, lemon zest and juice, and vinegar in bowl or mini food processor or blender and process until smooth. With machine running, gradually pour in oil until mixture emulsifies and forms a mayonnaise. Season with salt and pepper. Transfer mayonnaise to a bowl and, using a rubber spatula, fold in scallions and crabmeat until well combined. Combine bread crumbs and parsley in a shallow container. Form crab mixture into 8 patties about 3 inches wide and ¾-inch thick, and drop them into the bread crumb-parsley mixture; dredge on both sides. Fry half the crab cakes in about 2 tablespoons butter in large nonstick skillet over medium heat. Repeat for remaining crab cakes.

Mrs. Karen Tosten – Hattiesburg, Mississippi
Wife of Major (Ret.) William Tosten

Incredible Crab Imperial

WHITE SAUCE:

2 tablespoons butter	1 cup whole milk
2 tablespoons flour	

Melt butter in saucepan. Stir in flour. Cook for about 1 minute, stirring constantly. Slowly whisk in milk. Stir until thick and smooth. Let cool.

1 pound crabmeat (lump is great)	½ teaspoon Old Bay Seasoning
1 egg, beaten	½ teaspoon dry mustard
1 cup mayonnaise	1 teaspoon Worcestershire
1 cup cooled White Sauce (recipe above)	2 slices bread, torn into small pieces
2 teaspoons Durkee Famous Sauce (found near mustard)	Salt and pepper to taste
	⅔ cup crushed cornflakes

Preheat oven to 375°. Re-pick crab to remove any shell. Whisk egg, then add mayonnaise, White Sauce, Durkee Famous Sauce, seasoning, mustard, Worcestershire, bread, salt and pepper. Whisk until smooth. Fold in crab. Place in greased 9x9-inch casserole. Sprinkle top with crushed cornflakes. Bake 30 minutes. Can easily be doubled.

Mrs. Barbara McGee – Hampton, Virginia
Wife of Lt. Colonel (Ret.) Guy McGee

Mary Jane's Crab and Cheese Soufflé

*This recipe was given to my mother by her good friend Mary Jane Coleman.
It is wonderful for a brunch or as a side dish to a very special meal.*

8 slices bread, crust removed,
cubed
16 ounces Kraft Old English
Cheese, cubed, divided
1 (4-ounce) can mushrooms

1 pound crabmeat
1 pint half-and-half
½ cup butter, melted
6 eggs, well beaten

Preheat oven to 350°. Prepare 9x13-inch baking dish with Pam. Place
bread cubes on bottom of baking dish. Layer half of cheese on top of
bread. Layer all mushrooms and crab over cheese. Next sprinkle
remaining cheese over mushroom layer. Mix half-and-half, butter, and
eggs together. Pour over mushroom/crab layer. Place baking dish into
a larger dish or jellyroll pan. Pour boiling water into larger pan to create a water bath. Bake 1 hour, or until set.

Mrs. Karen Tosten – Hattiesburg, Mississippi
Wife of Major (Ret.) William Tosten

Eddie Rickenbacker, America's "Ace of Aces," was best
known as a World War I fighter ace and Medal of
Honor recipient. A flying ace or fighter ace is a military aviator credited with shooting down five or more
enemy aircraft during aerial combat. Rickenbacker's
26 victories during World War I constituted an
American record that stood until World War II. He
was also a race car driver and automotive designer, a
government consultant in military matters, and a pioneer in air transportation. During his
lifetime, Rickenbacker, who had a keen insight into technology and vision for future
improvements, worked with many influential civilian and military leaders. Rickenbacker,
along with other WWI pilots, developed important aviation principles that would serve
them in civil aviation and in WWII combat.

Crab and Shrimp Lasagna

8 lasagna noodles, cooked according to package
1 cup finely chopped onion
2 tablespoons olive oil
1 (8-ounce) package cream cheese, softened
1½ cups cottage cheese
1 egg, beaten
2 teaspoons dried basil
½ teaspoon salt
½ teaspoon pepper

¼ cup grated Parmesan cheese, divided
½ cup grated sharp Cheddar cheese, divided
2 (10¾-ounce) cans cream of mushroom soup
⅓ cup milk
⅓ cup dry white wine
1 (5-ounce) can crabmeat, drained
1 pound precooked shrimp

Preheat oven to 350°. Place 4 precooked lasagna noodles into 9x13-inch baking dish. Sauté onion in oil until clear; add cream cheese, cottage cheese, egg, basil, salt, and pepper. Mix well. Spread half of this mixture over noodles. Sprinkle with half the Parmesan and Cheddar cheeses. In a bowl, combine mushroom soup, milk, and wine. Gently stir in crabmeat and shrimp. Spoon half of this mixture over cheese layer. Repeat. Bake uncovered 45 minutes. Let stand 10–15 minutes to firm up before cutting and serving.

Mrs. Marty Holcomb – Athens, Georgia
Wife of Lt. Colonel Pete Holcomb

Shrimp Creole

2 pounds shrimp, cleaned,
  deveined
½ cup oil, divided
½ cup all-purpose flour
3 cups chopped onions
2 cups chopped celery
1 cup chopped green bell pepper
1 tablespoon minced garlic
1 (6-ounce) can tomato paste

1 (28-ounce) can crushed tomatoes
4 bay leaves
½ teaspoon thyme
Salt and pepper to taste
1 cup chopped green onions
½ cup minced parsley
Juice of 1 lemon
3 cups cooked rice

Lightly sauté shrimp in 3 tablespoons oil. Remove shrimp from pan. Add remaining oil, then add flour. Stir to make a roux. Reduce heat and add onions, celery, green pepper, and garlic. Cook and reduce until thickened. Add tomato paste and cook slowly a minute or so. Mix in tomatoes, bay leaves, thyme, salt and pepper, green onions, parsley, lemon juice, and shrimp. Simmer about 45 minutes. Serve over rice.

Mrs. Cathy Harvey – Georgetown, South Carolina
Wife of Lt. Colonel Joe Harvey

Easy-Fix Shrimp Scampi

1 pound angel hair pasta
4 cloves garlic, minced
½ cup butter
1½ pounds raw shrimp, peeled

3 tablespoons finely chopped
  parsley
1 teaspoon lemon juice

Cook angel hair pasta al dente, then drain. Sauté garlic in butter over medium heat for 1 minute. Add pasta, stirring until well coated. Add shrimp and cook about 5 minutes or until no longer pink. Add parsley and lemon juice. Serves 4.

Mrs. Billie Borders – Poquoson, Virginia
Wife of Major (Ret.) Jerry Borders

Coconut Shrimp with Orange Marmalade

2 cups shredded sweetened
coconut
2 cups bread crumbs
Kosher salt and freshly ground
black pepper

2 cups all-purpose flour
4 large eggs, beaten
24 large shrimp, peeled and
deveined
Vegetable oil, for frying

In a large bowl, combine coconut and bread crumbs, and season with salt and pepper. Place flour and eggs in separate bowls. Dredge shrimp in flour and shake off excess. Next, dip the shrimp thoroughly in egg and rub against side of bowl to lightly remove excess. Finally, coat shrimp thoroughly with bread crumb mixture. Lay shrimp on parchment-lined baking sheet or platter (so they do not touch) until ready to fry.

In a large Dutch oven, heat several inches of oil to 350°. Fry shrimp in batches until golden brown and cooked through, 3–4 minutes per batch. Be careful not to overcrowd shrimp in oil while frying. Drain on paper towels.

DIPPING SAUCE:
½ cup orange marmalade   1–2 tablespoons dark rum

Heat marmalade in small saucepan over low heat. Thin with rum as desired.

Mrs. Billie Neese – New Orleans, Louisiana
Wife of Lt. Colonel (Ret.) Robert Neese

Shrimp with Orange Liqueur

Delicious over rice or pasta, or in puffed pastry shells.

1 onion, sliced
3 cloves garlic, mashed
Oil for sautéeing
1 stick butter

24 shrimp, peeled
½ cup orange liqueur (Grand
    Marnier, Drambuie)

Sauté onion and garlic in cooking oil. Add butter, shrimp, and orange liqueur. Cook until shrimp are pink, about 3 minutes.

Colonel (Ret.) Ronald G. Noland – Baton Rouge, Louisiana

Angels on Horseback

2 (8-ounce) cans sliced water
    chestnuts
8 strips bacon, cut in thirds
24 medium-size fresh oysters

Garlic powder and seasoning
    salt to taste
Hot sauce (optional)

Stack 2 slices water chestnuts in center of a strip of bacon. Top with an oyster. Wrap each end of bacon over oyster, and secure with a toothpick. Bake in 350° oven until bacon is crisp. May be placed in broiler for faster cooking. If desired, splash with hot sauce.

Colonel (Ret.) Ronald G. Noland – Baton Rouge, Louisiana

Seared Sea Scallops
with Orange and Vermouth

2 tablespoons cooking oil,
divided
2 pounds sea scallops
½ teaspoon salt
⅛ teaspoon ground black
pepper

3 tablespoons butter
2 scallions, including green tops,
chopped
½ cup dry vermouth
1 teaspoon grated orange zest

In large nonstick frying pan, heat 1 tablespoon oil over moderately high heat until very hot. Dry scallops so they will brown nicely. Season with salt and pepper. Add half the scallops to pan and cook until browned, about 1 minute. Turn and cook until browned on second side, and just done, about 2 minutes. Remove from pan and add remaining tablespoon of oil; repeat with remaining scallops. Wipe out pan, then melt butter over moderate heat. Add scallions and cook, stirring for 1 minute. Add vermouth and orange zest. Cook until sauce thickens slightly, about 2 minutes. Add scallops and warm until heated through, about 1 minute.

Variations: Sear scallops with lemon and vermouth (use teaspoon of lemon zest in lieu of orange zest), or sear scallops with orange or lemon zest and white wine in lieu of vermouth.

Lt. Colonel (Ret.) Gloria Lewis – Hampton, Virginia
Wife of Colonel (Ret.) Howard J. Lewis

Blue Ribbon Crawfish Pie

This makes two pies–and you'll need two since it is so delicious.

1 large onion, chopped
¼ cup chopped green onions
2 ribs celery, chopped
2 cloves garlic, minced
½ green bell pepper, chopped
½ cup butter
1 (10¾-ounce) can cream of
  celery soup
4 tablespoons tomato paste
1 pound crawfish tails
¼ cup chopped parsley

½ cup seasoned bread crumbs
1 teaspoon salt
½ teaspoon red pepper
½ teaspoon black pepper
4 ounces fresh sliced mushrooms
1 egg, beaten
1 (8-ounce) package cream
  cheese, softened
Milk to mix
2 boxes Pillsbury ready-made
  pie crusts

Preheat oven to 350°. Sauté onions, celery, garlic, and green pepper in butter. Add soup, tomato paste, and crawfish. Cook 10 minutes, then turn off stove. Add parsley, bread crumbs, salt, red pepper, black pepper, mushrooms, egg, and cream cheese. Use milk to obtain desired consistency. Pour into 2 pie crusts and cover each with second pie crust. Brush top of pie crust with egg wash before baking. Bake 35–40 minutes.

Mrs. Frances Anderson – Pineville, Louisiana
Wife of Lt. Colonel (Ret.) Andy Anderson

High Flying Cakes

The **F-15E Strike Eagle** is a dual-role fighter designed to perform air-to-air and air-to-ground missions. (Previous models of the F-15 are assigned air-to-air roles only.) One of the most important additions to the F-15E is the rear cockpit, and the weapons systems officer. An array of avionics and electronics systems gives the F-15E the capability to fight at low altitude, day or night, and in all weather.

The F-15's superior maneuverability and acceleration are achieved through its high-engine, thrust-to-weight ratio and low-wing loading. It was the first U.S. operational aircraft whose engines' thrust exceeded the plane's loaded weight, permitting it to accelerate even while in vertical climb. Low-wing loading (the ratio of aircraft weight to its wing area) is a vital factor in maneuverability and, combined with the high thrust-to-weight ratio, enables the aircraft to turn tightly without losing airspeed.

Turtle Cake

1 (18¼-ounce) box German
  chocolate cake mix
1 (14-ounce) package Kraft
  caramels

¾ cup margarine
½ cup evaporated milk
1 cup chopped pecans
1 cup chocolate chips

Preheat oven to 350°. Mix cake mix as directed on package. Grease and flour a 9x13-inch pan. Pour half the batter into pan; bake 15 minutes. Melt caramels, margarine, and milk in saucepan. Pour over baked cake. Top with pecans and chocolate chips. Pour remaining cake batter over caramel and chocolate chip layers. Return pan to oven and bake 15 minutes longer.

ICING:

1 (8-ounce) package cream
  cheese, softened

½ box confectioners' sugar
3 tablespoons cocoa

Cream together and spread over cooled cake.

Mrs. Tammi Naman – Lincoln, Alabama
Wife of Major Kevin Naman

Sonic boom is an impulsive noise similar to thunder. It is caused by an object moving faster than sound—about 750 miles per hour at sea level. The Air Force has conducted faster-than-sound test flights since 1947, and today most Air Force fighter aircraft are capable of supersonic speed. Consequently, supersonic training flights that simulate actual combat conditions are necessary to ensure the success and survival of aircrews during wartime. However, Air Force procedures require that, whenever possible, flights be over open water, above 10,000 feet, and no closer than 15 miles from shore. Supersonic operations over land must be conducted above 30,000 feet or, when below 30,000 feet, in specially designated areas approved by United States Air Force Headquarters in Washington DC, and the Federal Aviation Administration.

Classic Coconut Cake

You can't beat the wonderful taste of this truly classic cake.

2 (6-ounce) packages frozen coconut

1 (8-ounce) carton sour cream

1 (18¼-ounce) box yellow cake mix

1½ cups granulated sugar

Combine coconut and sour cream; set aside. Bake cake as directed on package, using the 2 egg yolks from the Icing to replace one of the eggs. Split layers to make four. Spread coconut/sour cream mixture between layers while cake is still warm. Ice cake.

ICING:

2 egg whites (use yolks in cake)

¾ cup sugar

¾ cup white corn syrup

1 tablespoon water

¼ teaspoon cream of tartar

¼ teaspoon vanilla

1 (3½-ounce) can flaked coconut

Combine egg whites, sugar, corn syrup, water and cream of tartar in double boiler; cook, stirring constantly for 7 minutes after mixture begins to boil. Remove from heat; add vanilla. Ice cake; sprinkle with coconut.

Mrs. Tammi Naman – Lincoln, Alabama
Wife of Major Kevin Naman

One Bowl Chocolate Cake

3 cups all-purpose flour
2 cups sugar
2 teaspoons baking soda
½ teaspoon salt
⅔ cups cocoa

½ cup plus 2 tablespoons oil
2 tablespoons vinegar (yes, vinegar)
2 teaspoons vanilla
2 cups water

Preheat oven to 350°. Sift together flour, sugar, baking soda, salt, and cocoa. Then add oil, vinegar, vanilla, and water. Mix well. Pour into well-greased Bundt pan. Bake 45 minutes. Check with cake tester to make sure it comes out clean.

Note: This recipe will be very thin when mixed. It's a very moist cake. Let cake cool, then dust with powdered sugar.

Tech Sergeant (Ret.) Marie Guinee – Rockwood, Pennsylvania

Snickers Cake

1 (18¼-ounce) package chocolate cake mix, with pudding
¼ cup margarine, melted
1 tablespoon water

3 eggs, divided
4 regular-size Snickers Bars, chopped
1 (8-ounce) package cream cheese
1 pound powdered sugar

Preheat oven to 350°. Combine cake mix with margarine, water, and 1 egg. Press mixture into a greased 9x13-inch pan. Melt together Snickers Bars and cream cheese, then add remaining 2 beaten eggs. Stir in powdered sugar. Pour mixture onto crust. Bake 35–45 minutes. Take out of oven and let cool 30 minutes before serving.

Mrs. Lisa Hook – Muskegon, Michigan
Wife of Captain Patrick Hook

Chocolate Wacky Cake

1½ cups all-purpose flour
3 tablespoons cocoa (rounded)
1 cup sugar
1 teaspoon baking soda
½ teaspoon salt

6 tablespoons oil
1 teaspoon vinegar
1 teaspoon vanilla
1 cup water

Preheat oven to 350°. Sift together flour, cocoa, sugar, baking soda, and salt. Mix oil, vinegar, vanilla, and water together. Mix both dry and wet ingredients together. Pour into a greased 9x9-inch baking dish. Bake 35–45 minutes. Double recipe for 9x13-inch pan. Allow to cool, then frost with White Icing.

WHITE ICING:
⅞ cup powdered sugar
¼ cup margarine (regular, not light)

1 egg white
1 teaspoon vanilla

Beat in mixer until fluffy.

Note: For chocolate icing, add 3½ tablespoons cocoa.

Mrs. Tana Moran – Cincinnati, Ohio
Wife of Colonel (Ret.) Jack Moran

Dr. Pepper Chocolate Cake

I would like to thank my sister for sharing this recipe with me. All I know is that this is one of the best cakes I have ever tasted.

1 (18¼-ounce) box German
   chocolate cake mix
¾ cup vegetable oil
1 (5-ounce) box vanilla instant
   pudding

4 eggs
1 (12-ounce) can Dr. Pepper
   (room temperature)

Preheat oven to 325°. Mix cake mix, vegetable oil, and pudding mix together. Add eggs one at a time until all eggs are blended with cake mixture. Add Dr. Pepper. Mix well. Pour into 2 or 3 (9-inch-round) greased and floured cake pans. Bake 30–40 minutes. Allow cake to cool before frosting.

FROSTING:

1 (8-ounce) package cream
   cheese, softened
1 (1-pound) box powdered sugar
2 tablespoons vanilla

1 stick butter, softened
½ cup cocoa
1 cup finely chopped nuts

Mix cream cheese, powdered sugar, vanilla, butter, and cocoa together. Frost cake. Sprinkle nuts on top. If Frosting is too runny, chill in refrigerator before icing the cake. Cake is best stored in the refrigerator.

Staff Sergeant Robert W. Laughlin – Early, Texas

Signature Homemade Carrot Cake

2 cups vegetable oil
2⅔ cups sugar
5 eggs
2⅔ cups grated carrots
1⅓ cups chopped walnuts
⅓ cup raisins
1⅓ cups crushed and drained
   pineapple

⅔ cup sweetened coconut flakes
3½ cups all-purpose flour
1⅓ tablespoons baking soda
1⅓ tablespoons baking powder
2⅔ tablespoons cinnamon
1 teaspoon salt

Preheat oven to 350°. Grease 2 (10-inch) cake pans and set aside. In a large bowl, mix together oil, sugar, eggs, carrots, nuts, raisins, pineapple, and coconut. In another bowl, sift together flour, baking soda, baking powder, cinnamon, and salt. Add carrot mixture and blend. Pour batter into cake pans and bake 35–40 minutes, or until done. Remove from oven; cool 30 minutes.

Release cakes from pans and cool completely before cutting and frosting. Cut cakes in half. Assemble carrot cake one layer at a time. Finish carrot cake with a layer of cream cheese frosting on top. Do not frost side of cake. This gives the cake that special homemade country-style look. Garnish with toasted walnuts and coconut, if desired.

FROSTING:

2 (3-ounce) packages cream
   cheese, softened
¼ stick unsalted butter,
   softened
2 tablespoons vegetable
   shortening

1½ cups confectioners' sugar
1 teaspoon vanilla
1 cup chopped walnuts, toasted,
   for garnish (optional)
1 cup coconut flakes, toasted,
   for garnish (optional)

Beat together cream cheese, butter, and vegetable shortening for 15 minutes. Mixture must be very smooth and light. Add confectioners' sugar and vanilla and mix until smooth, about 3 minutes.

Master Sergeant Deb Marsh – Hubbard, Ohio

Delicious Carrot Cake

2 cups all-purpose flour
2 teaspoons baking soda
½ teaspoon salt
2 teaspoons cinnamon
3 large eggs
2 cups sugar
¾ cup vegetable oil

¾ cup buttermilk
2 teaspoons vanilla
2 cups grated carrots
1 (8-ounce) can crushed
 pineapple, drained
1 cup chopped pecans

Preheat oven to 350°. Grease 3 (9-inch) cake pans; line with wax paper. Lightly grease and flour wax paper.

Stir together flour, baking soda, salt, and cinnamon. Beat eggs, sugar, oil, buttermilk, and vanilla until smooth. Add flour mixture. Fold in grated carrots, pineapple, and pecans. Bake 25–30 minutes. Remove from pans, peel off wax paper, and cool completely. Frost with Cream Cheese Frosting.

CREAM CHEESE FROSTING:

1 (8-ounce) package cream
 cheese, softened
1 (3-ounce) package cream
 cheese, softened

¾ cup butter, softened
1 (1-pound) package powdered
 sugar
1½ teaspoons vanilla

Beat cream cheese and butter until smooth. Sift powdered sugar into cream cheese and butter mixture. Beat until fluffy. Stir in vanilla.

Mrs. Marty Holcomb – Athens, Georgia
Wife of Lt. Colonel Pete Holcomb

Cottage Pudding Cake

½ cup shortening
1⅓ cups sugar
2 teaspoons vanilla
2 eggs, well beaten

4½ cups all-purpose flour
8 teaspoons baking powder
1 teaspoon salt
2 cups milk

Preheat oven to 325°. Cream shortening, sugar, and vanilla. Add well-beaten eggs. Add flour, baking powder, and salt. Add milk. Pour into greased 9x13-inch cake pan. Bake 45 minutes. Serve with Lemon Sauce.

LEMON SAUCE:
6 tablespoons cornstarch
2 cups sugar
4 cups boiling water

12 tablespoons lemon juice
4 teaspoons grated lemon rind
4 teaspoons butter

Must mix cornstarch and sugar first, then add water. Cook 15 minutes, stirring constantly until thick. Remove from heat and add lemon juice, rind, and butter. Spoon Lemon Sauce over Cottage Pudding Cake.

Master Sergeant Deb Marsh – Hubbard, Ohio

From 1947–1969, the Air Force undertook Project Blue Book, an investigation into UFOs. Project Blue Book had two goals: to determine if UFOs were a threat to national security, and to scientifically analyze UFO-related data. Thousands of UFO reports were collected, analyzed, and filed. As the result of the Condon Report, which concluded there was nothing anomalous about any UFOs, Project Blue Book was ordered shut down in December 1969. This project was the last publicly known UFO research project led by the USAF. Of a total of 12,618 sightings reported to Project Blue Book, 701 remained "unidentified."

Pistachio Club Cake

1 (18¼-ounce) box yellow
cake mix
1 (3-ounce) package pistachio
instant pudding mix

1 cup cold club soda
½ cup cooking oil
1 cup chopped nuts
4 eggs

Preheat oven to 350°. Mix all ingredients at medium speed 4 minutes. Pour mixture into greased tube pan. Bake 55 minutes. Cool completely before cutting.

TOPPING:

1 cup cold milk
1 cup whipping cream

1 (3-ounce) package pistachio
instant pudding

Beat milk, cream, and pudding until Topping stands in peaks. Split cake 2 times and put Topping between layers and on top. Keep in refrigerator.

Master Sergeant Deb Marsh – Hubbard, Ohio

Chocolate Chip Cake

1 (18¼-ounce) box yellow
cake mix
1 (3-ounce) box vanilla instant
pudding
1 (3-ounce) box chocolate instant
pudding

1½ cups water
½ cup oil
4 eggs
¾ (12-ounce) package chocolate
chips

Beat first 5 ingredients 2 minutes; add eggs all at once and beat for 1 more minute. Add chocolate chips. Pour into greased and floured Bundt pan and bake for one hour. I don't use an icing or a glaze, but either one would be good.

Mrs. Billie Neese – New Orleans, Louisiana
Wife of Lt. Colonel (Ret.) Robert Neese

Oatmeal Chocolate Chip Cake

Note from the author: *I received a "typed" recipe from Mrs. Dorothy Hostetler. About a week later, I received an email with a recipe from Mrs. Melanie Hostetler. I wondered if they could be related, so I contacted Melanie and she told me that Dorothy Hostetler is her grandmother-in-law. They hadn't talked, so neither realized the other had submitted a recipe to me. Dorothy's husband JC flew a B-25 bomber in WWII with 62 missions. Their grandson Jacob is carrying on the proud bomber tradition in the family, currently flying a B-52. Melanie sent me these wonderful pictures of JC Hostetler to share with you.*

1¾ cups boiling water
1 cup uncooked oatmeal
1 cup lightly packed brown sugar
1 cup white sugar
½ cup butter, softened
2 extra large eggs
1¾ cups unsifted flour

1 teaspoon baking soda
½ teaspoon salt
1 tablespoon cocoa
½ (12-ounce) package chocolate
  chips
½ cup chopped walnuts or pecans

Preheat oven to 350°. Pour boiling water over oatmeal. Let stand until room temperature, about 10 minutes. Add brown sugar, white sugar, and butter; mix until well incorporated. Add eggs. Mix well. Sift together flour, soda, salt, and cocoa. Add flour mixture to oatmeal mixture. Mix well. Add chocolate chips and nuts to mixture. Pour into 9x13-inch pan. Bake 40 minutes or until tester comes out clean.

Note: This cake is so moist there is no need for frosting!

Mrs. Doris M. Hostetler – Aurora, Colorado
Wife of Lt. Colonel (Ret.) JC Hostetler and Grandmother of Lt. Jacob Hostetler

JC Hostetler

William's Birthday Banana Cake

2 sticks butter, softened
2 cups sugar
3 eggs
1½ cups ripe mashed bananas
(blend in blender)

2 teaspoons baking soda
1 cup milk
3 cups cake flour
1 teaspoon vanilla

Preheat oven to 350°. Cream butter; add sugar slowly and beat well. Add eggs one at a time. Then add bananas. Dissolve baking soda in milk. Fold in flour alternately with milk and vanilla. Pour into 3 greased and floured 9-inch cake pans. Bake 25 minutes or until done. Cool in pans 10 minutes before inverting onto wire racks. Cool completely before icing.

BANANA CAKE ICING:
1 (8-ounce) package cream
cheese, softened
1 (1-pound) box powdered
sugar, sifted

1 teaspoon vanilla

Mix cream cheese with powdered sugar. Add vanilla. Spread on cooled cake.

Mrs. Sara Tosten – Alexandria, Louisiana
Wife of Lt. Colonel (Ret.) Charles Tosten, Jr.

Bacardi Rum Cake

1 cup chopped pecans	4 eggs
1 (18¼-ounce) package yellow cake mix	½ cup cold water
	½ cup oil
1 (3-ounce) package vanilla instant pudding mix	¼–½ cup 80-proof dark rum

Preheat oven to 325°. Sprinkle nuts in bottom of greased and floured Bundt pan. Combine cake mix, pudding mix, eggs, water, oil, and rum in large mixing bowl. Beat at medium speed 2 minutes. Bake 60 minutes. Cool in pan 15 minutes. Turn onto cake plate. Glaze when cake has cooled ½ hour.

GLAZE:

½ cup sugar	¼ cup water
½ cup butter	¼–½ cup dark rum

Combine sugar, butter, and water in saucepan. Boil 5 minutes until mixture comes to soft-ball stage, stirring constantly. Remove from stove and add rum. Stir well. Glaze cake, pressing down on cake with spoon. (Or prick cake with toothpick or bamboo shish-kabob stick before adding Glaze.)

Mrs. Billie Neese – New Orleans, Louisiana
Wife of Lt. Colonel (Ret.) Robert Neese

Pumpkin Cake Roll

3 eggs
1 cup granulated sugar
⅔ cup pumpkin
1 teaspoon lemon juice
¾ cup all-purpose flour
1 teaspoon baking powder
2 teaspoons cinnamon
1 teaspoon nutmeg

½ teaspoon salt
1 cup finely chopped walnuts
1 cup powdered sugar plus more
   for sprinkling
1 (8-ounce) package cream
   cheese, softened
6 tablespoon butter, softened
1 teaspoon vanilla

Preheat oven to 375°. Beat eggs on HIGH speed of mixer for 5 minutes; gradually beat in sugar. Stir in pumpkin and lemon juice. Stir together flour, baking powder, cinnamon, nutmeg, and salt. Fold into pumpkin mixture. Spread in greased and floured 10x15x1-inch jellyroll pan. Top with walnuts. Bake 15 minutes. Turn out on towel sprinkled with powdered sugar. Starting at narrow end, roll towel and cake together; cool. Unroll.

For filling, combine powdered sugar, cream cheese, butter, and vanilla; beat until smooth. Spread over cake; roll. Chill. It is not as hard as it sounds, and is so nice for Thanksgiving and Christmas!

Mrs. Billie Neese – New Orleans, Louisiana
Wife of Lt. Colonel (Ret.) Robert Neese

Five-Flavor Tennessee Pound Cake

1 cup butter
½ cup shortening
3 cups sugar
5 eggs, room temperature,
  well beaten
3 cups all-purpose flour
½ teaspoon baking powder

1 cup milk
1 teaspoon vanilla extract
1 teaspoon coconut extract
1 teaspoon butter extract
1 teaspoon almond extract
1 teaspoon rum extract

Preheat oven to 325°. Cream butter, shortening, and sugar together. Add eggs one at a time. Mix well. Add flour and baking powder. Add milk and all 5 flavorings. Pour into tube pan. Bake 1½ hours. Test with cake tester for doneness. Cool in pan 15 minutes before turning onto cake platter.

Mrs. Barbara McGee – Hampton, Virginia
Wife of Lt. Colonel (Ret.) Guy McGee

Buttermilk Pound Cake

2 sticks butter, softened
2¾ cups sugar
4 eggs
3 cups all-purpose flour,
  sifted before measuring

¼ teaspoon baking soda
1 cup buttermilk
1 teaspoon vanilla
½ teaspoon almond extract

Preheat oven to 350°. Cream butter and sugar together 5–6 minutes. Add eggs one at a time. Do not overbeat. Dissolve soda in buttermilk. Add flour alternately with buttermilk and flavorings, ending with flour. Bake in a well-greased and floured Bundt pan 1 hour or until done. Cool 10 minutes. Invert onto wire racks.

Mrs. Sara Tosten – Alexandria, Louisiana
Wife of Lt. Colonel (Ret.) Charles Tosten, Jr.

Moth's Famous Cheesecake

Warning: This is not a low-cholesterol or low-calorie dessert! It tastes so good, people go back for more . . . .

1 stick butter	1 cup sugar
1 (12-ounce) box graham cracker crumbs	¼ teaspoon salt
	2 teaspoons vanilla extract
2 (8-ounce) packages cream cheese, softened	1 drop lemon juice
	1 pint sour cream
3 eggs	1 tablespoon flour

Preheat oven to 350°. Melt butter. Blend in graham cracker crumbs. Pat down on bottom and partly up sides (including the middle) of an angel food cake pan. Let cool. Beat cream cheese, eggs, sugar, salt, vanilla, and lemon juice until smooth. Add sour cream and flour. Mix well. Pour into crust. Bake 45–60 minutes. Top will be firm and just cracking. Chill.

Mrs. Cari Mansfield – Hampton, Virginia
Wife of Chief (Ret.) Rich Mansfield

The USAF has taken part in numerous humanitarian operations. Some of these include the Berlin Airlift, Operation Safe Haven, Operations Babylift, Newlife, Frequent Wind, and New Arrivals: Operation Provide Comfort, 1991 Operation Sea Angel, and Operation Provide Hope.

Oreo Zombie Ice Cream Cake

This cake is very decadent—we save it for special occasions like birthdays. The cake tastes best if it is assembled the day it is served, so the devil's food cake part is not frozen solid.

½ gallon cookies and cream
  ice cream
1 (18¼-ounce) box devil's
  food cake mix
1⅓ cups water
½ cup vegetable oil

3 eggs
1 jar Dove Milk Chocolate Ice
  Cream Topping
1 bag mini Oreo Chocolate
  Sandwich Cookies
1 (8-ounce) container Cool Whip

A least 1 day ahead, place plastic wrap in bottom of 3 different 9-inch cake pans, and spread ⅓ softened ice cream into each pan. Cover with more plastic wrap and place in freezer so ice cream can harden.

Prepare devil's food cake according to directions using 2 (9-inch) round cake pans. Remove cake from pans and cool completely. Then with large bread knife, cut each cake in half so you have 4 layers total. Place the first layer onto a cake platter. Then add a layer of the previously frozen ice cream. Top ice cream with a layer of ice cream topping. Add another layer of cake, ice cream, then topping. Then cake, ice cream, topping, and finally the last layer of cake.

Frost entire cake with a defrosted container of Cool Whip. Decorate cake with as many mini Oreos as you like. Place cake in freezer until you are ready to serve. Leave out 10–15 minutes before serving.

Mrs. Stephanie Miller – Tucson, Arizona
Wife of Lt. Colonel Stephen Miller

Éclair Cake

There are no calories if you close your eyes when you eat it!

1 (1-pound) box graham crackers
2 (3-ounce) boxes French vanilla instant pudding
3½ cups milk
1 (8-ounce) tub Cool Whip, thawed

Butter a 9x13-inch pan. Line bottom with 1 layer of crackers (do not crush). Mix pudding with milk, and beat at medium speed 2 minutes. Blend in Cool Whip. Pour half of mixture over crackers; top with another layer of crackers. Add remaining pudding mixture, then a third layer of crackers. Refrigerate 2 hours.

FROSTING:
6 tablespoons cocoa
2 teaspoons light corn syrup
2 tablespoons vegetable oil
2 teaspoons vanilla
3 tablespoons soft butter
1½ cups powdered sugar
3 tablespoons milk

Combine ingredients and beat until smooth. Spread over the "final" layer of graham crackers. Serve.

Master Sergeant Nelia Woods – Pasig City, Philippines

Afterburners:
Cookies & Candies

An **F-22 Raptor** in full afterburner during flight testing at Edwards Air Force Base, California.

The Raptor is the most advanced fighter aircraft in the world, combining a revolutionary leap in technology and capability with reduced support requirements and maintenance costs. In the air-to-air arena, the stealthy Raptor will be virtually unseen on radar, while its sophisticated array of sensors and advanced radar will allow it to reach out and strike adversary aircraft undetected from long range. The advanced software also enhances the Raptor's ability to deliver precision air-to-surface weapons on target, day or night, in any weather.

Sugar Cookie Cutouts

½ cup shortening
1 cup sugar
1 egg
3 cups all-purpose flour

¼ teaspoon salt
3 teaspoons baking powder
½ cup milk
1 teaspoon vanilla

Preheat oven to 350°. Thoroughly cream shortening and sugar. Add egg and beat well. Add sifted dry ingredients alternately with milk and vanilla. Mix thoroughly. You may wish to refrigerate for a couple of hours to make dough easier to handle.

Roll out on lightly floured surface. Cut with floured cookie cutters. Bake 10 minutes. (For crispier cookies, bake at 375°.) If desired, sprinkle with colored sugar before baking, or frost with Butter Frosting and decorate after baked cookies have cooled.

BUTTER FROSTING:

⅓ cup butter or margarine,
   softened
3 cups powdered sugar

Dash of salt
¼ cup milk
1½ teaspoons vanilla

Cream butter in small mixer bowl. Add sugar, salt, milk, and vanilla, beating on low until blended. Beat on HIGH until fluffy, about 2 minutes. Add a little more sugar, if needed for right spreading consistency. You may add food coloring, if desired.

Note: If adding decorations to cookies, do so shortly after frosting the cookies. Frosting will harden a bit as it sits.

Mrs. Gail Teigeler – Riverside, California
Wife of Lt. Colonel (Ret.) Thomas Teigeler

Sugar Cookies

3¼ cups all-purpose flour
1 teaspoon baking soda
1 teaspoon cream of tarter
¼ teaspoon salt
1 cup sugar

1 cup brown sugar
1 cup shortening
2 eggs
1 teaspoon vanilla
Additional sugar

Preheat oven to 350°. Sift flour, soda, cream of tarter, and salt together. Cream sugars and shortening together. Add eggs and vanilla. Mix in dry ingredients. Dough will be very heavy. Roll into walnut-size balls, then roll in additional sugar. Bake 10 minutes.

Mrs. Eleanor Eells, Rowlett, Texas
Tech Sergeant (Ret.) Robert Eells

Secret Kiss Cookies

1 cup margarine
½ cup sugar
1 teaspoon vanilla
2 cups all-purpose flour

1 cup finely chopped walnuts
1 (5¾-ounce) package chocolate
    kisses
Confectioners' sugar

Cream margarine, sugar, and vanilla until light and fluffy. Add flour and nuts, and blend on low speed. Chill dough. Remove foil from kisses. Using one tablespoon of dough, shape around a kiss, being sure to cover completely. Place on ungreased baking sheet.

Preheat oven 350°. Bake 12 minutes or until cookies are set but not brown. Cool slightly; remove to wire rack. While still warm, roll in confectioners' sugar. Cool. Store in tightly covered container. May roll again in sugar before serving, if desired.

Mrs. Tammi Naman – Lincoln, Alabama
Wife of Major Kevin Naman

Pinwheels and Checkerboards

2 cups all-purpose flour
1 teaspoon baking powder
½ teaspoon salt
⅔ cup butter or margarine, softened
1 cup sugar

1 egg
1 teaspoon vanilla extract
2 (1-ounce) squares unsweetened chocolate, melted
Milk for brushing checkerboards

Preheat oven to 375°. Mix flour, baking powder, and salt; set aside. Cream butter; gradually add sugar, and continue beating until light and fluffy. Add egg and vanilla; beat well. Gradually add flour mixture, mixing well after each addition. Divide dough in half; blend chocolate into one half.

PINWHEELS:

Roll chocolate and vanilla dough separately between sheets of wax paper into 8x12-inch rectangles. Remove top sheets of paper and invert vanilla dough onto chocolate dough. Remove remaining papers. Roll up as for jelly roll, then wrap in wax paper and chill until firm (at least 3 hours, or 1 hour in the freezer). Cut into ¼-inch slices and place on baking sheets. Bake 10 minutes, or until cookies just begin to brown around edges. Cool on racks. Makes about 5 dozen.

CHECKERBOARDS:

Set out small amount of milk. Roll chocolate and vanilla dough separately on lightly-floured board into 4½x9-inch rectangles. Brush chocolate dough lightly with milk and top with vanilla dough. Using a long sharp knife, cut dough lengthwise into 3 strips, 1½ inches wide. Stack strips, alternating colors and brushing each layer with milk. Cut lengthwise again into 3 strips, ½ inch wide. Invert middle section so the colors are alternated; brush sides with milk. Press strips together lightly to form a rectangle. Wrap in waxed paper and chill overnight.

(continued)

(Pinwheels and Checkerboards continued)

Cut into ⅛-inch slices, using a very sharp knife. Place on baking sheets. Bake at 375° about 8 minutes, or just until white portions begin to brown. Cool on racks.

Variation: Instead of chocolate, use food coloring to color half the dough.

Mrs. Cari Mansfield – Hampton, Virginia
Wife of Chief (Ret.) Rich Mansfield

Swiss Cinnamon Cookies

3 egg whites
3¼ cups powdered sugar
  (approximately), divided
3 cups walnuts, finely ground

1 tablespoon ground cinnamon
Chopped walnuts, colored sugars,
  candied cherries, etc., for
  garnish

Preheat oven 300°. In medium bowl, beat egg whites until foamy. Gradually beat in 2 cups sugar. Beat until mixture holds soft peaks, 3–4 minutes. Remove ¾ cup batter and set aside.

Mix walnuts, cinnamon, and ¾ cup more sugar into larger egg-sugar portion. Working with ⅓ of the dough at a time, roll out to ⅛-inch thickness on a pastry cloth or board heavily dusted with powdered sugar. Cut into desired shapes with cookie cutters. Place on greased or parchment-lined baking sheets. Spread reserved egg-sugar mixture ⅛ inch thick on top of each cookie, almost to the edges. Decorate immediately as desired. Bake in preheated 300° oven 12–14 minutes or until cookies are just set and very lightly browned. Remove to wire racks to cool completely. Store cookies in airtight container. Cookies can be securely wrapped and frozen up to 2 months. (Makes about 3 dozen cookies.)

Mrs. Cari Mansfield – Hampton, Virginia
Wife of Chief (Ret.) Rich Mansfield

Snickers Surprise Cookies

2 sticks butter, softened
1 cup creamy peanut butter
1 cup light brown sugar
1 cup sugar
2 eggs
1 teaspoon vanilla
3½ cups all-purpose flour

½ teaspoon salt
1 teaspoon baking soda
1½ (12-ounce) packages
  Snickers Miniatures
Powdered sugar (optional)
Chocolate chip pieces (optional)

Combine butter, peanut butter, and sugars using a mixer on medium to low speed until light and fluffy. Slowly add eggs and vanilla until thoroughly combined. Then mix in flour, salt, and baking soda. Cover and chill dough 2–3 hours.

Unwrap Snickers Miniatures. Preheat oven to 350°. Remove dough from refrigerator. Divide into 1-tablespoon pieces and flatten. Place a Snickers in the center of each piece of dough. Form dough into a ball around each Snickers. Place on a greased cookie sheet and bake 10–12 minutes. Let cookies cool on baking rack or wax paper. May sprinkle with powdered sugar and/or drizzle with melted chocolate, if desired.

Mrs. Gail Teigeler – Riverside, California
Wife of Lt. Colonel (Ret.) Thomas Teigeler

Chocolate Chip Cookies

1 cup granulated sugar	1 teaspoon salt
½ cup light brown sugar, firmly packed	1 teaspoon baking soda
	2¼ cups all-purpose flour
1 cup shortening	1 cup semisweet chocolate chips
1 tablespoon pure vanilla extract	1 cup chopped nuts (optional)
2 large eggs	

Preheat oven to 350°. Beat together sugar, brown sugar, and shortening. Add vanilla extract, eggs, salt, baking soda, and flour. Stir in chocolate chips and nuts, if desired. Drop mixture by rounded tablespoons onto ungreased baking sheets. Bake 9 minutes. Cool on wire rack. Makes approximately 3 dozen cookies.

Major Kimberly Tooman – Shamokin Dam, Pennsylvania

Chunky Chocolate Chip Cookies

1 cup butter or margarine, softened	2½ cups self-rising flour
	1 cup white chocolate chips
¾ cup sugar	1 cup semisweet chocolate chips
¾ cup brown sugar	1 cup milk chocolate chips
2 eggs	1 cup dark chocolate chunks
1 teaspoon vanilla	3 cups toasted pecans

Preheat oven to 375°. Combine butter and sugars. Add eggs and vanilla. Blend in flour. Add chips and pecans. Drop by teaspoon onto cookie sheet. Bake 8–10 minutes.

Mrs. Tammi Naman – Lincoln, Alabama
Wife of Major Kevin Naman

Peanut Butter Chocolate Chip Cookies

1 cup sugar
½ peanut butter (creamy or
  chunky)
½ cup evaporated milk

1 (6-ounce) package chocolate
  chips
1 cup coarsely chopped nuts

Preheat oven to 325°. In medium bowl, mix sugar and peanut butter until well blended. Stir in evaporated milk, chips, and nuts until well mixed. Drop batter by heaping teaspoonful 1½ inches apart on foil-lined cookie sheets. Spread batter evenly into 2-inch rounds. Bake 18–20 minutes or until golden. Cool completely on foil on wire racks. Peel foil from cookies. Makes about 3½ dozen cookies

Mrs. Cari Mansfield – Hampton, Virginia
Wife of Chief (Ret.) Rich Mansfield

Peanut Butter Cup Cookies

2½ cups all-purpose flour
⅓ cup unsweetened cocoa
  powder
1 teaspoon baking soda
½ teaspoon salt
1 cup butter, softened
¾ cup peanut butter

¾ cup light brown sugar
¾ cup white sugar
1 teaspoon vanilla
2 eggs
16–20 regular-size peanut butter
  cups, cut into eighths

Preheat oven to 375°. In a medium bowl, mix flour, cocoa powder, soda, and salt; set aside. In a large bowl, mix butter, peanut butter, sugars, and vanilla; beat in eggs. Stir in dry ingredients. Stir in peanut butter cups. Drop by teaspoon onto greased cookie sheets. Bake 9–10 minutes until bottoms are lightly browned. Do not overcook; they tend to darken as they cool. Makes about 6 dozen.

First Lt. Kelly Russell – Buffalo, New York
Wife of First Lt. Patrick Applegate

Colossal Cookies

This is a favorite in our house, and we joke that it can be eaten for breakfast because of all the oatmeal and peanut butter. And there is no mistake, there is no flour in this recipe.

½ cup butter or margarine,
    softened
1½ cups sugar
1½ cups brown sugar
4 eggs

1 teaspoon vanilla
2 cups chunky peanut butter
2½ teaspoons baking soda
6 cups old-fashioned oatmeal
1 cup semisweet chocolate chips

Preheat oven to 350°. Mix butter and sugars. Blend in eggs and vanilla. Add peanut butter and baking soda. Stir in oatmeal and chocolate chips by hand. Drop by ¼ cup 2–3 inches apart on ungreased cookie sheet. Flatten with fork. Bake 10–15 minutes or until slightly firm to the touch.

Mrs. Laurie Smith – Seattle, Washington
Wife of Lt. Colonel Bruce Smith

The United States Air Force Headquarters is located at the Pentagon building in Washington DC.

Banana Nut Cookies

2¼ cups cake flour
½ teaspoon salt
1 cup sugar
2 teaspoons baking powder
⅓ cup margarine, softened

2 eggs, beaten
½ teaspoon vanilla
1 cup mashed bananas
½ cup nuts

Mix together flour, salt, sugar, and baking powder. Beat margarine, eggs, vanilla, and bananas in mixing bowl. Add flour mixture to banana mixture. Stir well. Fold in nuts. Bake in preheated 350° oven 10–15 minutes.

Mrs. Eleanor Eells – Rowlett, Texas
Wife of Tech Sergeant (Ret.) Robert Eells

Chewy Chocolate Oatmeal Cookies

¾ cup shortening
1¼ cups firmly packed light
   brown sugar
1 egg
⅓ cup milk
2 teaspoons vanilla

3 cups quick oats, uncooked
1 cup all-purpose flour
½ teaspoon baking soda
½ teaspoon salt
1 (12-ounce) package chocolate
   chips

Preheat oven to 375°. Grease baking sheet or use nonstick baking sheet. Combine shortening, brown sugar, egg, milk, and vanilla in large bowl. Beat at medium speed of electric mixer until well blended. Combine oats, flour, baking soda, and salt into creamed mixture at low speed just until blended. Stir in chocolate chips. Drop rounded table-spoonfuls of dough 2 inches apart onto baking sheet. Bake 10–12 minutes or until lightly browned. Cool for 2 minutes on baking sheet. Remove cookies from baking sheet to wire cooling racks. Makes approximately 2 dozen cookies.

Mrs. Teri L. Mace – Mesquite, Texas
Wife of Staff Sergeant Nathaniel Mace

Swedish Oatmeal Cookies

1 cup sugar	1 cup oatmeal
1 cup brown sugar	1 cup flaked coconut
2½ cups all-purpose flour	½ cup chopped nuts
1 teaspoon baking powder	1 cup shortening, melted
1 teaspoon baking soda	2 eggs
¼ teaspoon salt	1 teaspoon vanilla

Preheat oven to 375°. Mix all dry ingredients together. Add shortening; mix well. Add beaten eggs and vanilla; mix well. Form into small balls and flatten with fork. Bake 10–15 minutes.

Mrs. Elaine Peterson – Abilene, Texas
Wife of Lt. Colonel (Ret.) Kenneth Harold Peterson

Lt. Colonel Harold Peterson was an Electronic Warfare Officer on a B-52 crew. He served in WWII, the Korean Conflict, and the Vietnam War. He was awarded the Bronze Star medal for meritorious service in military intelligence at Danang Air Base, Vietnam. (1923–1981)

Elaine and Harold

Walnut Freezer Roll

I have had this recipe about forty-five years and it is really great. The best part is that you can make it ahead and freeze it.

1 cup butter, softened	3 cups all-purpose flour
2 cups brown sugar	3 teaspoons baking powder
2 eggs	½ teaspoon salt
1 teaspoon vanilla	½ cup chopped walnuts

Preheat oven to 375°. Mix butter and sugar until light and fluffy; beat in eggs and vanilla. Sift flour, baking powder, and salt; beat into butter mixture. Stir in nuts. Wrap in foil, then refrigerate for several hours or until firm.

Divide dough in half and shape into 2 long rolls about 2 inches in diameter. Freeze, then when ready to bake, slice off cookies ⅛–¼ inch thick; bake on greased cookie sheet 8 minutes until light brown. Makes 7 dozen.

Mrs. Frances Anderson – Pineville, Louisiana
Lt. Colonel (Ret.) Andy Anderson

Walnut Balls with Chocolate Middles

1 cup California walnuts
⅔ cup powdered sugar, divided
1 cup butter or margarine, softened
1 teaspoon vanilla
1¾ cups all-purpose flour

Preheat oven to 350°. In a food processor or blender, process walnuts with 2 tablespoons powdered sugar until finely ground; set aside. In a large bowl, cream butter and remaining sugar. Beat in vanilla. Add flour and ¾ cup walnut mixture; mix until blended. Roll dough into about 3 dozen walnut-size balls. Place 2 inches apart on an ungreased cookie sheet. Bake 10–12 minutes or until just golden around the edges. Remove to wire racks to cool completely. Prepare Chocolate Filling.

CHOCOLATE FILLING:
3 (1-ounce) squares semisweet chocolate
½ teaspoon vanilla extract
2 tablespoon butter or margarine
2 tablespoon whipping cream
1 cup powdered sugar

Chop chocolate into small pieces; place in food processor or blender with vanilla. In small saucepan, heat butter and whipping cream over medium heat until hot; pour over chocolate. Process until chocolate is melted, turning machine off and scraping sides as needed. With machine running, gradually add powdered sugar; process until smooth.

Place generous teaspoonful of Filling on flat side of half the cookies. Top with remaining cookies, flat side down, forming sandwiches. Roll chocolate edges of cookies in remaining ground walnut mixture. Makes about 6 dozen.

Mrs. Cari Mansfield – Hampton, Virginia
Wife of Chief (Ret.) Rich Mansfield

Chocolate Pixies

¼ cup sweet butter
4 (1-ounce) squares unsweetened
  chocolate
2 cups all-purpose flour, divided
2 cups granulated sugar

4 eggs
2 teaspoons baking powder
½ teaspoon salt
½ cup chopped walnuts or pecans
Powdered sugar

In small saucepan over low heat, melt butter and chocolate; stir to blend. Cool. In large bowl, beat chocolate mixture, 1 cup flour, granulated sugar, eggs, baking powder, and salt until well mixed. Stir in remaining 1 cup flour and nuts. Cover and refrigerate until firm, 2 hours or overnight.

Preheat oven to 300°. Shape dough into 1-inch balls; roll in powdered sugar. Place 2 inches apart on greased cookie sheets. Bake 12–15 minutes or until firm to the touch. Remove to wire racks to cool. Makes about 4 dozen cookies.

Mrs. Cari Mansfield – Hampton, Virginia
Wife of Chief (Ret.) Rich Mansfield

One of the most significant events in the history of the U.S. Air Force Academy was the admission of women. On October 7, 1975, President Gerald R. Ford signed legislation permitting women to enter the United States service academies. On June 26, 1976, 157 women entered the Air Force Academy with the Class of 1980.

Amaretto Biscotti

2 cups all-purpose flour
2 teaspoons baking powder
½ teaspoon salt
1 stick unsalted butter, softened
1 cup granulated sugar

2 large eggs
¼ cup amaretto
1 teaspoon vanilla extract
½ cup slivered almonds, lightly
  toasted (optional)

Line 1 large baking sheet with parchment paper. Combine flour, baking powder, and salt in a small bowl. In a large bowl, cream together butter and sugar until fluffy. Add eggs, beating after each addition. Add dry ingredients, alternating with amaretto. Add vanilla and mix well. Fold in almonds. Divide dough into 2 equal pieces.

Preheat oven to 350°. On a lightly floured surface, roll each with your hands to make a log, about 12 inches in length, and 2 inches in diameter. (You can add some slivered almonds to the top, if desired). Place logs on the baking sheets, about 2 inches apart. Bake until golden brown and firm, about 30 minutes. Remove from oven and let cool completely on sheet. Reduce oven temperature to 300°. Transfer cookie log to a large cutting board and cut into ¾-inch-thick slices. Spread cookies on baking sheet. Bake, turning halfway through cooking, until firm and crisp, about 30 minutes. Remove from oven and transfer to a wire rack to cool.

If you want softer biscotti, cook 10 minutes one side and 10 minutes on other side.

Master Sergeant Deb Marsh – Hubbard, Ohio

Better Butter Squares

3 eggs, divided
1 (18¼-ounce) box yellow
  cake mix
1 stick butter, melted

1 (1-pound) box powdered sugar
1 (8-ounce) package cream
  cheese, softened

Preheat oven to 350°. Mix 1 egg, cake mix, and melted butter. Place in an ungreased 9x13-inch baking pan. Mix remaining eggs, powdered sugar, and cream cheese together. Spread this mixture on top of bottom layer. Bake uncovered 45 minutes, or until golden brown on top. Allow to cool before cutting into bite-size squares. Sprinkle with powdered sugar.

Mrs. Michelle Clark – New Orleans, Louisiana
Wife of Second Lt. Dwayne Clark

Barely Brown Butterscotch Bars

1 stick butter
1½ cups graham cracker
  crumbs
1 (14-ounce) can sweetened
  condensed milk

2 cups semisweet chocolate chips
1 cup butterscotch chips (peanut
  butter chips or white chocolate
  chips can be substituted)

Preheat oven to 350°. Grease sides of 9x13-inch pan. While oven is warming, place butter stick in the pan and warm in oven until butter is melted. Sprinkle graham cracker crumbs over butter. Pour condensed milk over crumbs. Sprinkle chips on top. Use a piece of wax paper to press down bars. Remove paper and bake 25 minutes or until condensed milk is light brown. Cool completely at room temperature or in the refrigerator before cutting.

First Lt. Kelly Russell – Buffalo, New York
Wife of First Lt. Patrick Applegate

Pumpkin Patch Bars

1 (18¼-ounce) box yellow
  cake mix
4 eggs, divided
½ cup butter, melted
1 (30-ounce) can solid-pack
  pumpkin (3 cups)
1 cup sugar, divided

½ cup firmly packed brown
  sugar
⅔ cup evaporated milk
1½ teaspoons cinnamon
½ cup chopped walnuts
¼ cup butter, softened

Preheat oven to 350°. Remove 1 cup dry cake mix; reserve. In small bowl, lightly beat 1 egg. In a large bowl, stir together remaining cake mix, melted butter, and beaten egg. Press into greased and floured 9x13-inch pan.

In a large bowl, lightly beat remaining 3 eggs. Stir in pumpkin, ½ cup sugar, brown sugar, evaporated milk, and cinnamon. Pour over cake mixture in pan. To cup of reserved cake mix, add remaining ½ cup sugar, nuts, and softened butter; mix until crumbly. Sprinkle over pumpkin mixture. Bake 50–60 minutes. Best when served warm.

Mrs. Diana M. Ratzburg – Las Vegas, Nevada
Wife of Senior Master Sergeant (Ret.) Herbert J. Ratzburg

Praline Candy Cookies

2 cups sugar
1 stick margarine
1 (5-ounce) can evaporated milk
¼ teaspoon vanilla extract

2 cups mini marshmallows
2 cups pecans
1¾ cups graham cracker crumbs

In heavy saucepan, combine sugar, margarine, milk, and vanilla extract. Cook at a slow rolling boil 8–10 minutes, stirring constantly. Remove pan from heat and add in the marshmallows, pecans, and cracker crumbs. Mix together until marshmallows melt. Spoon mixture onto wax paper until cool and firm to the touch.

Mrs. Jessica Kelly – Clarendon, Arkansas
Wife of Senior Airman Patrick Kelly

Chocolate Top Peanut Butter
Rice Krispies Bars

1 cup sugar
1 cup light corn syrup

1 cup creamy peanut butter
6 cups Rice Krispies cereal

Bring sugar and corn syrup to a boil; add peanut butter, stirring constantly until peanut butter is melted. Remove from heat and add rice cereal. Spread mixture into a greased cake pan; set aside.

FROSTING:

1½ cups chocolate chips
1½ cups butterscotch chips

Melt chocolate and butterscotch chips in a bowl in the microwave. Once melted, spread over top of rice cereal and let cool. Cut into bars to serve.

Mrs. Jenny Monroe – Morton Grove (Chicago), Illinois
Wife of Captain Timothy Monroe

Reese's Cup Brownies

These brownies have been to many Air Force potluck meals, and every time, someone asks me for the recipe.

2 (family-size) boxes Betty
   Crocker Fudge Brownies
½ cup water
1 cup vegetable oil

4 eggs
35 Mini Reese's Peanut Butter
   Cups

Preheat oven to 350°. Spray bottom of a 10x15-inch pan with Pam cooking spray. In a big bowl, stir both packages of brownie mix, water, vegetable oil, and eggs until well blended. Spread into pan. Bake 33 minutes or until toothpick comes out almost clean. Immediately after removing brownies from oven, place 5 rows of 7 pieces of Reese's Miniature Candy into brownies. While the brownies are still hot, cut them with a plastic knife and you will get nice clean edges.

Mrs. Stephanie Miller – Tucson, Arizona
Wife of Lt. Colonel Stephen Miller

Air Force bands are classified as premier bands and regional bands. There are two premier bands—The United States Air Force Band in Washington DC, and the United States Air Force Academy Band in Colorado. Ten regional bands are found at eight locations in the continental United States and operate from four locations overseas (Germany, Japan, Alaska, and Hawaii). Bands are organized so that they may be subdivided into several smaller musical units capable of performing autonomously. Some specialized performing units include: Air Force Strings, Airmen of Note (jazz), Ceremonial Brass (brass and percussion), Concert Band (symphonic wind ensemble), Max Impact (rock/pop), Silver Wings (country), and Singing Sergeants (vocal).

Hazel's Fudge

Growing up, I made this recipe every Christmas with my mom. Now I make it every Christmas with my daughters. Hazel Blanchard gave Mom the recipe years ago and it's a winner.

4½ cups sugar	3 cups chocolate chips
1 (12-ounce) can evaporated milk	1 teaspoon vanilla
½ pound butter (2 sticks)	1 (16-ounce) jar marshmallow fluff
Pinch of salt	1 cup chopped walnuts

Mix sugar, milk, butter, and salt in saucepan over medium heat and don't stop stirring. Wait until it comes to a boil and boil 9 minutes. Remove from heat. Then add chocolate chips, vanilla, and marshmallow fluff. Stir together thoroughly. Pour into buttered dishes; cut when set.

Mrs. Laurie Smith – Seattle, Washington
Wife of Lt. Colonel Bruce Smith

Peanut Butter Fudge

1 (12-ounce) can evaporated milk	1 cup chocolate chips (optional)
4 cups sugar	1 (12-ounce) package peanut butter chips
2 sticks butter	1 teaspoon vanilla

In 4-quart saucepan, heat evaporated milk and sugar to boiling. Add butter; cook, stirring constantly, for 6 minutes. Turn down heat, and add chips. Mix until melted. Add vanilla. Take off heat, and beat with electric mixer until fluffy. Pour into buttered 9x13-inch pan. Cut when firm.

Mrs. Barbara McGee – Hampton, Virginia
Wife of Lt. Colonel (Ret.) Guy McGee

Irresistible Buckeyes

1½ cups creamy peanut butter
½ cup butter, softened
1 teaspoon vanilla
4 cups powdered sugar

1 (6-ounce) package semisweet
  chocolate chips
2 tablespoons vegetable shortening

Line a baking sheet with wax paper and set aside. In a medium bowl, mix peanut butter, butter, vanilla, and powdered sugar with hands to form a smooth but stiff dough. Shape into balls using two teaspoons of dough for each ball. Place on prepared pan. Refrigerate. Melt shortening and chocolate together in the top of a double boiler. Stir occasionally until smooth. Remove chocolate from heat. Remove balls from fridge. Using a toothpick inserted into the ball, dip into chocolate to cover. Replace back on wax paper, chocolate side down. Remove toothpick and repeat. Refrigerate about 30 minutes to set.

Mrs. Carolyn Staley – San Carlos, California
Wife of Staff Sergeant Chad Staley

Irish Grandmother's Bourbon Balls

½ cup sugar
3 tablespoons light corn syrup
⅓ cup bourbon
1 cup finely chopped nuts

3 cups finely crushed vanilla
  wafers or honey graham crackers
Powdered sugar

Mix sugar, corn syrup, and bourbon until sugar is dissolved. Add nuts and crumbs. Mix well. Form into 1-inch balls; roll in powdered sugar. Store in airtight container one week before serving. Makes 4½ dozen.

Chief Master Sergeant (Ret.) David Williams – Layton, Utah

Wheaties Golf Balls

I make these every year for Christmas because my mom always did and it reminds me of home. I am still amazed that my mom had time to make Christmas cookies with seven of us running around: one girl and six boys! My mom never measures anything and when I called her years ago for the recipe, she gave it to me over the phone. I made it and gave some to our German landlord. The next day my mom called: "I forgot to tell you to add butter." I tasted the original cookies and they were hard as a rock! My landlord was probably wondering how we bit through them. Poor guy. At least we still get a Christmas card from him every year! Traveling around the world discovering new places is exciting, but it is always nice to have a little piece of home, especially at Christmastime .

½ cup butter
¾ cup sugar
2½ cups dates
1 tablespoon milk

½ teaspoon salt
1 teaspoon vanilla
4 cups crushed Wheaties cereal
½ pound flaked coconut

Combine butter, sugar, and dates in saucepan. Cook on medium low until dates melt and it become a syrup mixture, about 4 minutes. Add milk, salt, vanilla, and cereal to date mixture. Roll into golf-ball-size balls, then roll in flaked coconut.

Mrs. Jackie Gaffner – Waimea, Hawaii
Wife of Master Sergeant (Ret.) Kevin Gaffner

Brian's Chocolate Balls

These are wonderful around the holidays and are also delicious using mint Oreo cookies.

1 (20-ounce) bag Oreo cookies
1 (8-ounce) package cream
  cheese, softened

1 (1-pound) package melting
  chocolate (dark or white)

Crush Oreo cookies in a plastic bag using a rolling pin. Mix with cream cheese; roll into balls. Refrigerate for awhile to help them hold together better. Melt chocolate and dip Oreo balls a few at a time. Let them harden on wax paper.

Mrs. Billie Neese – New Orleans, Louisiana
Wife of Lt. Colonel (Ret.) Robert Neese

Never Fail Divinity

2½ cups sugar
½ cup water
½ cup white Karo syrup
2 egg whites, stiffly beaten

4 large marshmallows, chopped
1 teaspoon vanilla
1 cup chopped nuts

In saucepan, combine sugar, water, and syrup. Boil mixture to soft-ball stage (or 230° on candy thermometer). In large mixing bowl, beat egg whites until stiff. Pour half of syrup mixture over egg whites, beating constantly at HIGH speed on mixer. Return remaining syrup mixture to heat and continue to boil slowly until hard-ball stage (or 264°). Pour over egg white mixture and continue to beat. Add marshmallows, vanilla, and nuts; beat until thick or mixture begins to lose gloss. Drop by teaspoon onto wax paper.

Mrs. Tammi Naman – Lincoln, Alabama
Wife of Major Kevin Naman

Terrific Truffles

1½ (12-ounce) packages
semisweet chocolate chips
1 (14-ounce) can sweetened
condensed milk
3 tablespoons amaretto or
other almond liqueur

½ teaspoon almond extract
Finely chopped nuts (or flaked
coconut, chocolate or colored
sprinkles, unsweetened cocoa
powder, or colored sugar)
for garnish

In heavy saucepan over low heat, melt chocolate chips with condensed milk. Remove from heat; stir in amaretto and almond extract. Chill 2 hours or until firm.

Shape into 1-inch balls; roll in coating of choice. Chill 1 hour or until firm. Store covered at room temperature.

Variations:

Orange Truffles: Add 3 tablespoons orange-flavored liqueur; roll in finely chopped toasted almonds mixed with finely grated orange rind.

Vanilla Chocolate Truffles: Add 1 tablespoon vanilla extract.

Rum Truffles: Add ¼ cup dark rum; roll in coconut.

Bourbon Truffles: Add 3 tablespoons bourbon; roll in chopped nuts.

Mrs. Cari Mansfield – Hampton, Virginia
Wife of Chief (Ret.) Rich Mansfield

Chocolate Truffles

½ cup evaporated milk
¼ cup sugar
1 (12-ounce) bag chocolate chips

1 teaspoon almond extract
1 cup chopped almonds or
walnuts

Combine milk and sugar in saucepan. Cook on medium heat to a rolling boil. Boil 3 minutes, stirring constantly. Remove from heat. Stir in chocolate chips (I use Ghirardelli Milk Chocolate Chips) and extract until smooth. Chill 45 minutes, stirring every 15 minutes. Shape into 1-inch balls. Roll in nuts. Place in mini-size baking cups. Makes about 30 truffles.

Variation: As an alternative, finely chop the almonds and stir them in with the chips and extract. I load them in a cookie press and fill the baking cups.

Mrs. Diana Donnelly – Enterprise, Alabama
Wife of Lt. Colonel (Ret.) Robert Donnelly

Orange Dates

1 (8-ounce) container whipped
light cream cheese
1–2 teaspoons powdered sugar
½ teaspoon orange extract

1 teaspoon fresh or dried orange
zest
1 (1-pound) box or bag pitted
dates

Combine all above except dates; mix well, then split dates to stuff with cream cheese filling. Refrigerate until serving. Makes approximately 20 servings.

Mrs. Nancy Townsend – Colorado Springs, Colorado
Wife of Colonel Bruce Townsend

Almond Brittle

1 cup sugar
½ cup light corn syrup
⅛ teaspoon salt
1 cup coarsely chopped almonds
1 tablespoon butter

1 teaspoon vanilla extract
1½ teaspoons baking soda
¾ pound chocolate almond bark
  (optional)

In a 1½-quart microwave-safe bowl, combine sugar, corn syrup, and salt; mix well. Microwave on HIGH 4 minutes. Stir in almonds. Microwave on HIGH 4 minutes. Stir in butter and vanilla. Microwave on HIGH 1½ minutes. Stir in baking soda.

As soon as the mixture foams, quickly pour onto a greased metal baking sheet and spread with knife or spatula. Cool completely. Break into pieces.

If desired, melt chocolate almond bark and dip half of each piece into the chocolate. Place on wax paper to harden.

Mrs. Gail Teigeler – Riverside, California
Wife of Lt. Colonel (Ret.) Thomas Teigeler

Smooth Landings:
Pies & Desserts

Returning from a mission, an **E-3 Sentry** Airborne Warning and Control System (**AWACS**) comes in for a landing.

The aircraft provides all-weather surveillance, command, control, and communications needed by commanders of U.S. and NATO air defense forces. AWACS is a modified Boeing 707/320 commercial airframe with a rotating radar dome. The dome is thirty feet in diameter, six feet thick, and is held eleven feet above the fuselage by two struts. It contains a radar subsystem that permits surveillance from the earth's surface up into the stratosphere, over land or water. The radar has a range of more than 200 miles for low-flying targets and farther for aerospace vehicles flying at medium to high altitudes.

Light and Creamy Pumpkin Chiffon Pie

2 tablespoons unflavored gelatin
¼ cup cold water
3 eggs, separated
1 cup sugar, divided
1¼ cups pumpkin
½ teaspoon salt

½ teaspoon cinnamon
¼ teaspoon nutmeg
½ teaspoon ginger
½ cup milk
1 (9-inch) pie shell, baked

Dissolve gelatin in cold water. Beat egg yolks with ½ cup sugar; add pumpkin, salt, cinnamon, nutmeg, and ginger. Add milk and dissolved gelatin and water mixture. Pour into medium saucepan and cook until thickened, stirring constantly. Cool. Beat egg whites and remaining ½ cup sugar till stiff. Fold into cooled pumpkin mixture. Pour into pie shell. Refrigerate.

Mrs. Alice Taylor – Bann / Rheinland-Pfalz-Germany
Wife of Lt. Colonel (Ret.) Kerry Taylor

Peanut Butter Pie

1 (8-ounce) package cream
  cheese, softened
½ cup smooth peanut butter
4 ounces sweetened condensed
  milk

½ cup powdered sugar
5 ounces whipping cream,
  whipped, or Cool Whip
1 Oreo cookie crust

Mix cream cheese, peanut butter, sweetened condensed milk, and powdered sugar until creamy. Pour into Oreo cookie crust. Top with whipped cream or Cool Whip.

Mrs. Mary Ranger – St. Louis, Missouri
Wife of Colonel Kelly Ranger

Maple-Glazed Gingersnap Apple Pie

1 (9-inch) pie crust, (double
  crust), unbaked
6 cups thin apple slices, divided
½ cup sugar
¼ cup packed brown sugar
½ cup crushed gingersnap
  cookies
½ teaspoon cinnamon
½ cup black walnuts, chopped
¼ cup butter, melted
¼ cup maple syrup

Preheat oven to 375°. Line a 9-inch pie pan with bottom crust. Place
half the thinly sliced apples in crust; set aside. In mixing bowl, combine sugars, gingersnaps, cinnamon, nuts, and butter; sprinkle half
over apples in crust. Top with remaining apples and sugar mixture.
Roll out remaining pastry to fit top of pie. Cut a few slits in pastry,
place over apples, and seal. Cover loosely with foil and bake 35 minutes. Meanwhile, bring syrup to a gentle boil in a small saucepan.
Remove pie from oven; remove foil and brush hot syrup over pie and
into vents. Return pie to oven and bake, uncovered, 20 minutes longer.
Serve warm with vanilla ice cream.

Mrs. Amanda Lopez – Cincinnati, Ohio
Wife of First Lt. Lydell Lopez

*Amanda and Lydell with daughter
Isabelle in September 2005 when
Lydell came home from deployment.
Lydell is a B-52 Electronic Warfare
Officer for the 23rd Bomb Squadron,
stationed in Minot, North Dakota.
Amanda and Lydell met in college in
their hometown of Cincinnati, Ohio.*

Variable Cream Pie

⅓ cup flour
⅔ cup sugar
¼ teaspoon salt
2 cups scalded milk
3 egg yolks, slightly beaten
   (save whites)

2 tablespoons butter
1 teaspoon vanilla
1 (9-inch) pie shell, baked
3 egg whites
6 tablespoons sugar

Mix flour, sugar, and salt; gradually add milk. Cook over medium heat, stirring constantly, until mixture thickens and boils. Cook 2 minutes. Remove from heat. Add small amount of mixture to egg yolks to temper the yolks. Add rest of yolks to mixture and cook 1 minute; stir constantly. Add butter and vanilla. Cool slightly.

Preheat oven to 350°. Pour filling into baked pie shell. Cover with meringue made by whipping egg whites and sugar. Bake 12–15 minutes.

VARIATIONS:

Banana: Slice 3 bananas into pie shell before adding filling.

Chocolate: Increase sugar to 1 cup. Melt 2 squares unsweetened chocolate into scalded milk mixture.

Coconut: Add 1 cup moist, shredded coconut to filling mixture. Sprinkle ½ cup coconut over meringue before baking.

Major Rhonda Donze – Melbourne, Florida
Wife of Lt. Colonel (Ret.) Robert Donze

Ma's Lemon Meringue Pie

1 cup sugar
¼ cup flour
Pinch of salt
1 cup water, divided
3 eggs, separated (reserve whites
    for Meringue)

2 teaspoons lemon rind
¼ cup lemon juice
3 tablespoons butter
1 baked pie crust

Mix sugar, flour, and salt with ¼ cup water in saucepan. Beat egg yolks with remaining ¾ cup water; add to pan. Cook on low heat until thick. Place lid on pan and cook 10 minutes. Stir in rind, juice, and butter, and put in baked pie crust.

MERINGUE:

3 egg whites
½ tablespoon vanilla

5 tablespoons sugar

Preheat oven to 325°. Beat egg whites in glass bowl with vanilla. Add sugar one tablespoon at a time until stiff peaks form, 2–4 minutes. Spread on pie and bake 20–25 minutes until golden.

Mrs. Frances Anderson – Pineville, Louisiana
Wife of Lt. Colonel (Ret.) Andy Anderson

The National Museum of the United States Air Force (formerly the United States Air Force Museum) is located on Wright-Patterson Air Force Base, near Dayton, Ohio. More than 400 aircraft or "proud birds" and missiles are proudly on display, most of them indoors. Admission is free.

Blueberry Sour Cream Pie

My dear friend Teresa Rexing shared this recipe with me.

CRUST:

1 sleeve graham crackers   ⅓ cup butter, melted
⅓ cup sugar

Preheat oven to 400°. Finely grind graham crackers. Mix with sugar and melted butter. Press into bottom of 9-inch pie plate.

FILLING:

4 ounces cream cheese, softened   1 egg, beaten
¾ cup sugar   1 teaspoon vanilla
1 cup sour cream   ¼ teaspoon salt
3 tablespoons all-purpose flour   3 cups fresh blueberries

Beat cream cheese with sugar until fluffy. Add sour cream, flour, egg, vanilla and salt. Fold in blueberries and pour into pie crust. Bake until filling is just set, about 20 minutes. Sprinkle with Topping and bake 20 minutes more. Remove from oven. Let cool, then chill.

TOPPING:

¼ cup chilled butter   2 teaspoons sugar
8 tablespoons flour   ⅓ cup chopped pecans

Cut butter into mixture of flour and sugar. Add pecans, and sprinkle over pie.

Mrs. Karen Tosten – Hattiesburg, Mississippi
Wife of Major (Ret.) William Tosten

Elizabeth and Katie Tosten greet their dad William Tosten, B-52 EWO, at Eaker AFB, Arkansas, 1991.

Proven Pecan Pie

PIE CRUST:

1 ½ cups all-purpose flour   ½ cup shortening
Sprinkle of salt   Water (a little over ¼ cup)

Mix flour, salt, and shortening with a fork till little balls form. Add water a little at a time till mixture forms a ball that you can work with to roll out. Add a little flour to rolling surface and roll out 13-inch circle of dough to about ⅛–¼ inch thick. Put in pie pan and crimp top edges.

PIE FILLING:

¾ cup white corn syrup   ¾ cup chopped pecans
¾ cup white sugar   Whole pecans for making
3 extra large eggs   pattern (optional)
4 tablespoons butter, melted

Preheat oven to 325°. Mix (DO NOT BEAT) all ingredients except whole pecans. Pour into unbaked pie shell; top with whole pecans in circular pattern. Bake 50 minutes.

Major Kimberly Tooman – Shamokin Dam, Pennsylvania

Pecan Tassies

PASTRY:

1 (3-ounce) package cream
  cheese, softened

1 stick butter, softened
2 cups all-purpose flour

Mix Pastry dough with hands. Roll into a big ball. Cover with plastic wrap and chill 1 hour. Shape dough into 1-inch balls and press into ungreased mini muffin pans.

FILLING:

1½ cups light brown sugar
2 tablespoons butter, melted
2 teaspoons vanilla

Dash of salt
2 eggs, beaten
1⅓ cups chopped pecans

Preheat oven to 350°. Mix sugar, butter, and vanilla; add salt and beaten eggs. Fold in nuts. Fill mini muffin pan with nut mixture. Bake 20–25 minutes. Makes 18.

Mrs. De Edra Farley – Alpine, Texas
Wife of Captain Rich Farley

The United States Air Force Memorial honors the service of the personnel of the United States Air Force and its predecessors. The Memorial is located in Arlington, Virginia, on the grounds of Fort Myer near the Pentagon. The Memorial is 270 feet high and appears to be soaring—its array of stainless steel arcs against the sky evokes the image of "contrails of the Air Force Thunderbirds as they peel back in a precision 'bomb burst' maneuver." Only three of the four contrails are depicted, as the absent fourth evokes the missing man formation traditionally used at Air Force funeral fly-overs. The Memorial was dedicated on October 14, 2006, with approximately 30,000 people attending. The keynote address was delivered by President George W. Bush, a former F-102 Delta Dagger pilot.

Peach Cobbler

1 stick plus 2 tablespoons butter, softened, divided	1 cup sugar
	1 cup self-rising flour
1 (28-ounce) can sliced peaches in heavy syrup (reserve syrup)	¾ cup milk
	Syrup from canned peaches

Preheat oven to 300°. Warm 9x13-inch baking dish and melt 2 tablespoons butter in the bottom. Lay peaches in melted butter. In bowl, mix remaining 1 stick butter, sugar, flour, and milk. Pour over peaches. Pour syrup from canned peaches on top. Bake for 1 hour.

Staff Sergeant Christy M. Hardy – Douglas, Georgia
Wife of Staff Sergeant Christopher Hardy

Blueberry Buckle

2 cups all-purpose flour	¼ cup shortening
¾ cup sugar	¾ cup milk
2½ teaspoons baking powder	1 egg
¾ teaspoon salt	2 cups well-drained blueberries

Heat oven to 375°. Grease a 9x9x2-inch pan. Blend flour, sugar, baking powder, salt, shortening, milk, and egg together. Fold in blueberries. Spread in pan.

TOPPING:

½ cup sugar	½ teaspoon cinnamon
⅓ cup all-purpose flour	¼ cup butter, softened

Mix sugar, flour, cinnamon, and butter, and sprinkle over batter. Bake 45–50 minutes or until wooden pick inserted in center comes out clean. Serve warm. Makes 9–12 servings.

Master Sergeant (Ret.) Lin Howe-Young – Fruitport, Michigan

Apple Kuchen

½ cup margarine, softened
1 (18¼-ounce) package yellow
  cake mix
½ cup flaked coconut
2½ cups peeled, sliced
  cooking apples

½ cup sugar
1 teaspoon cinnamon
1 (8-ounce) carton sour cream
2 egg yolks

Preheat oven to 350°. Cut margarine into dry cake mix. Add coconut. Lightly pat into greased 9x13-inch pan. Bake 10 minutes. Arrange sliced apples on crust. Mix sugar and cinnamon together; sprinkle over apples. Blend sour cream and egg yolks and drizzle over top of apple mixture. Bake 25 minutes longer, until sour cream mixture is set.

Mrs. Eleanor Eells – Rowlett, Texas
Wife of Tech Sergeant (Ret.) Robert Eells

Pumpkin Bread Crumble

1 (14-ounce) can sweetened
  condensed milk
6 eggs, beaten
3 cups pumpkin
1 cup sugar
½ cup brown sugar
2 teaspoons cinnamon

1 teaspoon ground ginger
¼ teaspoon ground cloves
1 (18¼-ounce) package yellow
  cake mix
½ cup butter, softened
Cool Whip

Preheat oven to 325°. Combine condensed milk, eggs, pumpkin, sugar, brown sugar, cinnamon, ginger, and cloves. Pour into 9x13-inch baking dish. Mix cake mix and butter with pastry blender. Sprinkle cake mix topping over pumpkin mixture. Bake 1 hour or until cake tester comes out clean. Cool. Top with Cool Whip. Store in refrigerator.

Mrs. Cathy Harvey – Georgetown, South Carolina
Wife of Lt. Colonel Joe Harvey

Layered Butterscotch Delight

CRUST:

½ cup chopped pecans   1 stick butter, melted
1 cup all-purpose flour

Preheat oven to 350°. Combine all ingredients and spread into bottom of 9x13-inch baking dish. Bake 30 minutes.

FILLING:

1 (8-ounce) package cream   1 cup powdered sugar
  cheese, softened   ½ (8-ounce) container Cool Whip

Mix all ingredients until well blended and spread over cooled Crust.

PUDDING:

2¾ cups milk   1 (5-ounce) box butterscotch
1 (5-ounce) box vanilla instant   instant pudding mix
  pudding mix

Mix well and spread on top of Filling mixture. Top with remaining ½ container Cool Whip.

Staff Sergeant Christy M. Hardy – Douglas, Georgia
Wife of Staff Sergeant Christopher Hardy

Few schools in the country have an athletic program as extensive as the Air Force Academy's. The football team competes annually for the Commander-in-Chief's Trophy, which is emblematic of service academy football supremacy. The Air Force Falcons have won the trophy sixteen times, which is more than Army and Navy combined. The winner of the annual rivalry visits the White House to have the trophy presented by the president of the United States.

Kahlúa Chocolate Trifle

1 (18¼-ounce) box devil's food
  cake mix
2 (3-ounce) boxes chocolate
  instant pudding mix
3½ cups whole milk

½ cup Kahlúa
4–6 Heath bars
1 (16-ounce) carton Cool Whip,
  divided

Bake cake in a 9x13-inch pan, as directed on box. Prepare pudding mix with 3½ cups milk and ½ cup Kahlúa and set aside. Crush candy bars. In a large glass bowl, break ⅓ cake into bite-size pieces. Pour ⅓ pudding mix over cake. Spread ⅓ Cool Whip over that and sprinkle with ⅓ crushed candy bars. Continue layering. Chill several hours and serve.

Mrs. Billie Neese – New Orleans, Louisiana
Wife of Lt. Colonel (Ret.) Robert Neese

People Puppy Chow

½ cup butter or margarine
1 (12-ounce) package chocolate
  chips

1 cup peanut butter
1 (12-ounce) box Rice Chex
1 (1-pound) box powdered sugar

In a saucepan over low heat, melt butter, chocolate, and peanut butter. Stir until well combined. In a large bowl, pour chocolate and peanut butter mixture over cereal. Stir well. Sprinkle half the powdered sugar over cereal. Stir again. Let dry about 10 minutes. Finish by sprinkling other half of powdered sugar over cereal mixture.

Miss Katie Tosten – Blytheville, Arkansas
Daughter of Major (Ret.) William Tosten

Vanilla Ice Cream

1 quart half-and-half
2 (14-ounce) cans sweetened
  condensed milk

2 pints whipping cream
1 teaspoon vanilla

Mix all ingredients in large bowl. Refrigerate for several hours or until good and cold. Pour into ice cream maker and freeze.

Note: Many variations may be made to this recipe. Add chocolate, fruit, nuts, cookies, or candy to make it your very own favorite.

Mrs. Sara Tosten – Alexandria, Louisiana
Wife of Lt. Colonel (Ret.) Charles T. Tosten, Jr.

Oreo Torte

½ cup butter or margarine,
  melted
1 (20-ounce) package Oreos,
  crushed
1 (8-ounce) package cream
  cheese, softened

1 cup powdered sugar
2 (8-ounce) cartons Cool Whip,
  divided
1 (6-ounce) package chocolate
  instant pudding

Melt butter in 9x13-inch casserole dish in microwave. Stir in crushed Oreos (save a few for topping), and pat down in bottom. Put in freezer while preparing filling. Mix cream cheese and powdered sugar together until blended. Add 1 carton Cool Whip and blend together. Spread over cookie layer. Return to freezer. Mix pudding according to package directions. Spread on cream cheese layer. Refrigerate for at least 20 minutes or until pudding is set.

Frost with remaining Cool Whip and sprinkle with cookie crumbs. Keep refrigerated until ready to serve.

Mrs. Diana Donnelly – Enterprise, Alabama
Wife of Lt. Colonel (Ret.) Bob Donnelly

A Sampling of Famous Air Force Personnel

Paul W. Airey – First Chief Master Sergeant of the Air Force

Buzz Aldrin – Astronaut (Gemini 12 and Apollo 11–Second man to walk on the Moon)

William Anders – Astronaut (Apollo 8–first flight to orbit the Moon)

Michael P. Anderson – Astronaut (Killed in Columbia accident)

Clarence "Bud" Anderson – P-51 pilot and triple ace (Europe, World War II)

Henry "Hap" Arnold – First five-star General of the Air Force

Alonzo Babers – Airline pilot and former Olympic athlete

Esther Blake – First female member of the United States Air Force

Frank Borman – Astronaut (Gemini 7 and Apollo 8–first flight to orbit the Moon)

Boxcar Willie - Country music entertainer

Charles Bronson – Hollywood actor

Dale Brown – Author

George W. Bush – 43rd president of the United States

George Carlin – Actor and comedian

Johnny Cash – Country music singer

Harry Chapin – Singer/songwriter

Gordon Cooper – Astronaut (Mercury 9 and Gemini 5)

Michael Collins – Astronaut (Gemini 10 and Apollo 11)

Eileen Collins – Astronaut, first female space shuttle pilot and commander (STS-84, STS-93, STS-114)

James Gould Cozzens – Pulitzer Prize-winning novelist

Tom Daschle – Former U.S. Senator and floor leader (D-SD)

Benjamin O. Davis, Jr. – First African-American general in the Air Force

Charles Duke – Astronaut (Apollo 16)

Joe Engle – Astronaut (X-15 and space shuttle pilot)

Kelly Flinn – First female B-52 pilot

Tennessee Ernie Ford – Television comedian and recording artist

Nathan Bedford Forrest III – Great-grandson of Confederate general Nathan Bedford Forrest.

Joe Foss – Former marine ace and governor of South Dakota (Air National Guard)

Morgan Freeman – Actor

Theodore Freeman – Astronaut (killed in a jet plane accident)

Clark Gable – Actor

Marvin Gaye – Singer

Barry Goldwater – U.S. Senator, Republican Presidential Candidate in 1964

Lindsay Graham – U.S. Senator

Susan Grant – Novelist

Gus Grissom – Mercury astronaut (Mercury 4 and Gemini 3; later killed in Apollo 1 fire)

Michael Hayden – CIA Director

Chad Hennings – NFL player

Don Herbert – Television personality as "Mr. Wizard"

Charlton Heston – Actor; President of the National Rifle Association

LeRoy Homer – Airline pilot, co-pilot of United Airlines Flight 93 (hijacked 9-11-01)

Rick D. Husband – Astronaut (killed in *Columbia* accident)

James Irwin – Astronaut (Apollo 15)

John Hillerman – Actor

Bobby Jones – Champion amateur golfer

DeForest Kelley – Actor

Ron Kenoly – Christian music worship leader

Ivan Kincheloe – Air Force test pilot

Norman Lear – Television and motion picture producer

Curtis LeMay – Chief of Staff and vice presidential candidate

John Levitow – Enlisted recipient of the Medal of Honor

Jerry Mathers – Actor

Walter Matthau – Actor

T. Allen McArtor – Business executive and former FAA Administrator

Glenn Miller – Musician and director of the Band of the USAAF Training Command

Chuck Norris – Actor and martial artist

Robin Olds – Two-war flying ace

William H. Pitsenbarger – Enlisted recipient of the Medal of Honor

Greg Popovich – NBA head coach

Jody Powell – White House Press Secretary

Robin Quivers – Co-host of the *Howard Stern Show*

Ronald Reagan – Actor; 40th president of the United States

William Rehnquist – Former Chief Justice of the United States

R. Stephen Ritchie – Flying ace in the Vietnam War

Bob Ross – Painter

Eddie Rickenbacker – Famous WWI flying ace

Gene Roddenberry – Creator of *Star Trek*

James Salter – Novelist

Bob Schieffer – Host of *CBS Evening News*

Dick Scobee – Astronaut (killed in Space Shuttle *Challenger* disaster)

David Scott – Astronaut (Gemini 8, Apollo 9, and Apollo 15)

Lance Sijan – Medal of Honor recipient

Sinbad – Actor and comedian

Deke Slayton – Mercury and Apollo-Soyuz test project astronaut

Aaron Spelling – Film and television producer

Bill Stealey – Business CEO and co-founder of MicroProse

Jimmy Stewart – Actor

Hunter S. Thompson – Writer

Paul Tibbets – Pilot whose B-29 dropped the first atomic bomb

Harrison R. Thyng – Two-war ace and Senate candidate

Stephen W. Thompson – First person in U.S. military to shoot down an enemy aircraft.

George Wallace – Governor of Alabama; presidential candidate in 1968

Edward H. White II – Astronaut (first American to walk in space; later killed in Apollo 1 fire)

Heather Wilson – Member of Congress

Alfred Worden – Astronaut (Apollo 15)

Charles "Chuck" Yeager – First man to break the sound barrier

The Air Force Song
by Robert Crawford (1939)

"The U.S. Air Force" is the official song of the United States Air Force. It is informally known as "The Air Force Song," and is often informally referred to as "Off We Go," "Off We Go into the Wild Blue Yonder," or simply "Wild Blue Yonder." In 1947, the words "U.S. Air Force" in the title and lyrics replaced the original "Army Air Corps."

Off we go into the wild blue yonder,
Climbing high into the sun;
Here they come zooming to meet our thunder,
At 'em boys, Give 'er the gun! (Give 'er the gun now!)
Down we dive, spouting our flame from under,
Off with one helluva roar!
We live in fame or go down in flame. Hey!
Nothing'll stop the U.S. Air Force!

Minds of men fashioned a crate of thunder,
Sent it high into the blue;
Hands of men blasted the world asunder;
How they lived God only knew! (God only knew then!)
Souls of men dreaming of skies to conquer
Gave us wings, ever to soar!
With scouts before and bombers galore. Hey!
Nothing'll stop the U.S. Air Force!

Here's a toast to the host
Of those who love the vastness of the sky,
To a friend we send a message of his brother men who fly.
We drink to those who gave their all of old,
Then down we roar to score the rainbow's pot of gold.
A toast to the host of men we boast, the U.S. Air Force!

Off we go into the wild sky yonder,
Keep the wings level and true;
If you'd live to be a grey-haired wonder
Keep the nose out of the blue! (Out of the blue, boy!)
Flying men, guarding the nation's border,
We'll be there, followed by more!
In echelon we carry on. Hey!
Nothing'll stop the U.S. Air Force!

Index

The **T-38A Talon** is a twin-engine, high-altitude, supersonic jet trainer used in a variety of roles because of its design, economy of operations, ease of maintenance, high performance, and exceptional safety record. Air Education and Training Command is the primary user of the T-38A for joint specialized undergraduate pilot training. Air Combat Command, Air Force Materiel Command, and the National Aeronautics and Space Administration also use the T-38A in various roles.

Primarily Air Education and Training Command officials use the aircraft for undergraduate pilot and pilot instructor training. Student pilots fly the T-38 to learn supersonic techniques, aerobatics, formation, night and instrument flying, and cross-country navigation. More than 60,000 pilots have earned their wings in the T-38.

INDEX

BEST OF THE BEST STATE COOKBOOK SERIES

ALABAMA
(all-new edition)
(original edition)*

ALASKA

ARIZONA

ARKANSAS

BIG SKY
Includes Montana and
Wyoming

CALIFORNIA

COLORADO

FLORIDA
(all-new edition)
(original edition)*

GEORGIA
(all-new edition)
(original edition)*

GREAT PLAINS
Includes North Dakota,
South Dakota, Nebraska,
and Kansas

HAWAII

IDAHO

ILLINOIS

INDIANA

IOWA

KENTUCKY
(all-new edition)
(original edition)*

LOUISIANA

LOUISIANA II

MICHIGAN
(all-new edition)
(original edition out-of- print)

MID-ATLANTIC
Includes Maryland,
Delaware, New Jersey, and
Washington, D.C.

MINNESOTA

MISSISSIPPI
(all-new edition)
(original edition)*

MISSOURI

NEVADA

NEW ENGLAND
Includes Rhode Island,
Connecticut, Massachusetts,
Vermont, New Hampshire,
and Maine

NEW MEXICO

NEW YORK

NO. CAROLINA
(all-new edition)
(original edition)*

OHIO
(all-new edition)
(original edition out-of- print)

OKLAHOMA

OREGON

PENNSYLVANIA
(revised edition)

SO. CAROLINA
(all-new edition)
(original edition)*

TENNESSEE
(all-new edition)
(original edition)*

TEXAS

TEXAS II

UTAH

VIRGINIA

VIRGINIA II

WASHINGTON

WEST VIRGINIA

WISCONSIN

*Original editions only available while current
supplies last.

All BEST OF THE BEST STATE COOKBOOKS are 6x9 inches
and comb-bound with illustrations, photographs, and
an index. They range in size from 288 to 352 pages
and each contains over 300 recipes.

Retail price per copy $16.95.

To order by credit card, call toll-free
1-800-343-1583, visit **www.quailridge.com**,
or use the order form shown below.

NOTE: A free **Collect the Series Coupon Booklet** *is available upon request (call
1-800-343-1583). The coupons in this booklet offer a discount off the list price.*

⬛ Order Form

Send check, money order, or credit card info to:
QUAIL RIDGE PRESS • P. O. Box 123 • Brandon, MS 39043

Name _____

Address _____

City_____

State/Zip _____

Phone # _____

Email Address _____

❑ Check enclosed

Charge to: ❑ Visa ❑ MC ❑ AmEx ❑ Disc

Card # _____

Expiration Date _____

Signature _____

Qty.	Title of Book (State) or HOF set	Total

Subtotal _____

Mississippi residents add 7% sales tax _____

Postage ($4.00 any number of books) + $4.00

TOTAL _____